Nonveridicality and Evaluation

Studies in Pragmatics

Series Editors

Maj-Britt Mosegaard Hansen (*University of Manchester*)
Kerstin Fischer (*University of Southern Denmark*)
Anne Barron (*Leuphana University*)

VOLUME 11

The titles published in this series are listed at *brill.com/sip*

Nonveridicality and Evaluation

Theoretical, Computational and Corpus Approaches

Edited by

Maite Taboada
Radoslava Trnavac

BRILL

LEIDEN | BOSTON

Library of Congress Cataloging-in-Publication Data

Nonveridicality and evaluation : theoretical, computational and corpus approaches / Edited by Maite Taboada, Radoslava Trnavac.
pages cm. – (Studies in Pragmatics ; 11)
Includes index.
ISBN 978-90-04-25816-7 (hardback : alk. paper) – ISBN 978-90-04-25817-4 (e-book)
1. Subjectivity (Linguistics) 2. Grammar, Comparative and general. 3. Critical discourse analysis. 4. Computational linguistics. I. Taboada, Mar?a Teresa. II. Trnavac, Radoslava.

P299.S89N66 2014
415–dc23

2013035069

This publication has been typeset in the multilingual "Brill" typeface. With over 5,100 characters covering Latin, IPA, Greek, and Cyrillic, this typeface is especially suitable for use in the humanities. For more information, please see www.brill.com/brill-typeface.

ISSN 1750-368X
ISBN 978 90 04 25816 7 (hardback)
ISBN 978 90 04 25817 4 (e-book)

This book is printed on acid-free paper.

Contents

PART 3
Corpus Studies on Evaluation and Coherence in Nonveridical Contexts

Introduction

*Nonveridicality and Evaluation across Disciplinary Boundaries**

Maite Taboada and Radoslava Trnavac

1 Nonveridicality, Evaluation, and Coherence Relations

This volume brings together a diverse group of researchers with interests in areas with connection to evaluation in discourse. The papers contained in the volume address issues having to do with how evaluation and subjectivity are interpreted in context, the context being sometimes determined by the presence of nonveridical markers, and sometimes by other discourse phenomena such as coherence relations.

Evaluation and nonveridicality engage in an obvious interaction. Evaluation may be expressed as definitive, or it may be tempered by a nonveridical element, in which case it tends to have a weaker effect. Consider the difference between (1) and (2).

(1) He is a good student.
(2) He could be a good student.

The modal verb in (2) indicates that the positive evaluation is weakened, or downtoned, to a potentially negative appraisal of the student.

We use evaluation as an umbrella term that can be instantiated as Appraisal Theory (Martin & White, 2005), evaluation (Bednarek, 2006; Hunston & Thompson, 2000b), stance (Biber & Finegan, 1989), or subjectivity (Langacker, 1990; Lyons, 1982; von Fintel & Gillies, 2010). Nonveridicality (Giannakidou, 1998; Zwarts, 1995), or irrealis (Fleischman, 1995) refers to the expressions, such as modals and negation, that affect the truth conditions of elements in their scope, and, in particular, of evaluative elements.

Coherence relations are also of interest here because they interact with nonveridical markers to change the meaning of evaluation (Asher, Benamara, & Mathieu, 2009; Dancygier & Sweetser, 2005; Sanders & Sweetser, 2009; Trnavac & Taboada, 2012). In the next two examples, the fact that the positive

* Some of the papers in this volume were presented at a panel at the 12th Conference of the International Pragmatics Association in Manchester, July 2011. We acknowledge support from the Natural Sciences and Engineering Research Council of Canada (Discovery Grant 261104-2008 to Maite Taboada).

 | DOI: 10.1163/9789004258174_001

evaluations (*capture great dramatic moments* and *fun is good*) are embedded in a concessive and a conditional sentence respectively, affect the evaluation in subtle ways.

(3) … although he can capture great dramatic moments, he doesn't give anyone the idea on what type of film this should be.
(4) Fun is good, but only if you know when to stop.

We use evaluation here in a very loose way, encompassing aspects such as the study of attitude that the Appraisal framework proposes (Martin & White, 2005), subjectivity and point of view (Langacker, 1990), or opinion and sentiment (Pang & Lee, 2008). What they all have in common is a concern for how the speaker or writer involve themselves in the linguistic expression. Nonveridicality, or sometimes irrealis, is used to refer to statements that are not factual or true for diverse reasons, such as the presence of a negation, a modal, or an intensional verb.

We are well aware that the areas that we attempt to integrate—evaluation and nonveridicality—have very different theoretical foundations, the first one being approached from different perspectives in linguistics, including functional approaches (Martin & White, 2005); the second one being grounded in formal semantics (Zwarts, 1995). To this we add the study of coherence relations, again typically linked to functional approaches to language (Mann & Thompson, 1988), although not necessarily so (Asher & Lascarides, 2003). It is not our goal in this volume to fully integrate all these disparate areas. Rather, we see that they are all necessary to provide a clear understanding of evaluation in context, and thus shed light on the linguistic realization of evaluation.

In the following figure,[1] we show our understanding of the main concepts we explore. There is a clear interaction between evaluation, nonveridicality and coherence. First of all, evaluation overlaps with nonveridical phenomena, as shown in Example (2), although there are obviously evaluative instances that are veridical, as in (1). Second, evaluation and coherence relations interact in cases such as those shown in Examples (3) and (4). There are also coherence relations that are nonveridical, but not evaluative, the overlap at the bottom of the figure. We are interested in the shaded areas, where the three overlap. In those cases, we have expressions of evaluation that may be part

1 Modified from Trnavac and Taboada (2012).

of a coherence relation, such as a concessive relation, and at the same time contain nonveridical markers, such as the example in (5), where the modal verb *should* acts as a nonveridical operator.

(5) Fans of Gyllenhaal should best stay away from this film although she does a good performance.

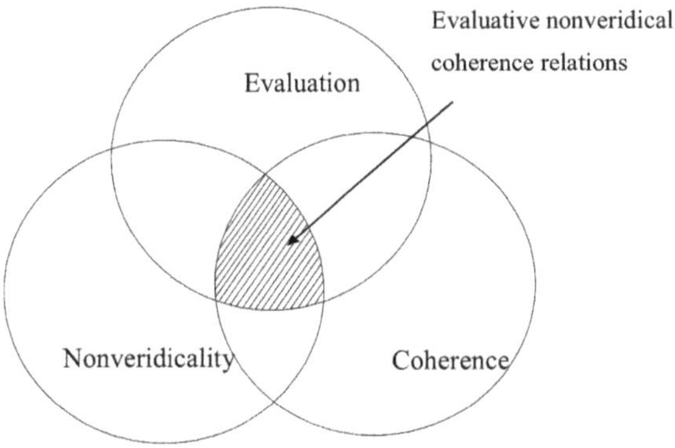

FIGURE 1 *Relationship between evaluation, nonveridicality and coherence*

We next attempt brief definitions of each of these aspects, before providing an overview of the papers in the volume in Section 4.

Montague (1969) defined nonveridicality in terms of non-existence while a more recent definition of nonveridicality proposed by Giannakidou (1995) and Zwarts (1995) suggests that veridical contexts are based on truth. Veridical operators express certainty and an individual's commitment to the truth of a proposition, whereas nonveridical expressions express uncertainty and lack of commitment. Nonveridicality, which incorporates the notion of irrealis, is formally distinguished from veridicality by positing a divide within the class of intensional verbs, depending on whether a truth inference is available, i.e., whether at least one epistemic agent is committed to the truth of the complement sentence. If a propositional attitude verb expresses such a commitment, it will be veridical and select the indicative; if not, it will be nonveridical and select the subjunctive (or infinitive if there is no formal subjunctive–indicative distinction). As proposed in Giannakidou (2009), among the first group (the group of weak intensional verbs) are assertives (*say, read, claim*), fiction verbs (*dream, imagine*), epistemics (*believe, think*), factive verbs (*be glad, know, regret*), semifactives (*discover, remember*). The second group (strong intensional verbs) contains the following verbs: volitionals (*want, hope, plan*), directives (*order, advise, suggest*), modals (*must, may*), permissives (*allow, forbid*), and negative verbs (*avoid, refuse*). Based on Giannakidou (1998, 2002, 2009), the following contexts are frequently analyzed as being nonveridical: modals, imperatives, questions, protasis of conditionals, habituals, the subjunctive, dyadic connectives (*or*, *if*, *only if*, *if* and *only if*, and *not p* or *not q*), as well as strong intensional verbs.

The term evaluation is much harder to pin down, and it has been used in very different approaches. Here we see it as an umbrella term encompassing work done within the Appraisal framework (Martin & White, 2005), studies of evaluation and affect in text (Bednarek, 2006; Hunston, 2011; Hunston & Thompson, 2000b), but also work in subjectivity and point of view, in that this work considers the speaker and writer as affective agents (Englebretson, 2007).

Finally, we want to introduce here the idea of coherence relations as important valence shifters (Polanyi & Zaenen, 2006) in the study of evaluation. Just like nonveridical markers affect the polarity and strength of evaluative statements, coherence relations, some of them in particular, as we have shown elsewhere for concessive and conditional relations (Trnavac & Taboada, 2012).

By coherence relations we mean the type of relations defined in Rhetorical Structure Theory (Mann & Thompson, 1988), but also in other theories (Asher & Lascarides, 2003; Sanders, 1997; Webber, Knott, Stone, & Joshi, 1999). In general, they refer to relations where two or more text spans are considered to be in one of a limited set of relations such as Cause, Concession, Condition, Elaboration, Purpose or Result. In most relations, a link is established between a main and a secondary part, the equivalents of the traditional main and subordinate clauses. Clearly, some of these relations will have an impact on the interpretation of evaluation, in similar ways to the impact created by nonveridical markers. For instance, a Condition relation will limit the extent of a positive evaluation. In Example (6), the positive evaluation is tempered by the condition that the reader has to be able to change their expectations about the author's typical style and previous books. This in effect downtones the positive evaluation contained in *interesting*.

(6) It is an interesting book if you can look at it without expecting the Grisham "law and order" style.

2 The Chapters in the Book

The volume contains contributions from two different types, theoretical and empirical. From a theoretical point of view, contributions reflect the interface between evaluation, nonveridicality and coherence. From empirical perspectives, the book contains contributions that use corpus methodology, qualitative descriptions of texts, and computational implementations. The volume is divided into three themes based on the linguistic perspectives adopted by the contributors.

2.1 *Theme One: Evaluation and Nonveridicality in Semantics*

The first thematic area includes three semantic studies which describe the interaction between nonveridicality and evaluation.

Giannakidou addresses the connection between nonveridicality and (non)-existence by analyzing the evaluative use of subjunctive in the relative clause in Greek. She shows that veridicality and nonveridicality are notions that are able to capture the behaviour of aspectual operators, such as the progressive and the perfective. In those cases veridicality and nonveridicality rely on the speaker's knowledge of whether an event is at least partially realized in the actual word. If an operator imposes knowledge of at least partial actualization, it is veridical as in the case of the progressive and the perfective. Another finding of the paper is that the subjunctive in the relative clause contributes epistemic weakening: A presupposition of epistemic uncertainty as to the existence of a referent of the NP it modifies. Epistemic weakening, according to Giannakidou, can be found in a nonveridical epistemic space since only such a space allows for the possibility that a referent may not actually exist. The background for this argument is the role of *optional* subjunctive, i.e., the subjunctive that is not selected. Giannakidou suggests that the function of the optional subjunctive is *evaluative*, and that the evaluative effect can be of two kinds: epistemic weakening, as in the case of the subjunctive relative clause, or expressiveness, as with subjunctive after emotive verbs in some Romance languages (as discussed in Giannakidou to appear). The important conclusion of the paper is that the subjunctive in the relative clause is evaluative, because it makes a subjective comment of the speaker on the existence or not of a referent, or an actualized event. The subjunctive affects locally the relative clause, and tampers with the strength of evaluation by weakening the speaker's convictions.

Goddard investigates the relation between nonveridicality and evaluation in the context of a semantic analysis of the English strong modals of "obligation"—*have to* and *must*—using the Natural Semantic Metalanguage (NSM) approach (Goddard, 2008; Goddard & Wierzbicka, 2002). *Have to* and *must* are characterized in the general literature as associated with an 'objective' vs. 'subjective' effect, respectively, properties connected with veridicality/ nonveridicality and with evaluation. The proposed semantic analysis demonstrates this effect. It is also argued that deontic *must* contains a component of negative evaluation that is not shared with *have to*, correlated with the perceived greater seriousness of *must*. Third, it is argued that deontic *must* includes a desiderative element, and that this helps account for distributional asymmetries with respect to combination with nonveridical operators such as *maybe*. The chapter proposes a set of NSM explications, i.e. reductive paraphrases, which give an intuitively satisfying account of the different nuances of meaning that separate the main English modals of necessity. Goddard shows how different aspects of the explications correlate with the different grammatical properties of the various expressions. Comparing the explications of the two necessity modals, Goddard concludes that neither of the two modals is simply an intensified version of the other. According to the author, despite the impression one has that *must* expresses a "stronger" message than *have to*, the relationship is not truly a scalar one.

The paper by Moeschler gives a coherent picture of negation in French, from a logical, semantic and pragmatic point of view. His contribution aims at answering questions that relate to the logical meaning of negation and its pragmatic meanings, the meaning of a negative sentence, the contribution of contexts in the computation of negation scope, and the relation between negation and events. The logical aspect is about the type of entailments between a negative sentence (NEG) and its corrective one (COR). In ordinary negation, the corrective sentence (COR) entails the negative one (NEG), whereas with metalinguistic negation, two situations arise: with upward negation, mainly with scalar predicates, COR entails the corresponding positive sentence (POS), whereas with a presuppositional negation, COR entails NEG and other entailed propositions. As for the semantic aspect, descriptive and metalinguistic negations display an asymmetrical behaviour: whereas descriptive is downward oriented, metalinguistic negation is upward oriented. It is argued that downward orientation of negation is the result of a semantic process, not a pragmatic one. The paper discusses the pragmatic and discourse aspects of the relation between NEG and COR as well. In the case of descriptive negation, the discourse relation is a Correction one. In the case of the metalinguistic negation, the relation between NEG and COR is a Contrast relation. The discourse relation between NEG and COR in presuppositional negation is Explanation. These three types of discourse relations and negation are made explicit by different connectives. In the final part of the paper, Moeschler investigates the issue of negation scope. He argues that the computation of negation depends on the type of contextual effects. In order to yield the right interpretation of negative utterances, contextual information should not only be consistent with the four types of properties (entailment, scope, discourse relation and connective), but also predict logical, semantic and pragmatic properties of the usages of negation.

In all, these three papers present radically different approaches to the study of phenomena that are traditionally considered as within the realm of irrealis or nonveridicality: mood, modality and negation. Although the approaches are all different, the papers in this section present potential approximations to the interaction between nonveridical phenomena (under whatever label) and evaluation.

2.2 *Theme Two: Evaluation, Nonveridicality and Coherence in Computational Applications*

The second theme addresses different computational approaches towards evaluation, coherence and nonveridicality.

Gros and Stede address the issue of nonveridicality and subjectivity (evaluation) by discussing the sub-genre of pathology reports in German and English in the light of annotated expressions of negation and their scope (i.e., the linguistic material that is being negated). They present Negtopus, a system for recognizing negation operators and their scopes in texts with medical diagnosis in English and German. The authors identify a number of shortcomings of the previous approaches that are mostly based on the *NegEx* algorithm and then provide results of their own comparative implementation, which for the German data contrasts a regular expression matching procedure (considering words and part of speech tags) with a different approach based on the output of a (genre-neutral) syntactic parser. Negtopus also relies on a lexical resource: a short list of closed-class items that have to be manually compiled for the target language, and a long list of domain-specific, open-class content words. The authors suggest learning these words from standard code book on the basis of extraction patterns. In the second part of the paper, the authors discuss the issue of whether the quality of state-of-the-art syntax parsing is sufficient to improve the results of the negation finding task, or whether it actually performs worse.

The work described in the paper of Benamara, Chardon, Mathieu, Popescu and Asher focuses on the interaction between evaluation and coherence relations. Part of the paper discusses the analysis of the interaction between evaluation and nonveridical markers, such as modality and negation. The authors follow the work of Asher and colleagues (Asher et al., 2009), where Segmented Discourse Representation Theory (SDRT, Asher & Lascarides, 2003) is used in order to obtain a deeper understanding of contextual polarity. The paper investigates how rhetorical relations interact with opinions, focusing on two specific genres: movie reviews and news commentaries. The authors propose a two-level annotation scheme: first at the segment level where each elementary discourse unit is annotated according to the opinion it conveys and then at the document level where the discourse structure of the document is built. The results show that segment-based opinion analysis is more appropriate to study opinions in discourse.

2.3 *Theme Three: Corpus Studies of Evaluation and Coherence in Nonveridical Contexts*

The third theme explores the relations between evaluation and coherence in nonveridical contexts from the empirical perspective of corpus linguistics.

Stukker and Sanders focus on subjectivity which is related to the broader concept of evaluation. The paper explores factors evoking deviant use of the Dutch causal connectives *dus* ('so'), associated with subjective causality and *daarom* ('that's why') associated with objective causality. Subjective causal relations, as nonveridical contexts, typically concern evaluation of aspects of reality (Pander Maat & Degand, 2001; Pit, 2003, pp. 116–123) regarding truth, desirability and quality. Stukker and Sanders investigate the difference between objective or external causal relations, and those that are perceived to be subjective or internal, construed by the speaker. It is well-known that some languages mark the distinction with different connectives. But one less well-documented fact is that counterexamples exist, where a subjective relation is marked with a prototypically objective marker, and vice versa. Stukker and Sanders propose that these apparent counterexamples are actually non-prototypical instantiations of the typical use of the connective. As an illustration of the above hypothesis, they explore two different sources of evidence that deviant usage events of the Dutch causal connectives *dus* and *daarom* are actually peripheral members of the same category their more conventional contexts of use belong to. The authors investigate the local, linguistic context of the causally related segments and the more global, primarily conceptual context of communicative goals of the discourse the causal relation belongs to. In addition, they investigate how patterns of distribution of *dus* and *daarom* across prototypical and less prototypical contexts of use might be affected by context factors.

The volume concludes with a paper framed in the tradition of Systemic Functional Linguistics (Halliday & Matthiessen, 2004), and more specifically within the Appraisal framework (Martin & White, 2005). Zappavigna examines microblogging and the popular Twitter service, focusing on how posts use the pattern of the conditional (nonveridical) phrase *RT if x* (retweet, or repost, if you fulfill a certain condition, such as liking a celebrity). She explores the relationship between *if-then* contingency patterns and retweeting practices. Using a 100 million word corpus of tweets she investigates the role of contingency in the way interpersonal bonds are proposed. According to the author, invitations to retweet a post are calls to re-share a bond. Under sharing a bond she understands a 'coupling' (Zhao, 2010) of evaluative and ideational meaning. Zappavigna explores how these calls for retweeting can be classified along Appraisal patterns, in particular expressions of Appreciation and Judgement.

3 Integration across Disciplinary Boundaries

The objective of this volume is to integrate various perspectives on the interaction between nonveridicality and evaluation from the point of view of theoretical semantics, computational and corpus linguistics. Another objective of the volume is to foster a dialogue between diverse areas of linguistics that approach similar phenomena using different terminology and methodologies. The starting hypothesis of the volume is that nonveridical markers to a certain degree alter the effect of evaluative statements. (Non)veridicality that expresses (un)certainty and (non)commitment of the epistemic agent to the truth of a proposition, is studied in formal semantics (Giannakidou, 1995, 1998, 1999, 2002, 2006, 2009; Montague, 1969; Zwarts, 1995). The work in formal semantics mostly discusses how selection of nonveridical markers is related to the number of distribution phenomena such as NPI licensing and free choice indefinites (Giannakidou, 1997, 1998, 2001), negation selection (Chatzopoulou, 2012), the use of genitive of negation in Russian (Partee & Borschev, 2004), among other phenomena. The paper of Giannakidou in this volume relates nonveridicality to evaluation through mood selection and the use of evaluative subjunctive in Greek. The separate markers of nonveridicality have been studied in many other areas of linguistics, including lexical semantics and pragmatics (see Goddard and Moeschler in this volume). Goddard in this volume links the use of necessity modals *have to* and *must* through their objective and subjective use, as well as through the negative semantics of *must*, to the notions of both (non)veridicality and evaluation. Moeschler addresses the question whether linguistic negation is connected to the truth conditions, and consequently to (non)veridicality and evaluation. In all three cases, and despite the very different theoretical perspectives the focus on nonveridicality and two subsumed phenomena, modality and negation, reveals how we can explore the same phenomenon from different points of view, and how the (non)veridicality spectrum relates to evaluation.

Nonveridicality has also been studied in the area of evaluation in discourse theory. Hunston and Thompson (2000a), for instance, propose that there are two aspects to evaluation: modality and something which is frequently called evaluation, or (attitudinal) stance. While modality, as part of what we call nonveridicality, tends to express opinions about propositions, such as their likelihood, and their expressions tend to be more grammaticalized, evaluation or (attitudinal) stance, on the other hand, expresses opinions about entities, and is mostly realized through adjectives (Bruce & Wiebe, 2000). Hunston and Thompson (2000a) note that there seem to be approaches that separate modality and evaluation as two distinct phenomena (Halliday, 1994; Halliday & Matthiessen, 2004; Martin, 2000; White, 2003). This includes some approaches to modality, such as those represented in Bybee and Fleischman (1995) or Facchinetti, Krug, and Palmer (2003). Other researchers combine the two expressions of opinion, often under one label: Biber and colleagues (Biber & Finegan, 1989; Conrad & Biber, 2000) use stance, and Stubbs (1986) refers to modality, but includes vague language and attitude.[2] This volume adopts an integrative approach towards study of evaluation and combines both grammatical and lexical approaches to evaluation.

Nonveridical markers in interaction with evaluation is currently a frequent topic in corpus linguistics (see Zappavigna in this volume) and in computational linguistics (Gros and Stede in this volume). Close to this line of research is the area of sentiment analysis (Asher, Benamara, & Mathieu, 2008; Asher et al., 2009; Chardon, Benamara, Mathieu, Popescu, & Asher, 2013a, 2013b) and coherence relations (Trnavac & Taboada, 2012) where it has been repeatedly shown that nonveridical markers in combination with discourse relations influence polarity of opinion (evaluation) (see Benamara et al. in this volume).

Nonveridical contexts have been studied in the area of subjectivity as well (see Stukker and Sanders in this volume) that is similar to a notion of evaluation. According to Bednarek (2006, p. 20) the difference between evaluation and subjectivity is one of emphasis and scope. Subjectivity is more speaker-centered and encompasses other linguistic phenomena than evaluation, since it may be broadened to include the speaker–hearer relationship.

By bringing different strands of linguistic research, this volume reflects a strong belief that fruitful study of the relation between nonveridicality and evaluation, and evaluation in general, needs truly interdisciplinary and combined theoretical and empirical approach.

2 For a more detailed review of literature on modality, nonveridicality, evaluation and similar phenomena see Trnavac and Taboada (2012).

4 Conclusions

This volume is unique in bringing authors that approach the innovative question of interaction between evaluation, nonveridicality and coherence from the perspective of different theoretical and empirical linguistic disciplines. The papers in the volume approach the question of the relation between nonveridicality and evaluation across a diverse group of European languages—English, German, Greek, French and Dutch. The variety of theoretical and empirical approaches to the topic of evaluation in linguistics are demonstrated on the grammatical, semantic, syntactic and discourse structures through introspective methods of formal and lexical semantics and pragmatics, as well as through various quantitative, statistical and annotation techniques. This volume represents the first attempt to integrate different formal, cognitive, computational and corpus perspectives in the study of an intriguing question of the interaction between nonveridicality and evaluation in linguistics.

Future work will need to expand on the impact that (non)veridical markers such as negatives, futures, subjunctives, modals, quasimodals, questions, and imperatives have on evaluative force in a sentence from theoretical (semantic and pragmatic), empirical, cross linguistic and contrastive perspectives. The second line of research will need to investigate how nonveridical markers and different coherence relations coupled with their nucleus-satellite structures (Mann & Thompson, 1988) affect evaluative content in discourse in terms of theory and its practical applications (the automatic extraction of opinion and sentiment analysis). The third line of research that is within the tradition of the Appraisal framework could explore how different forms of Engagement (Martin & White, 2005) expressing the author's/speaker's perspective serve to position the reader/listener vis-à-vis the attitudinal proposition conveyed. This interdisciplinary research will provide more precise methods in the future to characterize the relationship between evaluation and nonveridicality at the clause and discourse levels.

References

Asher, Nicholas, Benamara, Farah, & Mathieu, Yvette Yannick. (2008). Distilling opinion in discourse: A preliminary study *Proceedings of COLING* (pp. 7–10). Manchester, UK.

Asher, Nicholas, Benamara, Farah, & Mathieu, Yvette Yannick. (2009). Appraisal of opinion expressions in discourse. *Linguisticae Investigationes, 32*(2), 279–292.

Asher, Nicholas, & Lascarides, Alex. (2003). *Logics of Conversation*. Cambridge: Cambridge University Press.

Bednarek, Monika. (2006). *Evaluation in Media Discourse: Analysis of a Newspaper Corpus*. London: Continuum.

Biber, Douglas, & Finegan, Edward. (1989). Styles of stance in English: Lexical and grammatical marking of evidentiality and affect. *Text, 9*(1), 93–124.

Bruce, Rebecca F., & Wiebe, Janyce M. (2000). Recognizing subjectivity: A case study of manual tagging. *Natural Language Engineering, 5*(2), 187–205.

Bybee, Joan, & Fleischman, Suzanne (Eds.). (1995). *Modality in Grammar and Discourse*. Amsterdam and Philadelphia: John Benjamins.

Chardon, Baptiste, Benamara, Farah, Mathieu, Yvette Yannick, Popescu, Vladimir, & Asher, Nicholas. (2013a). Measuring the effect of discourse structure on sentiment analysis *Proceeding of the 14th international conference on Computational Linguistics and Intelligent Text Processing (CICLing)* (Vol. 7817 LNCS, pp. 25–37). Samos, Greece.

Chardon, Baptiste, Benamara, Farah, Mathieu, Yvette Yannick, Popescu, Vladimir, & Asher, Nicholas. (2013b). Sentiment composition using a parabolic model *Proceedings of the 10th International Conference on Computational Semantics (IWCS 2013)*. Potsdam, Germany.

Chatzopoulou, Katerina. (2012). *Negation in Greek: A Diachronic Perspective*. University of Chicago.

Conrad, Susan, & Biber, Douglas. (2000). Adverbial marking of stance in speech and writing. In Susan Hunston & Geoff Thompson (Eds.), *Evaluation in Text: Authorial Distance and the Construction of Discourse* (pp. 56–73). Oxford: Oxford University Press.

Dancygier, Barbara, & Sweetser, Eve. (2005). *Mental Spaces in Grammar: Conditional Constructions*. Cambridge: Cambridge University Press.

Englebretson, Robert (Ed.). (2007). *Stancetaking in Discourse: Subjectivity, Evaluation, Interaction*. Amsterdam: John Benjamins.

Facchinetti, Roberta, Krug, Manfred, & Palmer, Frank (Eds.). (2003). *Modality in Contemporary English*. Berlin: Mouton de Gruyter.

Fleischman, Suzanne. (1995). Imperfective and irrealis. In Joan Bybee & Suzanne Fleischman (Eds.), *Modality in Grammar and Discourse* (pp. 519–551). Amsterdam and Philadelphia: John Benjamins.

Giannakidou, Anastasia. (1995). On the semantic licensing of polarity items. In Anastasios-Phoevos Christidis, Maria Margariti-Roga & Argyris Arhakis (Eds.), *Studies in Greek Linguistics 15: Proceedings of the 15th Annual Meeting of the Department of Linguistics* (pp. 406–418). Thessaloniki: University of Thessaloniki.

———. (1997). *The Landscape of Polarity Items*. (Ph.D dissertation), University of Groningen.

———. (1998). *Polarity Sensitivity as (Non)Veridical Dependency*. Amsterdam and Philadelphia: John Benjamins.

———. (1999). Affective dependencies. *Linguistics and Philosophy, 22*(367–421).

———. (2001). Varieties of polarity items and the (non)veridicality hypothesis. In Jack Hoeksema, Hotze Rullmann, Víctor Sánchez-Valencia & Ton van der Wouden (Eds.), *Perspectives on Negation and Polarity Items* (pp. 99–127). Amsterdam and Philadelphia: John Benjamins.

———. (2002). Licensing and sensitivity in polarity items: From downward entailment to nonveridicality. In Maria Andronis, Anne Pycha & Keiko Yoshimura (Eds.), *Papers from the 38th Annual Meeting of the Chicago Linguistics Society. Parasession on Polarity and Negation*. Chicago: Chicago Linguistics Society.

———. (2006). *Only*, emotive factive verbs, and the dual nature of polarity dependency. *Language, 82*, 575–603.

———. (2009). The dependency of the subjunctive revisited: Temporal semantics and polarity. *Lingua, 119*(12), 1883–1908.

Goddard, Cliff (Ed.). (2008). *Cross-Linguistic Semantics*. Amsterdam: John Benjamins.

Goddard, Cliff, & Wierzbicka, Anna (Eds.). (2002). *Meaning and Universal Grammar-Theory and Empirical Findings* (Vol. I and II). Amsterdam: John Benjamins.

Halliday, Michael A.K. (1994). *An Introduction to Functional Grammar*. London: Arnold (2nd edition).

Halliday, Michael A.K., & Matthiessen, Christian M.I.M. (2004). *An Introduction to Functional Grammar* (3rd ed.). London: Arnold.

Hunston, Susan. (2011). *Corpus Approaches to Evaluation: Phraseology and Evaluative Language*. New York: Routledge.

Hunston, Susan, & Thompson, Geoff. (2000a). Evaluation: An introduction. In Susan Hunston & Geoff Thompson (Eds.), *Evaluation in Text: Authorial Distance and the Construction of Discourse* (pp. 1–27). Oxford: Oxford University Press.

Hunston, Susan, & Thompson, Geoff (Eds.). (2000b). *Evaluation in Text: Authorial Distance and the Construction of Discourse*. Oxford: Oxford University Press.

Langacker, Ronald W. (1990). Subjectification. *Cognitive Linguistics, 1*(1), 5–38.

Lyons, John. (1982). Deixis and subjectivity: 'Loquor, ergo sum?'. In Robert J. Jarvella & Wolfgang Klein (Eds.), *Speech, Place and Action: Studies in Deixis and Related Topics* (pp. 101–124). New York: John Wiley.

Mann, William C., & Thompson, Sandra A. (1988). Rhetorical Structure Theory: Toward a functional theory of text organization. *Text, 8*(3), 243–281.

Martin, James R. (2000). Beyond exchange: Appraisal systems in English. In Susan Hunston & Geoff Thompson (Eds.), *Evaluation in Text: Authorial Distance and the Construction of Discourse* (pp. 142–175). Oxford: Oxford University Press.

Martin, James R., & White, Peter R.R. (2005). *The Language of Evaluation*. New York: Palgrave.

Montague, Richard. (1969). On the nature of certain philosophical entities. *The Monist, 53*, 159–194.

Pander Maat, Henk, & Degand, Liesbeth. (2001). Scaling causal relations and connectives in terms of speaker Involvement. *Cognitive Linguistics, 12*(3), 211–245.

Pang, Bo, & Lee, Lillian. (2008). Opinion Mining and Sentiment Analysis. *Foundations and Trends in Information Retrieval, 2*(1–2), 1–135.

Partee, Barbara H., & Borschev, Vladimir. (2004). The semantics of Russian genitive of negation: The role and nature of perspectival structure. In Kazuha Watanabe & Robert B. Young (Eds.), *Proceedings of Semantics and Linguistic Theory (= SALT) XIV* (pp. 212–234). Ithaca, NY: CLC Publications.

Pit, Mirna. (2003). *How to Express Yourself with a Causal Connective: Subjectivity and Causal Connectives in Dutch, German and French*. Amsterdam: Rodopi.

Polanyi, Livia, & Zaenen, Annie. (2006). Contextual valence shifters. In James G. Shanahan, Yan Qu & Janyce Wiebe (Eds.), *Computing Attitude and Affect in Text: Theory and Applications* (pp. 1–10). Dordrecht: Springer.

Sanders, Ted. (1997). Semantic and pragmatic sources of coherence: On the categorization of coherence relations in context. *Discourse Processes, 24*, 119–147.

Sanders, Ted, & Sweetser, Eve (Eds.). (2009). *Causal Categories in Discourse and Cognition*. Berlin: Mouton de Gruyter.

Stubbs, Michael. (1986). 'A matter of prolonged field work': Notes towards a modal grammar of English. *Applied Linguistics, 7*(1), 1–25.

Trnavac, Radoslava, & Taboada, Maite. (2012). The contribution of nonveridical rhetorical relations to evaluation in discourse. *Language Sciences, 34*(3), 301–318.

von Fintel, Kai, & Gillies, Anthony S. (2010). *The subjectivity of conditionals in a new light*. Paper presented at the Annual Conference of the German Society for Linguistics (DGfS), Berlin.

Webber, Bonnie, Knott, Alistair, Stone, Matthew, & Joshi, Aravind K. (1999). Discourse relations: A structural and presuppositional account using lexicalised TAG *Proceedings of 37th Annual Meeting of the Association for Computational Linguistics* (pp. 41–48). College Park, Maryland.

White, Peter R.R. (2003). Beyond modality and hedging: A dialogic view of the language of intersubjective stance. *Text, 23*(2), 259–284.

Zwarts, Frans. (1995). Nonveridical contexts. *Linguistic Analysis, 25*(3/4), 286–312.

PART 1

Evaluation and Nonveridicality in Semantics

CHAPTER 1

(Non)veridicality, Evaluation, and Event Actualization: Evidence from the Subjunctive in Relative Clauses

Anastasia Giannakidou

1 Introduction: Referential Deficiency and Nonveridical Contexts

In recent works, veridicality and nonveridicality have been proposed to regulate a number of limited distribution phenomena such as NPI licensing, free choice indefinites (Giannakidou 1997, 1998, 1999, 2006, 2011b; Giannakidou and Quer 2013; Zwarts 1995, Bernardi 2001), mood selection and the so-called polarity subjunctive (Giannakidou 1998, 2009, 2011a, Quer 1998, 2001, 2009, Paducheva 1985, Marques 2004, 2010, Smirnova 2012), expletive negation (Yoon 2010), negator selection in Ancient Greek (Chatzopoulou 2012), the genitive of negation in Russian (Partee 1998, Borchev et al. 2008, Partee et al. 2012, Kagan 2009), to mention just some studies. These studies offer compelling evidence from a substantial number of languages that a big portion of limited distribution phenomena (known as *polarity*) are about referential deficiency (Giannakidou 1997, 1998)—or, 'low referentiality' (Partee 1998), 'referential vagueness' (Giannakidou and Quer 2013). Referentially deficient items (also known as 'weak' or anti-specific indefinites) favor generally nonveridical contexts.

The correlation of nonveridicality and referential deficiency has also been understood as *non-existence* e.g. for NPI-licensing in Chinese (Lin 1996) and Salish (Matthewson 1998). Matthewson (1998: 179), for instance, says that the NPI-determiners *ku ... a* and *kwel ... a* in St'at'imcet Salish "represent the notion of *non-assertion of existence*". Montague's own conception of veridicality (Montague 1969) relied on existence: if *I see a unicorn* is true, then a unicorn exists, hence *see* is veridical. Kamp (1999–2007: 6) talks about 'veridical perception' as "proper perception of the actual thing". Bhatt 1999 and Hacquard 2006 also talk about 'actuality entailment' when an event happened in the real world. My goal in the present paper is to address the relation of veridicality, existence, and actuality by studying a particular polarity item: the subjunctive relative clause. Examining this structure proves helpful not just from the perspective of veridicality, but also for understanding the role of the subjunctive.

 | DOI: 10.1163/9789004258174_002

I will argue that the subjunctive in the relative clause contributes a presupposition of epistemic uncertainty as to the existence of a referent for the NP it modifies, and I will call this *epistemic weakening*. Epistemic weakening can be done in a nonveridical epistemic space only—because only such a space allows for the possibility that a referent may not exist in the actual world. Epistemic weakening is a kind of *evaluation* (for more discussion see Giannakidou to appear). Overall, it is important to make the correlation between nonveridicality and evaluation, explored in great detail in the very important recent work of Trnavac and Taboada (2012).

TABLE 1 *Distribution of NPI, FCI, and any in nonveridical contexts*

	Environments	Any	Greek kanenas NPI	Greek free choice item
1.	Negation	OK	OK	*/#
2.	Questions	OK	OK	*/#
3.	Conditional (*if*-clause)	OK	OK	OK
4.	Restriction of *every/all*	OK	OK	OK
5.	(Non-antiadditive) DE Q	OK	??	??
6.	**Modal verbs**	OK, with FC	OK	OK
7.	**Nonveridical attitudes** (e.g. *want, insist, suggest, allow*)	OK, with FC	OK	OK
8.	**Imperatives**	OK, with FC	OK	OK
9.	**Habituals**	OK, with FC	OK	OK
10.	**Disjunctions**	*	OK	OK
11.	***isos/perhaps***	*	OK	OK
12.	***prin/before* clauses**	OK	OK	OK
13.	**Future**	OK, with FC	OK	OK
14.	***as if** clauses*	*	*	*
15.	Progressives	*	*	*
16.	Episodic perfective past sentences	*	*	*
17.	Positive existential structures	*	*	*
18.	Veridical attitudes (e.g. *believe, imagine, dream, say*)	*	*	*

Table 1 (from my earlier work) summarizes the empirical observation that limited distribution, referentially deficient expressions ('polarity items' such as negative polarity items, *any*, and free choice items) appear in nonveridical contexts.

Nonveridical contexts are contexts where the truth of a proposition *p* is open (i.e. *p* is *not* entailed or presupposed): questions, modal verbs and adverbs, imperatives, conditionals, the future, disjunctions, *before* clauses, and subjunctive selecting propositional attitudes such as *want, hope, suggest* are all nonveridical. Negative contexts are a subcase of the nonveridical: *not p* does not entail *p*, and we call them *antiveridical*. NPIs, FCIs, and *any* are admitted in nonveridical and antiveridical contexts, but are excluded in the last four rows, the veridical space.[1] In bold, we see nonveridical contexts that are not negative or downward entailing.

Giannakidou and Zwarts operate on a notion of nonveridicality that relies on truth, and the working question for our study here is: how exactly does veridicality correlate with existence? It is necessary to address this question because we hit upon the correlation at least three times, with: (a) the phenomenon of subjunctive in relative clauses; (b) the licensing of NPIs in determiner restrictions, where earlier work (Giannakidou 1998, 1999, Hoeksema 2008) showed that it depends not so much on monotonicity but on whether the restriction is non-empty; and (c) the non-licensing of NPIs and subjunctives with progressives:

(1) *O Janis **egrafe** olo to proi **kanena** grama.
The J. wrote.IMPERF.3sg all the morning **any** letter
'*John was writing any letter all morning.'

(2) *O Janis egrafe **ena** grama [pu **na** itan makroskeles].
The J. wrote.IMPERF.3sg **a** letter that Subj was long.
'John was writing a letter that was long.'

The subjunctive in Greek is expressed with the particle *na* (see Giannnakidou 2009, to appear, for discussion and references), and the subjunctive in the

1 For *any*, I adopt my earlier position that it is an NPI with a free choice implicature that gets cancelled in negative contexts (Giannakidou 1999, 2011a, Giannakidou and Quer 2013). The Greek NPI doesn't trigger this implicature and therefore never receives free choice readings. It is common crosslinguistically to tease NPIs and FCIs apart, but the 'fused' NPI is not that uncommon either (see Haspelmath 1997 for an overview).

relative clause is one of the polarity phenomena that have been discussed in the literature (Giannakidou 1998, Farkas 1985). The non-licensing of NPIs and the subjunctive with the progressive, that we see above, is surprising given the well-known accounts in the literature that render the progressive modal/intensional (Dowty 1979, Landman 1992, Sharvit 2003, Trnavac 2006, Boogart and Trnavac 2011). To appreciate the puzzle, note that NPIs and the subjunctive relative are otherwise licensed in modal and intensional contexts, as expected:

Modal intensional contexts with NPIs: Existential modals

(3) You may/can talk to any student.
(4) John could have talked to anybody.
(5) The committee should consider any of these candidates.

Modal verbs and volitional predicates

(6) I Ariaδni θa iθele na milisi me [opjonδipote/kanenan]
the Ariadne would like.3sg subj talk.1sg with FC-/NPI-
fititi.
student
'Ariadne would like to talk to any student.'

(7) Prepi na pendrefti enan andra [pou **na** exi pola
Must.2sg subj marry.3sg a man who subj have.3sg much
lefta].
money.
'She must marry a man who has a lot of money. (But we don't know if such a man exists.)'

(8) Thelo na agoraso mian obrela [pou **na** me prostatevi apo to kryo].
'I want to buy an umbrella that will protect me from the cold. (But I don't know if I can find such an umbrella.)'

(9) * I Roxani **idhe** enan andra [pu **na** exi pola lefta].
'Roxanne saw a man who had a lot of money.'

In (9) we see that without a nonveridical licenser, the subjunctive cannot be applied to the relative clause. So, the subjunctive in relative clauses is a licensed form, a polarity item. It appears in nonveridical contexts but not in progressives. But if progressives involve modality, and since all modal contexts are nonveridical (Giannakidou 1998, 1999) why don't we find NPIs and subjunctive relatives with progressives?

The answer will be that progressives, unlike modals, are veridical. Their veridicality arises because they make reference to *actual* events—albeit incomplete, partial ones. If I say *John was/is crossing the street*, then I, as a speaker, am committed to an event that I identify as John's event of crossing the street. Being committed to the event means that I know that John's crossing the street is (at least) partly realized in the actual world, the progressive is therefore veridical, and it is no surprise that it blocks NPs and the subjunctive.

Crucially, the progressive contrasts with *TRY* which allows NPIs and subjunctive relatives. We see this below, with the Greek verb *prospatho* 'try' in both perfective and imperfective:

(10) O Janis **prospathise/prospathuse** to proi na grapsi
The J. tried.perf.3sg/tried.imperf.3sg the morning subj write.3sg
kanena grama.
any letter
'John tried this morning to write a letter.'

(11) O Janis **prospathise/prospathuse** na grapsi ena grama
The J. tried.perf.3sg/tried.imperf.3sg subj write.3sg a letter
pu **na** itan makroskeles.
that SUBJ was long
'John tried this morning to write a letter that was.SUBJ long.'

These sentences contrast minimally with the ones in 1, 2 where the progressive blocks the licensing of *kanena* and the subjunctive. The contrast suggests that *TRY*, unlike the progressive, must be nonveridical—notice that it takes a subjunctive complement like nonveridical verbs do. This conclusion challenges the unification of TRY and the progressive (Sharvit 2003), and supports that the idea that TRY, unlike the progressive, does not involve necessarily physical action (Grano 2011). Kamp characterizes TRY as an operator of 'intentional activity', and part of the activity is understood as being 'in the head' (intentionality), not actualized or physical. I agree with these analyses, and capture TRY as an operator that conveys force (in the sense of Copley and Harley 2010, Giannakidou and Staraki 2013), i.e. it initiates an action path that may contain both purely mental, intentional acts (such as preparing for the event, making plans for it, etc.), as well as physical acts of realizing the specific event type embedded under TRY. This allows the speaker to still be uncertain about the actualization of the TRY event, hence TRY is nonveridical and allows for NPIs.

The paper goes as follows. In section 2, I lay out the basic ideas about mood selection and nonveridicality from my earlier work, in order to show that the subjunctive depends on a nonveridical licenser. Overall, I believe one can conceptualize the cases of selection as some kind of veridical and nonveridical agreement, with no semantic effect of the subjunctive itself. Then we move on to the subjunctive in relative clauses (section 3). Here the subjunctive has an evaluative, epistemic weakening affect. This effect is to express the speaker's attitude of uncertainty as to the existence of a referent. The discussion concludes with the progressive and TRY in section 4.

2 Mood Choice, (Non)veridicality, and Epistemic (Non)commitment

We start here with a commonplace observation: indicative is the mood of unembedded assertions, whereas the subjunctive is a 'dependent' mood, triggered by a higher element in the sentence. For instance, consider the following example from French:

(12) Le printemps est/*soit arrivé.
the spring is.IND/is.SUBJ arrived
'Spring has arrived'.

(13) a. Marc croit que le printemps est arrivé.
'Marc believes that spring has-IND arrived'
b. Marc veut que le printemps soit long.
Marc wants that the spring be-SUBJ long.
'Marc wants the spring to be long'.

We see that in the main clause, the subjunctive is impossible. When embedded, we say that the verb *croire* 'believe' selects the indicative, but *vouloir* 'want' selects the subjunctive. The choice here is a matter of selection in the sense that the use of a particular mood after a particular verb class is non-negotiable: an epistemic verb cannot appear with the subjunctive, and likewise a volitional cannot appear with the indicative. The patterns are quite robust across European languages (with the exception of Italian, see Giorgi and Pianesi 1997). I illustrate below with Greek, where the mood distinctions appear as particles external to the verb:

(14) O Pavlos nomizi oti/*na efije i Roxani.
the Paul thinks.3sg that.IND/that.SUBJ left.3sg the Roxani.
'Paul thinks that Roxanne left'.

(15) Thelo *oti/na erthi o Pavlos.
want.1sg SUBJ come.PNP.3sg the Paul.
'I want Paul to come'.

One of the central questions in the mood literature has been: why is the indicative the mood of unembedded assertions? And why is it selected by epistemic verbs, which are typically *irrealis* verbs? The choice of indicative with epistemic attitudes is inconsistent with the traditional *realis/irrealis* distinction, and indeed a fact that makes this distinction a non-starter. Traditional approaches to veridicality, such as e.g. Kartunnen 1971, Egre 2008—which identify veridical as 'true in the actual world'—are also challenged by the fact that verb meaning such as believe, think, dream select the indicative.

2.1 *(Non)veridicality: The Epistemic Substratum of Mood Choice*

In a number of works (Giannakidou 1994, 1998, 2009, 2011, to appear), I have been exploring the idea that mood selection is regulated by an epistemic version of (non)veridicality relativized with respect to individuals ('individual anchors'). Specifically, I have argued that the indicative reflects full commitment of an individual to a proposition (veridicality), whereas the subjunctive is selected when there is no full commitment (nonveridicality). Similar ideas in more recent literature say that "mood choice depends on the strength of epistemic commitment" (Smirnova 2012), or that "polarity subjunctives, unlike lexically triggered subjunctives, have the function to mark a high degree of epistemic uncertainty towards the proposition" (Aparicio 2012). This is my starting point here: mood selection is an epistemic phenomenon.[2]

A sentence, every sentence, is not true or false in isolation, but relative to an assessor, the *individual anchor* (Farkas 1992, Giannakidou 1998, 1999, 2011b). This means that every sentence is 'perspectival', and in an unembedded case, the sentence is true or false with respect to the speaker's perspective (see also

---

2 See Giannakidou 2011b and to appear for discussion of why the bouletic ordering approach to mood (Villalta 2008) fails to capture the correct correlations in mood distribution across languages. See also some comments in Portner and Rubinstein (to appear).

Harris and Potts 2009). To capture this idea of an individual's perspective, I used in Giannakidou 1997, 1998, 1999 the device of 'models of individuals'. Farkas 2003 uses the similar function "worldview". These models are epistemic spaces, i.e. sets of worlds, representing an individual's beliefs and knowledge:

(16) Epistemic model of an individual
A model M_E $(x) \in M$ is a set of worlds associated with an individual x representing worlds compatible with what x believes or knows.
GIANNAKIDOU 1999: 45

We can think of these models as the classical doxastic/epistemic functions we know from Hintikka's work, or as Kratzerian modal bases. Crucially, under normal circumstances, the epistemic models of individuals are *not* further structured by ordering sources—unlike modals, which typically are and therefore can only express full commitment in the *best, according to the ordering source*, worlds (see Giannakidou and Mari 2012 for recent detailed discussion of this). Commitment in a model means *universal truth in the model*, as is the case for an unembedded assertion. $M_E(s)$ represents the doxastic/epistemic status of the speaker.[3] A proposition *p* of an unembedded assertion will be evaluated as true or false with respect to this model:

(17) Truth in a model (= full commitment of an individual)
A proposition p is true in an epistemic model $M_E(x)$ iff $M_E(x) \subseteq p$:
$\forall w \, [w \in M(x) \rightarrow w \in \lambda w'. \, p(w')$

(18) a. John won the race.
b. $[\![$John won the race$]\!]$ = 1 iff $\forall w \, [w \in M_E(s) \rightarrow w \in \lambda w'.$ John won the race in w'$]$, where *s* is the speaker

This tells us that if the speaker decides in a context to truthfully assert the sentence *John won the race*, (s)he must be epistemically committed to the proposition the sentence conveys, i.e. she must believe that John won the race, which means that all worlds in her epistemic model are *John-won-the race* worlds. Hence: $M(s) \subseteq p$. Hence, unmodalized unembedded assertions expresses full speaker commitment, and are veridical:

3 The model remains a parameter of evaluation, and is not syntactically present (see my earlier work).

(19) Veridicality and Nonveridicality
(i.) A propositional operator *F* is veridical iff *Fp* entails or presupposes that *p* is true in some individual's model M(x); p is true in M(x), if $M(x) \subset p$; i.e., if all worlds in M(x) are p-worlds.
(ii.) If (i) is not the case, *F* is nonveridical.
(iii.) *F* is *anti*veridical iff *Fp* entails *not p* in some individual's model: iff $M(x) \cap p = \emptyset$.
GIANNAKIDOU 1998, 1999, 2011

A veridical modal space is homogenous, as we see—all worlds are *p* worlds. A nonveridical modal space, on the other hand, is not homogeneous: it contains *p* and *non-p* worlds:

(20) A modal space (a set of worlds) W:
(i.) Is *veridical* with respect to a proposition *p* just in case *all* worlds in W are *p*-worlds (*Homogeneity*).
(ii.) If there is at least one world in W that is a *non-p* world, *W* is nonveridical. (*Non-homogenous space*).

A nonveridical space is typically ordered by some other function (e.g. ordering sources of modals, desire as we see later), and this yields a partitioned domain. Nonveridical spaces are spaces where *p* and *not p* are live options, and propositions are non-resolved, decided, or *settled* (to use the phrasing from von Fintel and Gillies 2010).[4] Notice, crucially, that homogeneity and veridicality are not the same thing; this is so because the antiveridical space is homogenous: *not p*. Antiveridical spaces are *nonveridical*: when uttering a negative sentence, it is not the case that all worlds in the speaker's epistemic space are *p*-worlds. But believing or knowing *not p* does commit the speaker fully to *not p*.

4 See also Condoravdi's 2002 diversity principle, and Falaus's 'epistemic constraint' on PI *vreun* (cognate of *kanenas*) which is very similar, if not identical to nonveridicality: it requires that *vreun* appear in a sentence that "entails that the epistemic agent's doxastic alternatives include *non p*-worlds". Finally, the notion of 'undecidedness' suggested in a manuscript by Farkas (2003) is identical to (non)veridicality:

Let W_i be a set of worlds, and S a sentence with propositional content p,
(i) S is *positively decided* in W_i iff $W_i \subset p$. (ii) S is *negatively decided* in W_i iff $W_i \cap p = \emptyset$;
(iii) S is decided in S W_i iff either (i) or (ii); otherwise S is *undecided* in W_i.

Importantly, for this reason, negation in a main clause does not affect the mood: negation never triggers the subjunctive in an unembedded assertion. The subjunctive depends on partitioned, non-homogenous, nonveridical epistemic spaces.

Typically, volitional, future oriented, directive, and modal expressions (verbs, adverbs, the imperative, etc.), and the polarity licensing environments in Table 1 come with nonveridical spaces. Notice here also the use of NPIs with disjunction (21):

(21) I bike mesa **{kanenas/opjosdhipote} i** afisame to
either entered.3sg NPI/FCI OR left.1pl the
fos anameno.
light on
{Some person or other/ Anybody} could have come in OR we left the light on.

(22) *Bike mesa **kanenas/opjosdhipote ke (=and)** afisame to fos anameno.

(23) Did you see anybody?

Though questions seem common NPI licensers, the appearance of NPIs with disjunction (as opposed to conjunction) may strike one as not so common. However, we observe NPIs with disjunctions not just in Greek, but also in Romanian (Giannakidou 1994), and even English. In the example above we have *any*, with a free choice reading, but notice the example below, cited in Zwarts 1995 as a translation from Plato's *Protagoras and the Meno* [23: 146]:

(24) I hope no relative of mine *or any of my friends*, Athenian or foreign, would be so mad as to go and let himself be ruined by those people.

(*Any of my friends* is not in the scope of *no relative of mine*, another potential licenser). As Zwarts 1995 already noted, disjunction is nonveridical (*p or q* does not entail *p*, and does not entail *q*), but the conjunction is veridical (*p and p* entail both *p* and *q*), therefore the licensing of NPI should not come as a surprise if nonveridicality is the required property for licensing.

2.2 *Mood Selection Patterns: Dependency to Nonveridicality, but No Effect of Mood Itself*

Here I keep the discussion brief, as the topic has been discussed in detail in earlier works. The main selection patterns in Greek are as follows:

(25) *Indicative verbs*

assertives:	*leo*, 'say'; *dhiavazo*, 'read'; *isxirizome*, 'claim'
fiction verbs:	*onirevome*, 'dream'; *fandazome*, 'imagine'
epistemics:	*pistevo*, 'believe'; *nomizo*, 'think'
factive verbs:	*xerome*, 'be glad'; *gnorizo*, 'know'; *metaniono*, 'regret'
semifactives:	*anakalipto*, 'discover'; *thimame*, 'remember'

In the traditional 'realis' accounts, as I said earlier, it is impossible to explain why verbs like 'dream', 'imagine' would select the indicative, since clearly they do not imply truth in the actual world. However, these verbs opt for the indicative systematically, i.e., not just in Greek but also in most of the Romance languages. Importantly, factives in Greek as a class (cognitive as well as emotive) select the indicative.

In Giannakidou 1998, 1999, I argued that all indicative selecting verbs are veridical. For *x believes that p*, it must be the case that *x*, the main clause subject, is committed to the truth of the embedded proposition *p*, she believes it to be true. Consider the sentence below. Though the speaker might disagree, the subject believes *p* to be true. So, in the example below, it is Paul's epistemic model (i.e. the set of worlds compatible with what Paul believes) that is a subset of the worlds where *p* is true: M(Paul) $\subseteq$p. The speaker may believe or even know that what Jacob believes is false, but this is irrelevant for Paul's beliefs.

(26) $[\![$Jacob believes that Ariadne kissed Bill$]\!]$ = 1 iff
$\forall w\ [w \in M_E(\text{Jacob}) \rightarrow w \in \lambda w'.\ \text{Ariadne kissed Bill in } w']$

(27) Veridicality of the epistemic verb
If *believe* (*x, p*) is true in a context c, then $M_E\ (x) \subset p$ in c

(28) "*a* believes p" is true in w iff: $\forall w'$ in $Dox_a(w)$: p is true in w'
where $Dox_a(w)$ all the worlds that are compatible with what *a* believes
HINTIKKA 1969

So, *believe/think* expresses full commitment of the believer, and this makes them veridical: all worlds in M(Paul) are *p*-worlds. With *dream* and fiction verbs (*imagine, hallucinate*, etc. all indicative triggers), veridicality arises within the dream/fiction space: if *x dreams that p* is true then *p* must be true in the worlds compatible with *x*'s dreams.

(29) $[\![$Jacob dreamt that Ariadne kissed Bill$]\!]$ = 1 iff
$\forall w\ [w \in M_D(\text{Jacob}) \rightarrow w \in \lambda w'.\ \text{Ariadne kissed Bill in } w']$

(30) Truth in a dream space
A proposition p is true in a dream space $M_D(x)$ iff $M_D(x) \subseteq p$;
$M_D(x) \subseteq p$ iff: $\forall w\ [w \in M_D\ (x) \rightarrow w \in \lambda w'.\ p\ (w')]$.

So, when I dream or imagine something, as a dreamer, I am fully committed to the fictional reality of my dream. Fictional reality replaces the actual one. McCawley (1981) called these 'world creating' predicates for this reason. This can be understood as a kind of context shift: *dream* is veridical in the shifted context of the dreamer, and thus selects the indicative. Within the dream space, one can have moments of awareness that 'shift' her back to reality—as is the case, for instance, of being aware that one is dreaming. These can also be understood as model shifts (thanks to Oliver Bott for raising this question).

Factive verbs, as a class, are *strongly* veridical (Giannakidou 1999): they *presuppose* the truth of their complement; the sentence is part of the common ground, part of what speaker and hearer take for granted. So, the speaker's model, as well the subject's, only contain *p*-words:

(31) O Pavlos lipate pu efije i Roxani.
the Paul is-sad.3sg that left.3sg the Roxani
'Paul regrets that Roxanne left.'

(32) ⟦Paul regrets that Roxanne left⟧ = 1 iff
(i.) $\forall w\ [w \in M_E(\text{Paul}) \rightarrow w \in \lambda w'.$ Roxanne left in w']; and
(ii.) $\forall w\ [w \in M_E\ (\text{speaker}) \rightarrow w \in \lambda w'.$ Roxanne left in w']

Knowledge spaces are veridical: things that we know are true. All presuppositional, factive verbs are veridical and select the indicative (with the exception of *emotives* in some Romance languages, see Giannakidou to appear for a recent discussion).

It is important to recall that veridical verbs do not license NPIs, FCIs, or subjunctive relatives:

(33) a. *O Pavlos pistevi oti idhe {kanenan/opjondhipote}.
the Paul believe.3sg that saw.3sg NPI/FCI
*Paul believes that he saw anybody.

b. *Kseri oti aghorasa {kanena/opjodhipote} aftokinito.
know.3sg that bought.1sg NPI/FCI car
He knows that I bought any car.

c. *O Pavlos pistevi oti idhe mia gyneka pou na forai
Paul believes that he saw a woman [that SUBJ wear
kokino kapelo.
a red hat]

This correlation is found in most languages that possess NPIs, FCIs and subjunctive relatives (see e.g. Quer 1998 for Catalan and Spanish).

Now consider the verbs selecting subjunctive complements. These are the following:

(34) Subjunctive verbs

volitionals:	*thelo*, 'want'; *elpizo*, 'hope'; *skopevo*, 'plan'
directives:	*dhiatazo*, 'order'; *simvulevo*, 'advise'; *protino*, 'suggest'; *prospatho*, 'try'
modals:	*prepi*, 'must'; *bori*, 'may'
permissives:	*epitrepo*, 'allow'; *apagorevo*, 'forbid' (negative permissive)
negative:	*apofevgho*, 'avoid'; *arnume*, 'refuse'

Four are the core classes: volitional verbs, directives, negative verbs (including verbs of fear), and modals (epistemic, deontic, other flavors). It is clear that these verbs do not express certainty of the subject, but rather desire or wish, possibility, and more 'psychological' states such as fear, etc. These attitudes all involve epistemic uncertainty with respect to the outcome. Consider *want* as a representative case, but we also discuss *prospatho 'try'* at the end of the paper. The truth condition for *thelo* 'want' only requires that the intersection between M(x) and *p* be nonempty:

(35) a. O Pavlos theli na fiji i Roxani.
the Paul wants.3sg that leave.3sg the Roxani
'Paul wants that Roxanne leave.'

b. $[\![$Paul wants that Roxanne leave$]\!] = 1$ if
$\exists w\, [w \in M_E(\text{Paul}) \wedge w \in [w'. \text{Roxanne leave in } w']$

If *x wants p*, not all worlds in M(x) are *p*-worlds. In the doxastic model of the 'wanter' there are *p* and *non-p* worlds. *x wants p* requires that there is at least one world *w* in M(x) that is also a *p*-world. We can thus envision M(x) as partitioned into two sets, W1 and W2. W1 is the part that intersects with *p*. W2, is the part containing non-*p* worlds: therefore $W2 \cap p = \emptyset$:

(36)

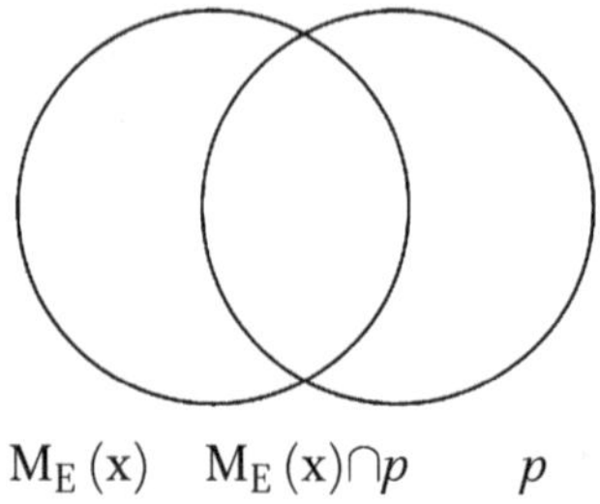

This places nonveridicality at heart of the truth condition for desire, and as I said, one can posit further psychological dimensions, as constraining ordering sources (e.g. bouletic, teleological, etc, as for example in Heim 1992). The important thing for mood choice is that a desire does not commit one to truth, and the choice to use subjunctive is determined by the epistemic non-commitment of the desirer. Overall, the important thing to retain is that nonveridicality arises whenever we have this partition within the epistemic model, and we have it with the other directive verbs such as "ask", "suggest", "hope" etc., as well as with modals, verbs of fear, and as I will argue in section 4, *try*.

This picture makes volitional and directive predicates epistemically very similar to disjunctions (that we discussed earlier). Subjunctive selecting verbs typically allow NPIs—in contrast to the indicative verbs that we saw earlier:

(37) I Ariaδni θa iθele na milisi me {opjonδipote/kanenan}
the Ariadne would like.3sg subj talk.1sg with FC-/NPI-
fititi.
student
'Ariadne would like to talk to any student'.

Overall, then, we see that veridicality and nonveridicality regulate mood choice in complement clauses and main clauses, as well as NPI licensing. In the complement clauses, the mood itself does not seem to contribute anything semantically—and as I argued in Giannakidou 2009, the mood particle is merely the place to introduce the lambda binder for the internal now. Depending on one's favorite theory of selection, one can simply say that, in selection, mood is a reflex of veridicality or nonveridicality marking, a kind of (non)veridicality agreement or concord with the higher, licensing element.

We can now proceed to address the role of subjunctive in relative clauses. We will see that in contrast to the selected subjunctive, the subjunctive in the relative clause actually has a semantic contribution: a presupposition of epistemic uncertainty.

3 The Subjunctive in Relative Clauses

3.1 *The Mood Alternation*

Typically, the subjunctive is allowed in the relative clause that modifies an indefinite QP which is in the scope of a nonveridical verb, e.g. *thelo* 'want' or *psaxno* 'look for':

(38) Theloume na proslavoume mia gramatea [pu **na** gnorizi
want.1pl subj hire.1pl a secretary that subj know.3sg
japonezika.]
Japanese.
We want to hire a secretary who knows Japanese. But it is hard to find one, and we are not sure if we will be successful.
Her name is Jane Smith.

(38') $\underline{\exists w\ [w \in M_E(s): \exists x \text{ secretary } (x, w)}\ \wedge$ speaks Japanese $(x, w) \wedge$ hire (we, $x, w)]$

This gives us a *de dicto*, narrow scope reading for the indefinite. There are worlds *w* where we find a secretary that speaks Japanese, but we do not know if the actual world will turn out to be a world with a secretary that speaks Japanese. Given our analysis of *want* earlier, the subjunctive statement says: there are doxastic alternatives *w* such that there is a secretary in *w* and she speaks Japanese. But there are also doxastic alternatives *w'* in M_E (s) where there is no such secretary, and it may turn out that the real world is one of those. So, we don't know, at the time of utterance, if there exists in the real world a secretary who speaks Japanese and that we can hire. Because we don't know that, the continuation *Her name is Jane Smith*, as indicated, is not permitted. The effect is similar to classical modal subordination.

Given this property of 'narrow scope', note that it is impossible to use the subjunctive without a nonveridical trigger:

(39) *I Roxani **idhe** enan andra [pu **na** exi pola lefta.]
(Roxanne saw a man who has a lot of money.)

In a positive veridical sentence, we are forced to talk about a man in the actual world; the subjunctive is impossible. With veridical propositional attitudes, again we have a bad result:

(40) *O Janis **pistevi/kseri** oti proslavame mia gramatea
The John believes/knows that hired.1pl a secretary.
[pu **na** gnorizi japonezika.]
that subj know.3sg Japanese
'John **believes/knows** that we hired a secretary who knows Japanese'.

The subjunctive in the relative clause appears also with negation:

(41) Dhen idha enan andra [pu **na** forai kokino kapelo.]
not saw.1sg a man that subj wear.3sg red hat
'I didn't see a man wearing a red hat'.

(41') $\underline{\forall w \in M(s)}: \neg\exists x\ [man(x,w) \wedge wear\text{-}red\text{-}hat\ (x,w) \wedge saw\ (I,x,w)$

Notice that the sentence is not generic, so we can't say it contains a modal operator (*pace* what is suggested by Partee 2008). Likewise, the genitive of negation in Russian is triggered in a purely episodic negation with exactly the same effect. Besides Greek and Romanian, this use of the subjunctive in relative clauses is found in other Romance languages and Russian (Borchev et al. 2007, Partee 2008, Kagan 2011).

Farkas 1985, in her dissertation on the Romanian subjunctive, characterized subjunctive relative clauses as 'intensional descriptions'. Given what we see here, clearly, the subjunctive triggering is not simply due to intensionality: veridical verbs are intensional but don't allow it, and negation allows it but is not intensional. In Giannakidou 1997, 1998, I suggested that the presence of the subjunctive indicates that "it is not known whether $\exists x$ [NP(x) & Relative clause (x)] exists".

The indicative relative (i.e. a relative clause without *na*) receives an interpretation independent of *thelo* "want", *de re*:

(42) Theloume na proslavoume mia gramatea [pu gnorizi
want.1pl subj hire.1pl a secretary that know.3sg
japonezika.]
Japanese
We want to hire a secretary that speaks Japanese.
OK: Her name is Jane Smith.
But I don't know if we'll find such a person.

Without subjunctive, the secretary exists in the actual world, the speaker has one in mind—as indicated in the logical form by adding the real world wo as an argument. In other words, the indefinite is interpreted 'specifically':

(42') $\exists x$ secretary(x, wo) $\wedge$ speaks Japanese (x, wo) $\wedge$ $\exists w \in \underline{M(s)}$ [hire (we, x,w)]

So, the speaker is certain that there exists an actual secretary who speaks Japanese, and the desire is to hire her. The uncertainty continuation *But I don't know if we'll find such a person*, as we see, is unacceptable. It appears then that the subjunctive-indicative alternation correlates with knowledge or non-knowledge of existence, and absence of subjunctive indicates existence in the actual world (or context). As a result, we cannot have referential definite descriptions being modified by subjunctive relatives:

(43) I Roxani theli na pandrefti {**enan**/***ton**} andra pu na
the R. want.3sg subj marry.3sg a/*the man that SUBJ
exi pola lefta.
has much money
'Roxanne wants to marry a man who has a lot of money'.

On the other hand, the subjunctive is *required* with verbs of creation: the speaker knows that there is no referent in the real world yet:

(44) Prepi na grapso mia ergasia [pu **na** ine pano apo 15
must.3sg subj write.1sg an essay that subj is more than 15
selidhes.]
pages
'I have to write an essay which has to be longer than 15 pages'.

(45) */#Prepi na grapso mia ergasia [pu ine pano apo 15 selidhes.]

Because the essay doesn't exist yet, I cannot use the indicative with creation verbs. Overall, then, it seems fitting to say that the use or not of *na* in the relative clause depends on what the speaker knows; in choosing *na*, the speaker signals that she is uncertain that a referent exists.

3.2 *The Subjunctive 'Evaluates': Epistemic Weakening*

So, the function of the subjunctive in the relative clause is to bring in the speaker's subjective point of view, in particular, her uncertainty about the existence of a value for the NP. I will call this *epistemic weakening* of the subjunctive. Epistemic weakening is both a nonveridical and evaluative effect in the sense that affects the strength of the initial evaluation of the sentence (see especially Trnavac and Taboada's 2012 conclusions, which I use as background here). The initial evaluation is the sentence without *na*, which conveys veridicality and certainty. Adding *na*, removes that certainty. But *na* can't introduce uncertainty on its own. Recall that without a nonveridical trigger, *na* is prohibited:

(46) I Roxani **idhe** enan andra [pu (***na**) exi pola lefta.]
'Roxanne saw a man who had a lot of money'.

The subjunctive has no effect here, and in fact it is unacceptable. Now, remember that we adopted a subjective stance on truth: every sentence is evaluated with respect to an individual and the main sentence is evaluated by the speaker. The speaker has a choice to use a subjunctive in the relative clause or not. In a positive unmodalized (veridical) sentence such as the one above, the speaker is committed to the existence of a man who has a lot of money. The subjunctive cannot be used to alter the speaker's commitments.

Trnavac and Taboada 2012, in a recent very insightful study, examine the interactions between nonveridicality and evaluative structure in corpora, and draw a number of useful conclusions. Two of these conclusions will be of relevance here: (a) they point out that a nonveridical device 'tampers with' the evaluative content of utterances, with the result of weakening the evaluation (TT: 2012: 316); and (b) nonveridical elements in the majority of cases modify polarity at the local level, i.e. level of the clause (TT: 2012: 317). Following up on these observations we can say that, although the use of the subjunctive itself in the relative clause cannot weaken the veridicality and create a nonveridical space, once in a nonveridical space, a speaker will choose to use the subjunctive to reflect her weakened certainty about the existence of a possible referent. (Recall that in the nonveridical context, the speaker also has the choice of indicative in case she is certain.)

I suggest to formulate this as the following presupposition:

(47) *Epistemic weakening* presupposition of the subjunctive in relative clauses [NP [SUBJ CP] will be felicitous in a context *c* iff:
There is at least one world *w* in M_E(speaker) such that it is not the case that ∃x NP(x) & CP(x) in *w*.

This presupposition excludes the subjunctive from a veridical space, since in this case *all* the worlds in M_E(x) would be worlds where the modified nominal receives a value, thus failing to meet the weakening presupposition. The same thing happens with veridical verbs, as we noted earlier: in every world, there is a secretary—maybe the same one, maybe different ones, it doesn't matter. Notice crucially that this shows that the phenomenon is not really about specificity, as one may think given the narrow scope observations, but about the speaker's commitment of existence. In choosing the subjunctive, the speaker simply doesn't have enough knowledge to support existence in all epistemic alternatives. She leaves the possibility open that there is a world with no value. With nonveridical verbs, we have *non-p* worlds, and in these worlds the indefinite may receive no value. By being partitioned into *p* and *non-p* spaces, nonveridical models thus satisfy the presupposition of the subjunctive.

This gives us a very simple account of the 'polarity', i.e. limited distribution, of the subjunctive in the relative clause: its distribution is restricted by the presupposition of epistemic weakening, and nothing special needs to be said regarding the polarity status of the subjunctive itself. I consider this to be an appealing result. And notice that, in agreement with Trnavac and Taboada, the effect is local: subjunctive weakening will impact the relative clause. However, notice also that the requirement is imposed on the non-local model, the speaker's—though since the models are not syntactically present, but mere parameters of evaluation, one could maintain that locality has a limiting effect only in syntactic objects. Clearly, locality in this syntactic sense is met, since *na* influences the relative clause.

We move on now to address one final puzzle: the non-use of the subjunctive in the progressive, but its use with *try*.

4 Nonveridicality, Event Actualization, and *Trying*

In this final section, we examine the impossibility of NPIs/subjunctive relative clauses with the progressive, and their well-formedness with TRY. I discuss the progressive and imperfective first (4.1) and show that the progressive is veridical because it involves physical realization, i.e. actualization of the specific event type described by the VP; I then compare the progressive with TRY (4.2), in order to show that the latter is nonveridical, i.e. it does not impose event actualization. The arguments will rely on recent work by Kamp (1999–2007), Grano (2011), and Giannakidou and Staraki (2013).

4.1 *The Veridicality of the Progressive: Knowledge of Partial Event Realization*

We start with the basic puzzle:

(48)

*O	Janis	**egrafe**	olo	to	proi	**kanena**	grama.
The	J.	wrote.IMPERF.3sg	all	the	morning	any	letter.

'*John was writing any letter all morning'.

(49)

*O	Janis	egrafe	**ena**	grama	[pu	**na**	itan	makroskeles].
The	J.	wrote.IMPERF.3sg	a	letter	that	Subj	was	long.

Intended: 'John was writing a letter that was long'.

In my earlier work, I claimed that the progressive is veridical, but given what we just said about the presupposition of the subjunctive, we have an obvious puzzle: if from *John was writing a letter* we cannot conclude that a letter exists in the actual world, the subjunctive should be OK. Additionally, there is very well-known literature that makes a case for a modal dimension in the progressive: Dowty 1979, Landman 1992 claim that the progressive is intensional (it involves *inertia* worlds and continuation branches), Sharvit 2003 modifies that analysis by restricting the event progression to *realistic* continuation branches; Trnavac 2006, Boogart and Trnavac 2011 posit a connection between imperfective aspect and modal, counterfactual readings, and epistemic modality, and much other work assumes a semantics of the progressive that involves *possible* completion in some branch or other as the event progresses (see Pinon 2008, Grano 2011 for more recent overviews). All these could be used to argue for a 'nonveridical' analysis of the progressive, but the subjunctive and NPI licensing facts require the progressive to be veridical, and entail some sort of action and existence.

Consider an explicitly modal approach to PROG, e.g. Sharvit's (2003):

(50) For any event e, property of events P, and world w, e $\in$ PROG(w)(P) iff:
  a. e is an event in w; and
  b. for any *realistic continuation branch* C for e relative to w, there is an event e′ and a world w′ such that ⟨e′, w′⟩ is in C and e′ $\in$ P(w′). (Sharvit 2003: 414)

The idea here is that in order to evaluate a sentence such as *Mary was crossing the street* (*when a bus hit her*), we build a continuation branch based on the evaluation world and the ongoing event given by the VP. We stay in the evaluation world until Mary gets hit by a bus, at which point we shift to a maximally similar world in which a bus does not hit her and *which is a reasonable option*, and continue to trace the progression of the event. Under normal circumstances, the continuation branch will contain an event in which Mary successfully crosses the street, and so the sentence is judged true. In a sentence like *Mary was landing on the moon* (*when the phone rang*), on the other hand, we have a non-realistic evaluation branch and therefore the sentence is judged to be false—or true only in a fictional/dream context.

The important thing is clause *a*, that an event (given by the VP) is physically realized in a world. This physical realization, although completion is lacking, suffices to give us veridicality: a rational speaker chooses to use PROG [*cross the street*] when she knows that there is an *actual*, ongoing event *e* of crossing the street. So, all worlds compatible with her beliefs, knowledge and perceptions, are worlds where the street is physically being crossed, though the event may not be completed. Likewise, in degree based approaches of the progressive (Piñón 2008), progressive events are realized, in the actual world, to a degree higher than zero. This again makes the progressive *actual.*

It appears, then, that when we consider events, the veridicality of the sentence correlates with actualization, and actualization is physical realization in the actual world of the event. The progressive is thus an actualization function —I will call it ACTUAL—that when it applies to VP creates veridicality:

(51) *Actualization operators are veridical*
(i.) When an eventuality *P* is *actualized, P* is at least partially physically realized in the actual world.
(ii.) Actualization happens with actualization functions (ACTUAL).
(iii.) Application of *ACTUAL* to *P* entails veridicality:
[x *ACTUAL* (*P*)] is true if: $\forall w\ [w \in M_E$ (speaker) $\rightarrow w \in \lambda w'.\ P(x)$ in $w']$.

ACTUAL refers abstractly to functions like the progressive (PROG), the perfective, and the past tense. In choosing any of these functions, the speaker knows that there is some physical realization of the event *P*. This knowledge renders the sentence with PROG veridical. This explains why the progressive patterns with the perfective past in being a bad context for NPIs, subjunctives, and other polarity items (recall Table 1). Lacking a result doesn't have any implications: an actualized event can be a complete one (perfective) or an incomplete, open-ended one (progressive).

In earlier work, I suggested a special definition for veridicality and nonveridicality for temporal operators:

(52) **Giannakidou 2002 (23):** *(Non)veridicality for temporal/interval operators*
Let F be a temporal/aspectual operator; t an instant or an interval.
(i.) F is *veridical* iff for Fp to be true at a time t, p must be true at a (contextually relevant) time $t' \leq t$. Otherwise F is *nonveridical.*
(ii.) If Fp is true of an interval t, then F is veridical iff for some and possibly all (contextually relevant) $t' \subseteq t$, p is true at t'. Otherwise, F is nonveridical.

Clause (i) was intended to capture veridicality of the past and nonveridicality of the future, and relied on p being true at a time prior to equal to the utterance time. This rendered the past veridical and the future nonveridical, but it required a difference definition for nonveridicality. This now doesn't seem necessary, since in (51), we rely simply on the veridicality of the speaker's knowledge. This seems to me a better analysis, not in the least because it allowed us to capture veridicality *globally*, as a property of sentences containing actualization operators. With *Past p*, the speaker knows that p is true, therefore the past is veridical. The future is not veridical, since at the time of utterance the speaker does not know p to be true (Giannakidou 1998, Giannakidou and Mari 2012, 2013, see also earlier work by Copley 2002).

Before closing this section, I wanted to address the 'modality' of the imperfective. In Greek, unlike English, progressive readings are conveyed with the imperfective aspect. This is typically the case in Romance and Slavic languages too. A recurring observation is that the imperfective also has modal uses, i.e. it is the form that allows counterfactual readings in conditionals (for Greek see Iatridou 2000, Giannakidou and Mari 2012), and allows modal readings with present imperfectives (including future readings, such as *O Janis fevgi avrio* 'for all I know, John is leaving tomorrow'). In recent, quite detailed work, Boogart and Trnavac 2012 suggest that languages differ with respect to how strongly their imperfectives are 'linked' to modality—and Boogart and Trnavac correlate this further with sequence of tenses: in languages with sequence of tense (Romance, Germanic), we have a "perspectivized" function of imperfective past tense in indirect speech, which is an intermediate step between "objective" (temporal, aspectual) use of imperfective aspect and "subjective" (modal) readings of imperfective aspect. Greek and Slavic, on the other hand, do not have sequence of tenses, and this would mean that the link to modality might be weaker in Romance languages, and that Greek in that respect is closer to Slavic languages. In other words, if the link between modality and progressive aspect in Greek is weaker, that could be part of the explanation why subjunctive does not occur with progressive in Greek. However, as far as I know, the distribution of the subjunctive in relative clauses doesn't differ much between Greek and the Romance languages, and Romance subjunctive is also not allowed with the progressive. Since there is no empirical difference, it becomes difficult to make the case for a correlation of the strength between modality and the imperfective, on the one hand, and NPI/subjunctive licensing on the other.

Finally, it is not entirely clear to me that the common observation that imperfective aspect conveys modality is correctly captured. Regarding the counterfactual readings, consider the following classical case:

(53) I Ariadne tha efevge tora.
The Ariadne FUT leave.imperf.past.3sg now.
Ariadne would leave now.
a. Ala dhen efije telika.
'But she didn't actually leave.'
b. Ke pragmati, ine sto treno.
'And indeed she is in the train.'

The counterfactual reading is cancellable. But not so with the past perfect:

(54) I Ariadne tha ixe fiji
The Ariadne FUT had.3sg left.PERF.past.
Ariadne would have left.
Ke pragmati, ine sto treno. '#And indeed she is in the train'.

So, the past perfect indeed compositionally conveys counterfactuality. But for the imperfective, it is reasonable to assume that the counterfactual reading is not a genuine compositional reading—in the sense that it is not derived from the meaning of past and imperfective. Rather, it is an implicature that we get because we are not using the *perfective* past. We can imagine the hearer thinking that if the speaker knew that Ariadne left, they would have used the perfective form, a stronger one which conveys completion of the event. They didn't, therefore the speaker must not know for sure that Ariadne left, hence the counterfactual inference. So, in this case too, the use of imperfective aspect correlates with speaker uncertainty (nonveridicality), but the uncertainty is created by pragmatic reasoning, and not from inherent nonveridicality of the imperfective.[5]

4.2 *TRY, (Non)veridicality, and Intentional Activities*

Prospatho 'try' contrasts with the progressive in that it allows NPIs and subjunctive relative clauses. We mentioned this at the beginning of the paper, recall the examples below, with the Greek verb *prospatho* 'try' in both perfective and imperfective version:

(55) O Janis **prospathise/prospathuse** to proi na grapsi
the J. tried.perf.3sg/tried.imperf.3sg the morning subj write.3sg
kanena grama.
any letter.
John tried this morning to write a letter.
Speaker bias: but he didn't manage to write a word.

(56) O Janis prospathise/prospathuse na grapsi ena grama
the J. tried.perf.3sg/tried.imperf.3sg subj write.3sg a letter
pu na itan leptomeres.
that was detailed.
John tried this morning to write a letter that was.SUBJ detailed enough.
Speaker bias: but he didn't manage to write anything close to that.

These sentences contrast minimally with the progressive ones where *kanena* and the subjunctive are blocked. The contrast suggests that *try*, unlike the progressive, must be nonveridical—notice that it takes a subjunctive complement like nonveridical verbs do—and challenges analyses unifying TRY with progressive (Sharvit 2003). The contrast seems to support the competing idea that TRY is an 'intentional activity' that involves both *mental* and physical action (Kamp 1999–2007, Grano 2011). Notice also that the uses of the NPI and the subjunctive relative clause impose a bias in the context for a non-realization reading (we return to this soon).

5 Crucially, the imperfective as GEN is indeed nonveridical (see Giannakidou 1995, 1997), since from "generally p" the speaker does not know if p is *actually* true. GEN may even be modal. As is obvious, this differing behavior of GEN (and the ensuing pattern of NPI-licensing) challenges the unification of the two uses of the imperfective, and makes it, in my view, undesirable to attribute them to a single semantics. In the view I sketched above, the imperfective can be understood as *non-perfective*, and in this sense it has a variety of uses, which need not be unified by a single overarching function.

The existence of the incremental theme has been central to the discussion of TRY. Sharvit (2003b) argues that *try* is different from *want*, in that it entails existence of the theme:

(57) a. John wanted to cut a tomato, but there were no tomatoes to cut.
b. John tried to cut a tomato, #but there were no tomatoes to cut.

(58) a. Mary wanted to push a cart, but there were no carts to push.
b. Mary tried to push a cart, #but there were no carts to push.
SHARVIT 2003: 405

She then goes on to say: "Intuitively, it seems that *try* differs from its cousins *want, expect, believe*, etc. in that it doesn't simply express an attitude of some individual toward some 'proposition', *but that it also expresses some activity* ... This required 'action' is extensional, in the sense that it has to go on in the actual world for the sentence to be judged true" (Sharvit 2003: 407). 'Extensional action' renders *try* an actualization operator, akin to the progressive. But then, the non-licensing of NPIs and subjunctive relatives with TRY becomes a problem.

But is TRY really an actualization operator? (I am using here TRY for the item crosslinguistically.) Grano 2011 suggests that *try* does not necessarily involve physical action and does not always imply the physical existence of the incremental theme. He offers the following cases; notice crucially the contrast with the progressives:

(59) John tried to find a book, but there was no book.

(60) a. John was eating an apple. → Part of the apple was consumed.
b. John tried to eat an apple. But there was no apple, so no apple was consumed.

(61) Context: John is severely injured and cannot move his arm:
a. # John was raising his arm.
b. John tried to raise his arm. (But he didn't.)

These examples are problematic for the assumption that *TRY* involves action like the progressive, and show that, although we tend to think of TRY as involving physical action, in fact it need not. According to Kamp (Kamp 999–2007: 1), TRY (as well as FAIL, SUCCEED) is a device for intentional activity, and is one of the cases that indicate "conceptual continuity which often exists between things we *intend* to find or do or make, and the events in the real world that result when we try to realize those plans and intentions." In *x TRY P*, where *P* is a predicate of events, an agent *x* has the intention or a plan to set a path for action that will count as P, but what Kamp seems to be saying is that there is a conceptual continuum between the plan/intention and the action—a continuum that includes pure intention as well as action. Grano 2011, likewise, proposes that *try* P, unlike the progressive, contains a preparatory phase of the event that need not involve physical action P, but just mental action (e.g. planning, etc.).

I will follow here Copley and Harley 2010 and Giannakidou and Staraki 2013 in capturing the conceptual continuum between intention/planning (mental action) and physical action as an action path characterized by *force*. Forces are, in the most obvious case, physical forces, i.e. contact forces that result in change in the spatiotemporal properties of the object (i.e. in movement or rest, etc). Forces, in this physical sense, can also be understood as 'tendencies' (in the sense of Aristotle, e.g. in *Physics*), or gravitational forces; but forces can also be *psychological forces*, i.e. desires, intentions, and, as Giannakidou and Staraki suggest, abilities. Psychological forces are not ontologically identical to physical forces: intentions are not physical themselves. Having a desire by itself does not necessarily entail acting on the desire—and I may well have desires that I know cannot be acted upon. So, although desires and intentions are forces, they do not involve action themselves, physical or mental, and are therefore nonveridical.

Kamp describes the difference between intentional verbs like *try* and pure volitionals as follows: "The situation is different with verbs such as *want, wish*, and *desire*. These verbs do not claim the existence of an intention, you can wish or desire to open the door without having an actual intention to that effect. [...] In the semantic contribution of the *to*-complements of these verbs, we do not want any intention at all, in particular we do not want the one that comes from the action verb" (Kamp 1999–2007: 63). In other words, *want* is a nonveridical verb without intention for action, but TRY is a novneridical verb with intention for action.

TRY is a device that triggers a transition from pure intention (psychological force) to an *action path*. The TRY path thus includes physical force, i.e. actions of an agent in order to materialize the intention, but also an initial stage of mental force where no physical action has taken place. If we go back to the injured person example, trying to raise her hand, we see that it is possible for a TRY-path to refer exclusively to this initial stage of intention, without physical realization at all. Likewise, the biased Greek examples with the NPIs focus the sentence almost exclusively to the initial stage of intention/preparation: the speaker imagines a situation in which John was sitting on his desk, maybe reading old letters that he wrote, thinking about what to write, making a mental map of what needs to be included or excluded, but not actually engaging in physical letter writing. Or maybe John put some scribbles on the paper, or words on the screen—material that in the view of the speaker (because of their mistakes, incoherence, or randomness), do not count as actual realization of 'write a letter'. So, part of the TRY path involves purely mental force, the intention to do P, and it is possible to override actualization as not really counting as trying P.

The progressive thus involves physical action, it is, as I said in section 4.1, an actualization operator. TRY isn't. Notice that the two contrast sharply also in cases of direct negation of the action:

(62) a. John *tried* to write a letter, but he didn't.
b. John *wanted* to write a letter, but he didn't.
c. #John was writing a letter, but he didn't.

(63) a. John *tried* to talk to Ariadne, but he didn't manage [to talk to Ariadne].
b. John *wanted* to talk to Ariadne, but he didn't manage [to talk to Ariadne].
c. #John was talking to Ariadne, but he didn't manage [to talk to Ariadne].

Try follows the nonveridical pattern with the verb *want*. But the progressive simply does not allow for the event not happening. I will briefly summarize this in the truth condition below, where TRY initiates a path for action that contains non-physical action:

(64) *Try* as force operator
$[[x\ try_{Force}\ (P)\ ]]$ is true at time t in w iff:
(i.) there is an action path characterized by the event predicate P;
(ii.) an action path is a sequence of actions S ($\langle s_{init}, \ldots \rangle$) in order to bring about P;
(iii.) The initial action s_{init} is pure intention to bring about P.

(65) *TRY is nonveridical*
TRY P does not imply that the speaker knows that P is at least partly realized.

In other words, TRY is not ACTUAL. The truth condition renders TRY does not attribute to the speaker the knowledge that P is physically realized, since, but clause (iii), TRY P includes a stage where the eventuality *P* has no physical dimension yet. We must conclude then, that a uniform analysis of TRY and the progressive, in terms of both comprising physical realization of an event is not desirable. Instead, we need to distinguish the two by acknowledging that TRY does not entail physical realization. This analysis renders TRY, in contrast to the progressive, nonveridical, and explains why TRY, unlike the progressive, is a licenser for NPIs and subjunctive relative clauses. At the same time, it explains why TRY is different from nonveridical volitional predicates such as *want, wish* which involve no intention, and therefore no force or action.

5 Conclusions

In this paper, we used NPIs and the subjunctive relative clause as a diagnostic for studying the relation between (non)veridicality, existence and event actualization. We found that veridicality and nonveridicality are fundamentally epistemic notions that appear to be able to capture the behavior of aspectual operators too, such as the progressive, the perfective, and the meaning of verbs like TRY. In these cases, veridicality and nonveridicality rely on the speaker's knowledge of whether an event is at least partially *actualized*, i.e. physically realized in the actual world. If an operator imposes knowledge of at least partial actualization, it is veridical. The progressive and the perfective are such operators. But intentional verbs like TRY are nonveridical because they allow a stage of pure intention in their truth condition, and are therefore not homogenous.

Another important finding was that that the subjunctive in the relative clause contributes *epistemic weakening*: a presupposition of epistemic uncertainty as to the existence of a referent for the NP it modifies. Epistemic weakening can be done in a nonveridical epistemic space only—because only such a space allows for the possibility that a referent may not actually (i.e. in the real world) exist. The weakening presupposition of the subjunctive in the relative clause supports the correlation between nonveridicality and evaluation, observed in the very important recent work of Trnavac and Taboada (2012). Just as predicted in that work, we found the subjunctive to 'tamper' with the strength of evaluation by weakening the speaker's convictions.

Acknowledgement

I wish to thank Rada Trnavac and Maite Taboada for inviting me to prepare this paper for the Workshop on *Veridicality, Evaluation, and Discourse Coherence*.

I am also very grateful for their detailed and helpful comments on a previous version of this manuscript, which helped me to re-direct the paper in the dimension of epistemic evaluation, which connects really nicely with their own work. Many thanks also to the audience of workshop for their feedback—especially to Hans Kamp for his very helpful suggestions and more recent discussions here in Chicago. Some of this material was presented at the TRAIT workshop on *Categories*, at the University of Wroclaw, Poland, and I wanted to thank that audience too for their insightful comments, especially Malte Zimmermann, Mikhail Kissine, and Oliver Bott. Many thanks also to Barbara Partee for continuing discussions on nonveridicality and the subjunctive relative clause, and to Tommy Grano, for discussions on the progressive and *try*.

References

Ambar, Manuela. 1999. "Infinitives vs. Participles". In Esthela Trevino e José Lema (eds.)*Semantic Issues in Romance Syntax*, Current Issues in Linguistic Theory. Amsterdam-USA: John Benjamins, pp. 1–20.

Aparicio, Helena. 2012. Polarity subjunctives, epistemic modals, and (non)veridicality. Ms. University of Chicago.

Bernardi, R. 2002. *Reasoning with Polarity in Categorial Type Logic*. PhD thesis, U Utrecht.

Bhatt, R. (1999). *Covert Modality in Non-Finite Contexts*. PhD. University of Pennsylvania.

Boogaart, R. and R. Trnavac 2011. "Imperfective aspect and epistemic modality". In Cognitive Approaches to Tense, Aspect, and Epistemic Modality. In Patard, Adeline and Frank Brisard (eds.), 217–248.

Borschev, Vladimir, Paducheva, E.V., Partee, Barbara H., Testelets, Yakov, and Yanovich, Igor. 2008. Russian genitives, non-referentiality, and the property-type hypothesis. In Formal Approaches to Slavic Linguistics: The Stony Brook Meeting 2007 (FASL 16), eds. Andrei Antonenko, John F. Bailyn and Christina Bethin, 48–67. Ann Arbor: Michigan Slavic Publications.

Chatzopoulou, K. 2012. *Negation in Greek: a diachronic perspective*. PhD thesis, U Chicago.

Condoravdi, C. 2002. Temporal interpretations of modals: modals for the present and modals for the past. In D. Beaver, S, Kaufmann, B. Clark and L. Casillas (eds.) *The Construction of Meaning*, 59–88. CSLI Publications, 2002.

Copley, Bridget. 2002. *The semantics of the future*, PhD thesis, MIT.

Copley, B. and H. Harley. (2010). An ontology for a force-dynamic treatment of events. Ms. Paris 8, and University of Arizona.

Dowty, David R. 1979. *Word Meaning and Montague Grammar. The Semantics of Verbs and Times in Generative grammar and Montague's PTQ*. Reidel, Dordrecht.

Espinal, M.T. 2002. Licensing expletive negation and negative concord in Catalan and Spanish. *Catalan Working Papers in Linguistics.*

Falaus, A. 2009. Polarity items and dependent indefinites in Romanian. Doctoral Dissertation, Université de Nantes.

Farkas, D.F. 1985. *Intensional Descriptions and the Romance subjunctive mood.* Garland, NY.

———. 2002. Extreme non-specificity in Romanian In: C. Beyssade, R. Bok-Bennema, F. Drijkoningen & P. Monachesi (eds.). *Romance Languages and Linguistic Theory 2000*. Amsterdam: John Benjamis, 127–151.

———. 2003. Notes on Mood. Lecture presented at ESSLI.

Von Fintel, K and A. Gillies. 2010. Must ... stay ... strong! Nat Lang Semantics (2010) 18: 351–383.

Giannakidou, A. 1994. The semantic licensing of NPIs and the Modem Greek subjunctive. In De Hoop H. et al. (eds) Language and Cognition 4:55–68, Yearbook of the Research Group for Theoretical and Experimental Linguistics, University of Groningen.

———. 1997. *The Landscape of Polarity Items*. Ph.D. thesis. U Groningen.

———. 1998. *Polarity Sensitivity as (Non)veridical Dependency*. Amsterdam and Philadelphia: John Benjamins.

———. 1999. Affective dependencies. *Linguistics and Philosophy* 22: 367–421.

———. 2001. The meaning of free choice. *Linguistics and Philosophy* 24: 659–735.

——— 2002. Licensing and sensitivity in polarity items: From downward entailment to nonveridicality. In: M. Andronis, A. Pycha & K. Yoshimura (eds.). *Proceedings of the Annual Meeting of the Chicago Linguistics Society* (= *CLS*) *38*. 29–53.

——— 2006. *Only*, emotive factive verbs, and the dual nature of polarity dependency. *Language* 82, 575–603.

——— 2009. The dependency of the subjunctive revisited: Temporal semantics and polarity. *Lingua* 119(12), 1883–1908.

———. 2011a. Nonveridicality and mood choice: subjunctive, polarity, and time. *Tense across Languages*, ed. by Renate Musan and Monika Rathert. Berlin: Mouton de Gruyter. 59–90.

———. 2011b. Negative polarity items and positive polarity items. In von Heusinger, Maienborn, and Portner (ed.), *Semantics: An international Handbook of Natural Language Meaning* (*second edition*). Berlin: Mouton de Gruyter. 1660–1711.

———, to appear. The epistemic basis of mood: selection, nonveridical weakening, and emotive verbs. To appear in *Tense, Mood, and Modality: New Perspectives on Old Questions*, ed. by Blaszack, J., D. Klinek-Jankowska, Kryzstof Mygdalski, and Anastasia Giannakidou. With Chicago University Press.

Giannakidou, Anastasia and Alda Mari. 2012. The future as epistemic and evidential: evidence from Greek and Italian. To appear in Lingua.

Giannakidou, Anastasia and Josep Quer. 2013. Exhaustive and non-exhaustive variation with anti-specific indefinites: free choice and referential vagueness in Greek, Catalan and Spanish. In press, Lingua.

Giannakidou, A. and E. Staraki, 2013. Ability, action, and causation: from pure ability to force. To appear in Mari et al. (eds), *Genericity*, OUP.

Giannakidou, Anastasia & Suwon Yoon 2011. Referential vagueness and negative polarity: evidence form Greek and Korean. To appear in CLS 38.

Giannakidou, Anastasia and Frans Zwarts. 1999. Temporal, aspectual operators and (Non)Veridicality. Ms.

Giorgi, Alessandra, and Fabio Pianesi. 1997. *Tense and Aspect: from Semantics to Morphosyntax*. Oxford University Press.

Grano, Thomas. 2011. Mental action and event realization in the semantics of *try*. SALT 21: 426–443.

Hacquard, V. (2006). *Aspects of Modality*. PhD thesis. MIT.

Harris, Jesse and Chris Potts. 2010. Perspective shifting with appositives and expressives. *Linguistics and Philosophy* 32: 523–552.

Haspelmath, Martin. 1997. *Indefinite Pronouns*. Oxford University Press: Oxford.

Heim, I. 1992. Presupposition projection and the semantics of attitude verbs. *Journal of Semantics* 9, 183–221.

Holton, David, Peter Mackridge, and Irene Philippaki-Warburton. 1997. *Greek: A comprehensive grammar of the modern language*. Routledge: London.

Hoeksema, J. 2008. There is no number effect in the licensing of negative polarity items: a reply to Guerzoni and Sharvit. *Linguistics and Philosophy* 31 (4):397–407.

Iatridou, Sabine. 2000. The grammatical ingredients of counterfactuality. *Linguistic Inquiry* 31: 231–270.

Kagan, Olga. 2009. Genitive of negation: a modal account. Ms. Hebrew University of Jerusalem.

Kamp, Hans. 1999–2007. Intentions, plans, and their execution: turning objects of thought into entities in the external world. Ms.

Kratzer, A. 1991. Modality. In Semantics: An International Handbook of Contemporary Research, edited by Arnim von Stechow & Dieter Wunderlich, pp. 639–650. Berlin: de Gruyter.

Klecha, P. 2011. The meanings of predictive expressions. Ms. University of Chicago.

Landman, F. 1992. The Progressive. *Natural Language Semantics* 1: 1–33.

Lee, Chungmin 1999. Types of NPIs and nonveridicality in Korean and other languages. In: G. Storto (ed.). *Syntax at Sunset 2* (= *UCLA Working Papers in Linguistics*) *3*, LA, CA.

Lin, Jo-Wang 1996. *Polarity Licensing and Wh-Phrase Quantification in Chinese*. Ph.D. Dissertation. University of Massachusetts, Amherst.

Marques, Rui. 2004. On the system of mood in European and Brazilian Portuguese. Journal of Portuguese Linguistics 3 (2004), 89–109.

———. 2010. On the selection of mood in complement clauses. in Hogeweg et al. *Crosslinguistic semantics of tense, aspect and modality*. Benjamins.

Matthewson, Lisa 1998. *Determiner Systems and Quantificational Strategies. Evidence from Salish*. The Hague: Holland Academic Graphics.

McCawley, James D. 1981. *Everything linguists always wanted to know about logic, but were ashamed to ask*. University of Chicago Press, Chicago.

Montague, R. 1969. On the nature of certain philosophical entities. *The Monist* 53, 159–194.

Paducheva, Elena V. 1985. *Vyskazyvanie i ego sootnesennost' s dejstvitel'nost'ju* (*The Utterance and its Correspondence with Reality*). Nauka, Moskow.

Partee, Barbara H. 2008. Negation, intensionality, and aspect: Interaction with NP semantics. In: S. Rothstein (ed.). *Theoretical and Crosslinguistic Approaches to the Semantics of Aspect*. Amsterdam: John Benjamins, 291–317.

Partee, Barbara H. & Vladimir Borschev 2004. The semantics of Russian genitive of negation: The role and nature of perspectival structure. In: K. Watanabe & Robert B. Young (eds.). *Proceedings of Semantics and Linguistic Theory (= SALT) XIV*, Ithaca, NY: CLC Publications, 212–234.

Partee, Barbara H., Borschev, Vladimir, Paducheva, Elena V., Testelets, Yakov, and Yanovich, Igor. 2011. Russian Genitive of Negation alternations: The role of verb semantics. Scando-Slavica 57.2: 135–115.

Piñón, Chris. 2008. Aspectual composition with degrees. In Louise McNally & Christopher Kennedy (eds.), Adjectives and Adverbs: Syntax, Semantics, and Discourse, 183–219. Oxford: Oxford University Press.

Quer, Josep 1998. *Mood at the Interface*. Ph.D. Dissertation. University of Utrecht.

———. 2001. Interpreting mood. *Probus* 13: 81–111. Quer, Josep. 2009. Twists of mood: the distribution and interpretation of the indicative and the subjunctive. *Lingua* 119: 1779–1787.

Rubinstein, Aynat, and Paul Portner. to appear. Mood and contextual commitment. Proceedings of SALT 22.

Sharvit, Yael (2003). "Trying to be Progressive: the Extensionality of Try", *Journal of Semantics* 20: 403–445.

——— (2003). Embedded Tense and Universal Grammar, *Linguistic Inquiry* 34: 669–681.

Smirnova, A. 2012. The semantics of mood in Bulgarian, To appear in CLS 48.

Trnavac, R. 2006. *Aspect and subjectivity in Modal constructions*. PhD thesis, Un. of Leiden.

Trnavac, Radoslava, and Maite Taboada. 2012. The contribution of nonveridical rhetorical relations to evaluation in discourse. In *Language Sciences* 34: 301–318.

Villalta, Elizabeth. 2008. Mood and gradability: an investigation of the Subjunctive Mood in Spanish. *Linguistics and Philosophy* 31:467–522.

Yoon, Suwon. 2010. *NOT in the Mood: the Syntax and Pragmatics of Evaluative Negation*. PhD thesis, U. of Chicago.

Zwarts, Frans. 1995. Nonveridical contexts. *Linguistic Analysis* 25, 3–4: 286–312.

CHAPTER 2

Have to, *Have Got to*, and *Must*

NSM Analyses of English Modal Verbs of 'Necessity'

Cliff Goddard

1 Orientation

A tremendous amount has been written about modal verbs in English and in other languages (e.g., Palmer 1986, 1990; Coates 1983; Frawley ed. 2006; Perkins 1983; Traugott 1989; Krug 2000; Warner 1993; Biber 2004; Bybee & Fleischman eds. 1995; Myhill 1995, 1996; Myhill & Smith 1992; Stubbs 1988: Ch. 8; van de Auwera & Plungian 1998; Fachinetti, Krug & Palmer eds. 2003; Depraetere & Reed 2007). We need not review this literature in any detail, but it will be helpful to highlight the differences in the assumptions and approach of previous work as compared with the NSM approach.

The mainstream research tradition, which can perhaps be traced to Lyons (1977), is based on classification. The meanings or uses of modal verbs are classified in terms of two principal dichotomies: (a) necessity vs. possibility and (b) deontic vs. epistemic. The first pair of concepts, as Huddleston and Pullum (2005: 55) point out, are "the key concepts of modal logic", reminding us of the extent to which the study of formal logic has shaped linguistic approaches to modal verbs. It is normally assumed by linguists that the meanings of the terms "necessity" and "possibility" are self-evident and require no further explanation. Huddleston and Pullum's explanation of the second pair of concepts is also representative of the mainstream: *epistemic* is "concerned with what is necessary or possible given what we know (or believe)", while *deontic* is "concerned with what's required or permitted ... [with] authority and judgement". Some analysts recognise an additional category of 'dynamic', particularly for certain uses of *can*. Another widely used term is 'root modality', which is used in place of either deontic (non-epistemic) or dynamic, or both.

Such classification schemes can be further elaborated in two ways: (a) by distinguishing different types or domains of necessity and/or possibility, e.g. objective vs. subjective, social vs. logical, participant-internal vs. participant-external, and (b) by adding scalar qualifications (such as strong, mild, or weak) to indicate different degrees of modal strength. Not surprisingly, a good

 | DOI: 10.1163/9789004258174_003

TABLE 1 *Semantic primes—English exponents*

I, YOU, SOMEONE, SOMETHING~THING, PEOPLE, BODY	Substantives
KIND, PART	Relational substantives
THIS~IT, THE SAME, OTHER~ELSE	Determiners
ONE, TWO, MUCH~MANY, LITTLE~FEW, SOME, ALL	Quantifiers
GOOD, BAD	Evaluators
BIG, SMALL	Descriptors
THINK, KNOW, WANT, DON'T WANT, FEEL, SEE, HEAR	Mental predicates
SAY, WORDS, TRUE	Speech
DO, HAPPEN, MOVE, TOUCH	Actions, events, movement, contact
BE (SOMEWHERE), THERE IS, BE (SOMEONE'S)~BELONG, BE (SOMEONE/SOMETHING)	Location, existence, possession, specification
LIVE, DIE	Life and death
WHEN~TIME, NOW, BEFORE, AFTER, A LONG TIME, A SHORT TIME, FOR SOME TIME, MOMENT/IN ONE MOMENT	Time
WHERE~PLACE, HERE, ABOVE, BELOW, NEAR, FAR, SIDE, INSIDE	Space
NOT, MAYBE, CAN, BECAUSE, IF	Logical concepts
VERY, MORE	Intensifier, augmentor
LIKE~AS~WAY	Similarity

Notes: · Primes exist as the meanings of lexical units (not at the level of lexemes). · Exponents of primes may be words, bound morphemes, or phrasemes. · They can be formally complex. · They can have combinatorial variants (allolexes, indicated with ~). · Each prime has well-specified syntactic (combinatorial) properties.

deal of the conventional literature is devoted to attempting to clarify these classifications, to debating the merits of alternative systems, and to grappling with cases that do not fit neatly or cleanly into the system. (For recent reviews of the terminology, see Nuyts 2006; Depraetere & Reed 2007, 277–280.)

The NSM approach (Wierzbicka 1996; Goddard 1998; Goddard & Wierzbicka eds. 2002; and other works) differs from the mainstream in two related ways. First, the NSM approach does not attempt to classify meanings (from the outside, as it were), but to paraphrase them. An NSM explication for a sentence like *I must ring my mother*, for example, attempts to "say the same thing" in a paraphrase composed of maximally simple, intelligible, and translatable words (semantic primes), thereby laying bare the semantic content of the original sentence. Second, no specialist or technical terms are allowed in formal NSM semantic explications, on the grounds that to do so inevitably leads to unacceptable abstractness and obscurity. In the main body of this chapter, I propose explications (systematic reductive paraphrases) for sentences like *I must ring my mother*, *I have to ring my mother*, and *I've got to ring my mother*. The explications will be phrased exclusively in a subset of NSM semantic primes. Semantic primes are a mini-lexicon of 65 putatively indefinable meanings, listed in Table 1.

Table 1 is presented in its English version, but comparable tables have been drawn up for many languages, including Russian, French, Spanish, Chinese, Japanese, Malay, Korean, Lao, Mbula, and East Cree, among others. Cross-linguistic research suggests that semantic primes have lexical exponents in all or most languages, and equally that they can be combined according to a common mini-grammar which has analogues in all or most languages (Goddard & Wierzbicka eds. 1994, 2002; Peeters ed. 2006; Goddard ed. 2008). To the extent that expressions composed in semantic primes are transposable across languages the NSM metalanguage can serve as a stable and essentially language-neutral medium for cross-linguistic semantics. There is a large body of descriptive empirical work in the NSM framework on many aspects of lexical and grammatical semantics, with literally hundreds of published explications. Key references and important collective works, in addition to those already mentioned, include the following: Harkins and Wierzbicka eds. (2001)

and Wierzbicka (1992, 1997, 1999, 2006a). Additional references can be found at the NSM homepage: http://www.griffith.edu.au/humanities-languages/school-languages-linguistics/research/natural-semantic-metalanguage-homepage.

The NSM explications in this study consist of a series of components phrased entirely in the metalanguage of semantic primes. It can be observed that some words in the explications (in particular, the verbs) adopt variant forms as required by the rules of English grammar; for example, verbs shift to a past tense form in contexts where there is a prior time reference. Likewise, grammatical function words such as complementising *to* (with WANT) appear freely as required by English grammar. These morphological features, and, indeed, the normal English word order, are not essential parts of the Natural Semantic Metalanguage, but simply aspects of its English-specific instantiation. When an explication is transposed into Chinese or Russian, for example, these particular features would disappear and be replaced by others appropriate to the language concerned. Despite these variations, however, the meaning expressed by each component is preserved under translation. More detail on the grammar of the NSM metalanguage is available in Goddard and Wierzbicka eds. (2002) and Goddard ed. (2008).

The validity of NSM explications can be tested on the basis of two main conditions. The first is substitutability in a broad sense: explications have to make intuitive sense to native speakers when substituted into their contexts of use, and to generate the appropriate entailments and implications. The second condition is well-formedness: they have to be framed entirely in semantic primes or molecules[1] and conform to the syntax of the Natural Semantic Metalanguage. In addition, explications have to conform to a coherence condition. In other words they have to make sense as a whole, with appropriate chains of anaphora, co-reference, causal links, etc. In relation to the substitutability condition, NSM semantics makes extensive use of linguistic corpora, and, more recently, of internet searches using the Google search engine (though these have to be undertaken with due caution, cf. Goddard 2009; Wierzbicka

1 NSM theory recognises that in certain areas of the lexicon it is not possible to paraphrase meanings exclusively into combinations of semantic primes. Rather it is necessary to employ certain relatively simple, but still complex, word-meanings in combination with semantic primes. For example, when explicating physical activity verbs such as *eat* and *walk* (Wierzbicka 2009b; Goddard 2011) it is necessary to employ 'mouth' and 'feet' as semantic molecules. No semantic molecules are necessary for the purpose of this chapter.

2009a).[2] Though there are some heuristics, there is no mechanical procedure for NSM analysis. Published explications, including those proposed in the present chapter, have usually been through a dozen or more iterations over several months.

Coming now specifically to the topic of modal verbs, it should be noted that NSM accepts one modal expression—CAN—as a universal semantic prime. NSM researchers have long claimed that CAN is both semantically irreducible (i.e. impossible to paraphrase in simpler terms) and universally expressible in the languages of the world (whether as an auxiliary verb, an inflectional category, a modal particle, or whatever). As discussed in previous work (e.g. Wierzbicka 1996), this position clashes with the standard assumption that there is a sharp distinction between the 'can of possibility' (e.g. *Something bad can happen*) and the 'can of ability' (e.g. *I can't do it now*). Against this, NSM researchers have pointed out that this supposed distinction is one which the great majority of languages from around the world, including English, refuse to recognise in their lexicons. English is typologically typical in having a single expression that is employed in both contexts. In the NSM view, then, the word CAN means the same thing in both 'possibility contexts' and 'ability contexts'. I will not discuss this issue further here.[3] The main points for our purposes are that CAN is claimed to be a semantic prime and that it is therefore available to be used in explications for other modal expressions. In particular, the combination CAN'T NOT (DO) will be a recurring one in our explications, roughly corresponding to the notion of necessity.

Before we begin, three final observations should be made. First, there are significant semantic differences between modal meanings and usage even among European languages, such as German, English, French, and Scandinavian languages (cf. Palmer 1986, 33–39). Second, it is well known that the modal system of English has been in a state of considerable flux over the past three or four centuries. In the area of obligation/necessity, an important aspect has been the rise, first, of the semi-modal *have to* and, much later, of the construction *have got to* (Visser 1963–1973, cited in Tagliamonte 2004; Krug 2000, 53–115; Smith 2003; Mair & Leech 2007). Third, certain differences in patterns and

2 All the examples adduced in this chapter are naturally occurring, taken from personal observation by the author, from the Cobuild Wordbank of English, or from the internet. Sources for publicly available examples are given the Appendix.

3 This is not to deny that some uses of English *can* are language-specific, cf. *I can see your house from here ≈ I see your house from here.*

frequencies of modal usage have been documented between British English and American English (e.g., Myhill 1996; Jankowski 2004; Smith 2003; Mair & Leech 2007) and between more localised regional varieties. Australian English too has its own characteristic usage patterns (Collins 2005). For the time being, however, I am going to assume that these differences are matters of usage preferences (perhaps linked with different communicative styles in their respective speech communities). I will attempt to develop semantic explications that are applicable across standard English generally in the mainstream Anglo-English communities of discourse.

2 *Have To*

Although *have to* is a semi-modal rather than a full modal verb in the grammatical sense, it is an appropriate place to start for several reasons. First, according to corpus studies, in deontic uses *have to* is the most common of the various modals of necessity and obligation found in contemporary English (Myhill 1996; Krug 1998, 2000; Smith 2003). Second, the apparent equivalents of English *must* in other European languages are (seemingly) often closer to *have to* than to *must*, both in grammar and in meaning. German *müssen*, for example, has the same range of tense options as a regular verb, and it lacks the heightened sense of urgency or importance conveyed by *must*, as opposed to *have to*; cf. *Aber er müsste* 'but he had to'. The third reason is that there is a convenient starting point for discussing the semantics of *have to* in NSM terms—namely, the proposal that it simply means CAN'T NOT (DO).[4]

I would like to argue that while CAN'T NOT (DO) is certainly one crucial component of the meaning expressed by *have to*, there are also two other aspects to it. First, there is a component that presents the CAN'T NOT component as part of an objective situation, cf. Palmer's (1990, 113–114) intuition that *have to* expresses "neutral or circumstantial necessity"; and second, there is a component that presents the CAN'T NOT component as potentially 'knowable'. A schema for *have to* with 'verbs of doing' is given in [A].

4 Some NSM work (e.g. Goddard 2000; Wierzbicka 1998) has used the expression *have to* in semantic explications, on the assumption that it was a portmanteau for CAN'T NOT. This assumption is now rejected. Using *have to* in semantic explications also creates translation problems in languages such as Russian, which have several non-identical near equivalents (cf. Gladkova 2007), and in languages like Yankunytjatjara (Goddard 1996), which have no equivalent to *have to*.

[A] *Someone X has to do something (VP):*
  a. it is like this:
  b.   this someone X can't not do something (VP)
  c. someone can know this

The rationale for the three-part structure will become clear as we consider examples. Consider an affirmative first-person present-tense example, like (1a) below, noting that as well as implying some kind of objective or circumstantial necessity, the sentence conveys the impression that the speaker is pretty confident that he or she can fulfill the requirement. If the speaker had any significant doubts about it, then an alternative like (1b) would usually be more appropriate.

(1a) *I have to finish this before 5:00.*
(1b) *I'm supposed to finish this before 5:00.*

Sentence (1a) can be explicated as shown in [B] below. The framing clause ("it is like this: --") in (a) conveys an objective perspective. It presents what follows as a 'situation'.[5] There are two interconnected aspects to this situation: (b) its content 'I can't not do this', and (c) the fact that 'someone can know this'. The combined effect of these components seems to model or mimic both the content and the tone of the original sentence.

[B] *I have to finish this by 5:00.*
  a. it is like this:
  b.   I can't not do this [finish this by 5:00]
  c. someone can know this

For the examples considered so far, it might seem that the component (c) could come in a simpler form than the proposed 'someone can know this'. It might seem that it could be phrased not in terms of potential knowability, but in terms of the subject's actual knowledge; e.g. as 'someone knows this'. To see the need for the 'can know' formulation, consider a sentence like *I didn't know that I had*

5 In the expression 'it is like this', the word 'it' is a substantive (or quasi-substantive) manifestation of semantic prime THIS. NSM theory hypothesises that the semantic prime THIS can occur universally not only in specifier-type positions, but also as an independent nominal (Goddard & Wierzbicka 2008).

to do it, where the *have to* clause is embedded under a main verb that implies a lack of knowledge. For example:

(2) *Probably one of the most common comments that you get from many taxpayers is: 'I didn't know that I had to do it'.*

This sentence can be explicated as in [C] below. The whole explication is transposed into the past tense (see below), but the main point of relevance is the (c) component. Formulated as it is, in terms of potential knowability, the component is both semantically acceptable and intuitively plausible.

[C] *I didn't know that I had to do it*
a. I didn't know (at that time) that it was like this:
b. I couldn't not do it
c. someone could know this

Questions such as *Do I have to ...?* are also very common in corpora. A similar approach will work with these sentences. For example, someone who asks *Do I have do it?* is asking, essentially, 'Is it like this?—I can't not do it, someone can know this'.[6]

Now consider some imperative sentences. As shown in [D1] and [D2], the same scheme of explication works for them.

(3a) *You have to come inside now.*
(3b) *You have to believe me.*

[D1] *You have to come inside now.*
a. it is like this:
b. you can't not do this [come inside now]
c. someone can know this

[D2] *You have to believe me.*
a. it is like this:
b. you can't not think about it like this [i.e. believe me]
c. someone can know this

6 It would take us too far afield to cover the semantics of questions adequately; see Goddard (2002) for an NSM approach to yes/no questions.

Notice that in the sentence being explicated in [D2], the verb (*believe*) is a verb of thinking, rather than a verb of doing. The scheme also works for verbs of happening, as shown in [E].

[E] *You don't have to die of breast cancer.*
a. it is not like this:
b. this can't not happen [you die of breast cancer]
c. someone can know this

Now let us consider some past-tense examples, where, as noted by many observers (e.g. Palmer 1990, 114), there is often a factive implication. Sentence (4a), for example, strongly implies that the subject did leave her children behind; (4b) strongly implies that she did vacate the room; (4c) strongly implies that the astronauts did the paperwork after they got back. As shown by the material in parentheses, to deny this implication induces anomaly.

(4a) *She had to leave her children behind* (*?but she didn't*).
(4b) *She had to vacate the room* (*?but she didn't vacate it*).
(4c) *The moon astronauts had to do paperwork when they returned* (*?but they didn't do it*).

Past-tense sentences like those in (4) above can be modelled by adding a past-time reference adjunct to the top component, so that 'it is like this: --' becomes 'it was like this at that time (some time before I say this): --'. Naturally (in English), this also triggers a change in the morphological tense of the subsequent components. The factive implication follows naturally, given that there was a situation in which the subject couldn't not undertake the action and that this was knowable at the time. Some sample explications follow.

[F1] *She had to leave her children behind.*
a. it was like this at that time (some time before I say this):
b. she couldn't not do this [leave her children behind]
c. someone could know this

[F2] *The moon astronauts had to do paperwork when they returned.*
a. it was like this at that time (some time before I say this)
b. the moon astronauts couldn't not do something [do paperwork when they returned]
c. someone could know this

The semantics of tense cannot be dealt with fully here, but the main point for our purposes is simply that the framing component 'it is like this: --' is compatible with an explicit temporal adjunct.[7]

Some past-tense sentences, such as those in (5a) and (5b) below, require a slightly more elaborate treatment. They are 'subjectivised', depicting how a protagonist was thinking about a situation. As one might expect, this is particularly common with a first-person subject, as in personal narratives, reminiscences, and the like.

(5a) *I had to find a job. I couldn't use father's money anymore.*
(5b) *They felt that homosexuals must not remain second-class citizens forever, and someone had to do something.*

As shown in [G], it is a simple matter to model the subjective framing of such a sentence, while the content of the modal expression remains the same. Notice also how the explication conveys the same determined tone as the original sentence.

[G] *I had to find a job.*
a. I thought like this at that time (some time before I say this):
b. it is like this:
c. I can't not do this [find a job]
d. someone can know this

Turning now to sentences in which *have to* appears in the future tense, it appears that in many cases the modal content is also subjectivised. Consider sentences like:

(6a) *I'll have to finish this by 5:00.*
(6b) *You'll have to do it tomorrow.*

7 As a matter of detail, it can be noted that most "present tense" sentences lack any such time specification. That is to say, a sentence like *I have to do it* is "timeless", just as a sentence like *This is big* is timeless. The former does not mean the same as 'I now have to do it' (which would imply a contrast between conditions as they are now, and conditions at some other time), just as the latter does not mean the same as 'this is now big' (which would imply that at some other time it was not big).

In natural text, examples like these are often introduced by expressions such as "Well, in that case …", or by a conditional such as "If I'm going to have time …", or by an epistemic expression such as *I guess* or *I suppose*—i.e., they typically occur in contexts where the speaker's judgement is provisional, tentative, or conditional. Often the speaker appears to be thinking it through as he or she speaks. Some examples follow.

(7a) *He'll probably want to play, but I'll have to monitor how he feels.*
(7b) *Unfortunately, I've misplaced my son's list, so I'll have to do it all over again.*
(7c) *Looks like I'll have to order carefully because so many of the dishes incorporate pork, but a couple of things look appealing.*
(7d) *Guess I'll have to wait until Ian and Sofie find me another house.*

According to explication [H], sentences like these are subjectivised relative to the corresponding versions with plain *have to*. They represent the content of a *have to* sentence as the speaker's current point of view:

[H] *(In that case), you'll have to do it tomorrow.*
a. I think like this now:
b. it is like this:
c. you can't not do it tomorrow
d. someone can know this

The claim is then, that in such contexts the future tense morphology does not correspond to future time reference in a literal sense. From an inspection of corpus examples, it appears that the great majority of future-tense subject sentences with *will have to* are of this subjectivised kind. This is not to say that plain future-tense sentences, referring simply to future obligations, are impossible. They are not, as shown by the following examples, but they seem to be comparatively rare.

(8a) *If I want to stay here for more than three months, I'll have to make a short trip to New Zealand, or somewhere else close, to get my visa renewed.*
(8b) *In the future, people will have to use videoconferencing to meet, because international travel will be too expensive.*

Plain future sentences can be explicated using the same approach as we used with past-tense sentences; shifting the time-reference of the top clause to the future (triggering concomitant morphological changes to the subsequent components).

[I] *In the future, people will have to use videoconferencing to meet.*
a. in the future (i.e., at some time after I say this) it will be like this:
b. people can't not do something [use videoconferencing to meet]
c. someone can know this

I have argued in this section that sentences with *have to* share a semantic invariant, which can be captured as follows: a situational frame ("it is like this: --"), a component stating that the subject "can't not do (think, say, etc.) something", and a component representing this content as knowable ("someone can know this"). In addition, the interpretation of many *have to* sentences is subjectivised in the sense that the semantic content of *have to* appears as an implied thought or attitude attributed to a protagonist.

Whether the knowability component implies actual knowledge by the subject of the sentence is determined contextually according to overall semantic plausibility. Some rough generalisations are possible with reference to the person category of the subject, the tense of the verb, etc. For example, declarative past-tense sentences with first-person or third-person subjects generally support the inference that the subject actually had such knowledge. This inference does not work, for obvious reasons, with interrogative counterparts of such sentences. With second-person subjects, "someone can know this" generally does not imply that the subject had the knowledge, not only for imperatives but even for declaratives, because it is not very likely that the speaker would want to attribute certain knowledge to an addressee. The overall plausibility of the inference to actual knowledge can also be influenced by factors such as the epistemic phrases and adverbs, and, in the case of embedded clauses, the nature of the matrix verb.

I hope to have shown how the invariant semantic of English *have to* can be captured in a substitutable reductive paraphrase.

3 *Have Got To*

From a formal point of view, the expression *have got to* (*'ve got to*) is closely related to *have to*, and on this basis we can also expect their meanings to be similar. There is an intriguing puzzle in the fact that unlike *have to*, *have got to* (*'ve got to*) lacks tensed forms.

Many sentences with *have got to*, particularly when the verb depicts an action, sound urgent, seeming to imply that something has to be done soon. For example:

(9a) *I've got to go.*
(9b) *I've got to finish this by 5.*
(9c) *You've got to listen to me.*
(9d) *You've got to help me.*

On inspecting a large number of examples, however, one sees counterexamples, even with action verbs. For example:

(10a) *'Twould be nice to give Pigeon his swansong in the World Cup, but the selectors have got to do what is best for the team.*
(10b) *You've got to remember that voting is not compulsory in America.*

Also, the form *'ve got to* is often used in giving advice, and there may be no clear time reference in mind for the projected action.

(11a) *You've always got to be positive. I'm not the only person to go through these situations. You've got to think about it. You've got to take time and have a strong family behind you as well, which I do.*
(11b) *"That's the way, young Robbie", the Premier recalled Keating as saying: "In this life you've got to go out to stand in the middle of the freeway and defy them to run you down". "And that's what you have got to do", Carr said.*

I propose that the semantic component in question does not relate to the urgency of the action in the sense of something that must be done soon. Rather it relates to the pressing nature of what is being said (from the speaker's point of view). This appears as component (d) in the explications below, which caps the explication with the speaker's comment that "I/you can't not think about this now". This component makes the meaning expressed sound pressing and immediate. It also ties the utterance to the present, which may explain why the *have got to* locution lacks past and future tense forms.

[J1] *I've got to go now.*
a. it is like this:
b. I can't not do this [go now]
c. someone can know this
d. I can't not think about this now

[J2] *You've got to help me.*
a. it is like this:
b. you can't not do this [help me]
c. someone can know this
d. you can't not think about this now

Consistent with these explications is the fact that a sentence like *I've got to mow the lawn* is well suited to a 'one-off' situation, such as when the speaker is talking about the immediate situation, but is less common and less felicitously used to convey a generic or habitual obligation. (My thanks to Peter Collins for this observation.)

The same explicatory format works for stative or durative predicates too, if the reference to "do something" in component (b) is switched to "be like this".

[K] *You've got to be strong.*
a. it is like this at this time:
b. you can't not like be this [strong]
c. someone can know this
d. you can't not think about this now

4 *Must*

Must is usually compared with *have to*, but *must* has no tense forms, which would be very puzzling if there was hardly any semantic difference between them. Some writers have suggested that *must* implies greater speaker involvement than *have to* (Coates 1983, 33), or that it is more subjective (Lyons 1977; Perkins 1983), participant-internal (van der Auwera & Plungian 1998), or 'discourse oriented' (Palmer 1990). As far as I know, however, there have been no attempts to explain how such putative semantic differences might be correlated with the grammatical differences between the two expressions.

We need to distinguish several different contexts for the use of *must*. The easiest and most intuitive place to start is with what I will term "personal" deontic uses—i.e., when one particular person issues a *must* utterance with a view to influencing someone (possibly him or herself) to do something. I will deal with these below, then turn to what I call "public directives", such as the use of *must* on public signs, in policy documents, and so on.

4.1 *"Personal" Deontic Uses*

Unlike their counterparts with *have to*, personal deontic sentences with *must* clearly seem to imply the speaker's wanting. For example, one says things to oneself like *I must call my mother today* or *I must pay that bill* to urge oneself on and to remind oneself, as it were, that I really want to do it. The implication that 'I want to do it' is strong enough that it induces anomaly to simultaneously deny it, as in (12a), compared with *have to* in (12b). Another interesting property of deontic *must* is that it is incompatible with *maybe*, as shown in (13). *Must* also usually seems to imply a higher degree of importance or seriousness than *have to*.

(12a) ?*I must do it, but I don't want to.*
(12b) *I have to do it, but I don't want to.*
(13) ?*Maybe you must come inside now.*

I would suggest the following explications. The lack of the "it is like this" component (and its replacement by an "I want" perspective) is consistent with the view that *must* sentences are not as 'objective' as *have to* sentences. Note that the proposed explications do not involve any provision for time reference. This accounts for the lack of tensed verb forms.

[L1] *I must call my mother today.*[8]
 a. I want to do something [call my mother today]
 b. it will be bad if I don't do it
 c. I can't not do it

[L2] *Must pay IPrA fee by 15 April* (a note to myself):
 a. I want to do something [pay my IPrA fee by 15 April]
 b. it will be bad if I don't do it
 c. I can't not do it

When the subject is in the second person, the explication also works well. The combination of the speaker's wanting ("I want you to do"), the element of seriousness ("it will be bad if you don't do it"), and the message that "you can't

8 It may be worthwhile at this point to recall that an explication is not a description of reality, but a paraphrase of the speaker's meaning. Sometimes a speaker who thinks, for example, *I must call my mother*, actually does not want to call his or her mother. This doesn't prevent the speaker from saying to him or herself 'I want to do it'.

not do it" seems to model the insistent or demanding quality of such utterances quite nicely.

[M1] *You must come inside now*:
  a. I want you to do something [come inside now]
  b. it will be bad if you don't do it
  c. you can't not do it

[M2] *You must believe me*:
  a. I want you to think about it like this [i.e. believe me]
  b. it will be bad if you don't think about it like this
  c. you can't not think about it like this

It might be thought that this style of explication would not work for uses of *must* in social routines, such as *You must try some of my pie*, but it still seems appropriate once we take into account the rhetorical exaggeration of such sentences.

The content of the proposed explications accounts for the otherwise curious fact that *must* sentences are incompatible with *maybe*, cf. **Maybe you must come inside now*. This follows because one aspect of the message conveyed by *must* is that 'I want (you) to do it', and it would not make sense for a speaker to express uncertainty (via *maybe*) about what he or she wants.

A well-known difference between *must* and *have to* concerns how they respond to negation. A sentence like *You don't have to come*, for example, does not impose any obligation on the addressee: rather, it says that there is no such obligation. A sentence like *You mustn't come*, on the other hand, does impose an obligation—an obligation not to come. The explications below show how this works semantically:

[N1] *You mustn't come*:
  a. I want you not to do something [come]
  b. it will be bad if you do it
  c. you can't do it

[N2] *(I) Mustn't grumble*:
  a. I want not to do something [grumble]
  b. it will be bad if I do it
  c. I can't do it

These examples of personal deontic *must* have had first- and second-person subjects. *Must* also commonly occurs with third-person subjects, primarily in what I will term public directives and public pronouncements. Often in these contexts there is no obvious personal deontic source. This has led some observers to the view that sometimes *must* simply expresses "neutral necessity" (Palmer 1990, 113–115), which would mean that it overlaps semantically with *have to*. In my view, however, it is possible to paraphrase these apparently neutral uses in such a way as to preserve a distinction between *must* and *have to*, and at the same time show the relationship between the personal (deontic) and public uses of *must*.

4.2 Must *in Public Directives*

Must often appears on public signs and notices, in official directives in memos and policy documents, and in public statements by commentators and experts. For example:

(14a) *All visitors must report to the school office.*
(14b) *Staff travelling overseas* **MUST** *forward a form "Request For Approval to Travel On Official University Business" (A8) to Accounts Payable.*
(14c) *Applicants must be over 18.*

I suggest that such expressions differ from personal uses of deontic *must*, insofar as they depend on special cultural presuppositions. Public signs, for example, presuppose the existence of some authorities with the power to make binding rules about how people can act in the places in question. Cultural assumptions like these are not part of the message expressed by a public directive itself, but they are part of the 'semiotic scaffolding' needed to interpret the message properly.

For example, the message in (14a) above appeared on a notice displayed near the front gate of my son's primary school. In my view, the content of the message can be explicated as in [O]. Overall, it is very much the same as for regular deontic *must*, except that component (a) is phrased as "someone in this place wants them to do something" (rather than "I want them to do something", as it would be in a personal deontic usage). Part of the idea is that public signs are deictically tied to their location (in this case, of course, the words *visitors* and *school* are spatial words).

[O] *All visitors must report to the school office.*
a. when people visit this place, someone in this place wants them to do something [report to the school office]
b. it will be bad if they don't do it
c. they can't not do it

An observer from a very different culture to our own (a hunter-gatherer society, for example) would find it hard to understand the content of explication [O], even if this hypothetical cultural outsider understood the meanings of words like *school* and *office*. This is because the message takes for granted the idea that a school is a special place, regulated by its own local authorities, such as the school principal and the Education Department (and similarly for hospitals, airports, etc.).

As for organisations, they are analogous to places in some ways, but an organisation is primarily a collective entity, made up of the people who are its staff, along with their established ways of doing things. Generally speaking, there is a boss or some similar source of authority who is in a position to lay down, or at least give backing to, internal regulations. At my university, one finds sentences with *must* occurring profusely in statements of university policies and procedures. The example in (14b) above concerns the need for staff to lodge an A8 form with approval signatures and itinerary information, prior to any official travel. It can be explicated as follows:

[P] *Staff travelling overseas **MUST** forward a form "Request For Approval to Travel On Official University Business" (A8) to Accounts Payable.*
a. when people working in this place want to travel overseas, someone in this place wants them to do something [forward an A8 form to Accounts Payable beforehand]
c. it will be bad if they don't do it
d. they can't not do it

Given that we can recognise assumptions about the existence of people in authority in institutions and organisations, other "official-sounding" sentences, such as Kempson's (1977, 73), *The report you send in must be as simple as possible*, should not be a problem.

4.3 Must *in Public Pronouncements*

A somewhat different class of public uses of *must* are public pronouncements by expert commentators and political figures. They are typically found in newspapers, on television and in other media, and seem to be directed to the "public at large".

(15a) *A first step is that Australia must recognise its indigenous languages.*
(15b) *Lecturers must block extremism.*
(15c) *Social Scientists Must Help Policy Makers Respond to Climate Change, Report Says.*

Sentences like these are embedded in culture-specific genres that presuppose interpretative assumptions such as the importance of public debate and the existence of a public space in which experts and other interested parties are entitled to make pronouncements ('calls') in the interests of the public good. We understand that such sentences express a public message from an important person of some kind. If we assume the existence of cultural scripts spelling out these assumptions, it becomes plausible that the content of these *must*-sentences follows a similar pattern as for regular deontic *must*. For example:

[Q] *Australia must recognise its indigenous languages.*
someone says this:
a. I want people in Australia to do something [recognise its indigenous languages]
b. it will be bad if they don't do it
c. they can't not do it

A similar class of examples are quasi-generic sentences such as *101 books you must read before you die*, which appear in magazines or newspapers, heading lists, or feature articles that give recommendations from an expert of some kind. Similar usage is found in derived expressions like *a must-see musical, a must-read book, a must-have fashion*, and in the expression *It's a must.*

5 Review and Prospectus

This chapter has proposed a set of NSM explications, or reductive paraphrases that, as I see it, give an intuitively satisfying account of the different nuances of meaning that separate the main English modals of necessity. I have sought to show how aspects of the explications correlate with the different grammatical properties of the various expressions. The explications are framed in a formal and highly constrained metalanguage. In this final section I will recap the main claims and findings and consider some broader issues.

Let us review the following pair of explications, noting that the combination CAN'T NOT (DO)—roughly equating to necessity, is found in both. From an intuitive point of view, the presence of the "it is like this" frame in [R] corresponds to the objective quality of *have to,* while the presence of "I want" in [S] corresponds to the subjective quality of *must*. The [S] explication includes a reference to negative consequences, correlating with the perceived greater seriousness of *must*.

[R] *You have to tell him the truth:*
a. it is like this:
b. you can't not do this (tell him the truth)
c. someone can know this

[S] *You must tell him the truth:*
a. I want you to do this (tell him the truth)
b. it will be bad if you don't do it
c. you can't not do it

From a grammatical point of view, the fact that the framing expression "it is like this" in [R] is compatible with a temporal specification allows such sentences to be transposed into past and future tenses, while the absence of a similar option in [S] is consistent with the lack of tense options for *must*. It has been shown that the difference in interpretation under negation (i.e., that *You don't have to* ... denies obligation, whereas *You must not* ... imposes an obligation not to do something) falls out naturally from the proposed explications. It has also been shown that the explications account for a range of distributional facts, such as the relative oddness of *must* in sentences like *I ?must/have to do it, but I don't want to* and *Maybe you ?must/have to do it*.

As for the contrast between *have to* and *have got to* (*'ve to*), I have proposed that for the latter, the extra component 'I/you can't not think about this now' be added to explication [R]. This accounts for an additional sense of urgency attaching to such sentences, while at the same time tying the sentences to the speech context, which helps to account for their lack of past- and future-tense options.

Comparing the two explications above, it will be clear that neither of the two main English necessity modals (*must* and *have to*) is simply an intensified version of the other. Despite the impression one has that *must* expresses a stronger message than *have to*, the relationship is not a truly scalar one. Rather, the semantic configuration of each verb is qualitatively different. The impression of different degrees of strength derives from the nature of the qualitative differences.[9]

The present study is confined to a selection of modals of necessity in present-day English. Future work should extend the analysis to modal expressions in other languages, taking into account that modal meanings can be expressed in

9 *Should* is sometimes positioned as a "weak" marker of obligation or deontic necessity, but the semantic content and structure of *should* is quite different from both *have* and *must*. I would advance the following explication for *You should apologise*: '(a) I think like this: it will be good if you do this [apologise], it will be not good if you don't do it, (b) if someone thinks about it well, they can think the same'. The only alignment with *must* and *have to* is the component 'it will not be good if ...', which partly aligns with 'it will be bad if ...' for *must*.

various ways, such as by particles, adverbs, and by full verbs, rather than modal verbs or verbal auxiliaries. In my view, the prospects must be rated as good, since NSM is a proven technique for cross-linguistic semantics (cf. Harkins & Wierzbicka eds. 2001; Peeters ed. 2006; Goddard ed. 2008). In particular, the reductive paraphrase technique allows for much better delicacy and precision than approaches which rely on abstract labels and scales.

Another important project would be an extended exploration into the culture-historical evolution and development of the English modal system. On general principles, one would expect the distinctive and high-frequency modal verbs of English to be connected somehow with aspects of Anglo culture, i.e. with the social values and characteristic modes of social interaction found in mainstream English-speaking culture. In cross-linguistic perspective, it is surely a striking fact that some languages, such as the languages of Europe, have elaborate and highly grammaticalised systems of modal verbs, while other languages (such as Australian Aboriginal languages, for example) not only have no modal verbs, but generally seem much less concerned with expressing modal-like meanings across the board.

At a more fine-grained level of detail, it should be possible to inquire into the different "modal profiles" of particular languages. Wierzbicka (1998, 269–271) has made a case that the German-specific modal *dürfen* 'be allowed to' does a lot of culture-related "work" in German discourse—work which can be linked with widespread social attitudes in German-speaking society. Is there any cultural-historical explanation for the fact that English developed a contrast between the "strong" modal meanings expressed by *must* and *have to*, whereas German, for example, gets by with a single modal *müssen* (cognate with *must*, but apparently closer in meaning to contemporary English *have to*)? As noted by a number of scholars (Myhill 1996; Biber 2004; Burridge 2002), one would expect changes in the modal system to be a sensitive indicator of changes in societal attitudes and interactional styles. Investigating these factors may help bring to light ways in which social and cultural changes can motivate or drive processes of language change.

Interestingly, according to historical corpus studies (e.g. Myhill 1996; Krug 2000), *have to* and *have got to* have extended their frequencies greatly in recent times, while concomitantly deontic *must* has been on the decline, especially in interpersonal contexts. In view of the explications presented in the present study, it is tempting to hypothesise, with Smith (2003, 263) and others, that the increasing "democratisation of discourse" and the increased value placed on individual freedom of action have contributed to this decline. The message expressed by *must* smacks too much of "personal pressure" to be appealing to modern sensibilities (Wierzbicka 2006b). The more objective and quasi-factual mode of presentation of *have to* seems much less personally confronting: objective factors—*have to* seems to say—leave you with no choice. The added urgency conveyed by *have got to* (*'ve got to*) also seems to chime with the time-pressure of the late twentieth century.

Much more work remains to be done on these and other questions in the contrastive study of modality—across different varieties of English, across different languages, or across different historical periods. To make progress, however, will require a more sensitive and precise method of semantic description than that provided by conventional systems of categorising modal meanings.

In the framework of the present volume, it should be pointed out that the expression of modality, and its analysis through explications, should be considered part of the study of evaluation, as modal expressions convey evaluative meaning. This study shows how modality can be studied within a different theoretical perspective than, for instance, that of Giannakidou or Moeschler (this volume), where mood and negation (and modals) are part of a larger concept of nonveridicality.

Acknowledgements

The chapter has had a long gestation. The explications were developed in collaboration with Anna Wierzbicka. For corpus work and valuable suggestions I am grateful to my research assistant Vicki Knox. I would like to thank Qian (Jennifer) Zhu, with whom I had valuable discussions about contrastive modal semantics of English and Chinese. I received helpful feedback from Brian Byrne and Peter Collins. Needless to say, any remaining faults are my own responsibility. This research was supported by the Australian Research Council.

Appendix: Sources of Examples

The other examples are from personal observation.

(2) Joint Statutory Committee of Public Accounts and Audit, 28/07/06, Hansard.
(4a) http://www.wareenvillage.org/ss_amey.html, accessed 30/01/09.
(4b) http://chuculain.livejournal.com/, accessed 30/01/09.
(4c) http://www.cynical-c.com/?p=7168, accessed 30/01/09.
(5a) http://australiannetwork.com/livingenglish/stories/ie-ep37/htm, accessed 30/01/09.

(7a) Cobuild Word Bank of English.
(7b) http://humans.scienceboard.net/?m=200708, accessed 1/04/09.
(7c) http://www.donrockwell.com/index.php?showtopic=3083&pid=38393&mode=threaded&start=, accessed 1/04/09.
(7d) http://pjf.id.au/blog/?count=5&position=91/, accessed 1/04/09.
(10a) http://www.alphamagazine.com.au/archives/2007/02/pigeons_last_ro.php, accessed 2/08/07.
(10b) ABC radio morning 4/08/07.
(11a) Soccer star Harry Kewell, discussing his attitude to recovering from serious injury. http://news.ninemsn.com.au/article.aspx?id=143325/, accessed 1/04/09.
(11b) Former NSW Premier Bob Carr, 22 May 2002, http://www.steptothefuture.com/page.php?id=3&nid=11, accessed 2/08/2007.
(15a) Aboriginal lawyer Noel Pearson, in an opinion piece in *The Australian* newspaper, 10/03/2007.
(15b) BBC news headline, attributed to UK Universities Secretary John Denham, 17/09/07; http://news.bbc.co.uk/2/hi/uk_news/education/6998418.stm.
(15c) Chronicle of Higher Education, http://chronicle.com/daily/2007/09/2007091403n.htm.

References

Biber, Douglas. "Historical patterns for grammatical marking of stance: A cross-register comparison." *Journal of Historical Pragmatics* 5, no. 1 (2004): 107–136.

Burridge, Kate. "Changes within Pennsylvania German grammar as enactments of Anabaptist world view." In *Ethnosyntax*, 207–230. Oxford: Oxford University Press, 2002.

Bybee, Joan, and Suzanne Fleischman, eds. *Modality in Grammar and Discourse*. Amsterdam: John Benjamins, 1995.

Coates, Jennifer. *The Semantics of the Modal Auxiliaries*. London: Croom Helm, 1983.

Collins, Peter. "The modals and quasi-modals of obligation and necessity in Australian English and other Englishes." *English world-wide* 26, no. 3 (2005): 249–273.

Depraetere, Ilse, and Susan Reed. "Mood and modality in English." In *The Handbook of English Linguistics*, 269–290. Oxford: John Wiley and Sons, 2007.

Fachinetti, Roberta, Manfred Krug, and Frank Palmer, eds. *Modality in Contemporary English*. Berlin: Mouton de Gruyter, 2003.

Frawley, William, ed. *The Expression of Modality*. Berlin: Mouton de Gruyter, 2006.

Gladkova, Anna. "Semantic analysis of several Russian modal verbs." Presentation at NSM Semantic Workshop, Australia National University, Canberra, April 2007.

Goddard, Cliff. *Pitjantjatjara/Yankunytjatjara to English Dictionary*. Revised 2nd ed. Alice Springs: Institute For Aboriginal Development, 1996.

———. "'Cultural scripts' and communicative style in Malay (Bahasa Melayu)." *Anthropological Linguistics* 42, no. 1 (2000): 81–106.

———. "Yes or no? The complex semantics of a simple question." In *Proceedings of the 2002 Conference of the Australian Linguistic Society* (2003): http://www.als.asn.au.

———. "*Not taking yourself too seriously* in Australian English: Semantic explications, cultural scripts, corpus evidence." *Intercultural Pragmatics* 6, no. 1 (2009): 29–53.

———. *Semantic Analysis*. 2nd ed. Oxford: Oxford University Press, 2011.

Goddard, Cliff, ed. *Cross-Linguistic Semantics*. Amsterdam: John Benjamins, 2008.

Goddard, Cliff, and Anna Wierzbicka. "New semantic primes and new syntactic frames: 'specificational BE' and 'abstract THIS/IT.'" In *Cross-Linguistic Semantics*, 35–58. Amsterdam: John Benjamins, 2008.

Goddard, Cliff, and Anna Wierzbicka, eds. *Semantic and Lexical Universals—Theory and Empirical Findings*. Amsterdam: John Benjamins, 1994.

———. *Meaning and Universal Grammar—Theory and Empirical Findings. Volumes I and II*. Amsterdam: John Benjamins, 2002.

Harkins, Jean, and Anna Wierzbicka, eds. *Emotions in Crosslinguistic Perspective*. Berlin: Mouton de Gruyter, 2001.

Huddleston, Rodney D., and Geoffrey Pullum. *A Student's Introduction to English Grammar*. Cambridge: Cambridge University Press, 2005.

Jankowski, Bridget. "A transatlantic perspective of variation and change in the English deontic modality." *Toronto Working Papers in Linguistics* 23, no. 2 (2004): 85–113.

Kempson, Ruth. *Semantic Theory*. Cambridge: Cambridge University Press, 1977.

Krug, Manfred. "*Gotta*—The tenth central modal in English? Social, stylistic and regional variation in the British National Corpus as evidence of ongoing grammaticalization." In *The Major Varieties of English*, 177–191. Växjö: Växjö University Press, 1998.

———. *Emerging English Modals: A Corpus-Based Study of Grammaticalization*. Berlin: Mouton de Gruyter, 2000.

Lyons, John. *Semantics: Vol. 2*. Cambridge: Cambridge University Press, 1977.

Mair, Christian, and Geoffrey Leech. "Current changes in English syntax." In *The Handbook of English Linguistics*, 318–343. Oxford: John Wiley and Sons, 2007.

Myhill, John. "Change and continuity in the functions of the American English modals." *Linguistics* 33 (1995): 157–211.

———. "The development of the strong obligation system in American English." *American Speech* 71, no. 4 (1996): 339–388.

Myhill, John, and Laura A. Smith. "The discourse and interactive functions of obligation expressions." In *Modality in Grammar and Discourse*, 237–292. Amsterdam: John Benjamins, 1992.

Nuyts, Jan. "Modality: Overview and linguistic issues." In *The Expression of Modality*, 1–26. Berlin: Mouton de Gruyter, 2006.

Palmer, F.R. *Mood and Modality*. Cambridge: Cambridge University Press, 1986.

———. *Modality and the English Modals*. 2nd ed. Harlow, England: Longman, 1990 [1979].

Peeters, Bert, ed. *Semantic Primes and Universal Grammar. Evidence from the Romance Languages*. Amsterdam: John Benjamins, 2006.

Perkins, Michael R. *Modal Expressions in English*. London: Frances Pinter, 1983.

Smith, Nicholas. "Changes in the modals and semi-modals of strong obligation and epistemic necessity in recent British English." In *Modality in Contemporary English*, 241–266. Berlin: Mouton de Gruyter, 2003.

Stubbs, Michael. *Text and Corpus Analysis*. Oxford: Blackwell, 1998. [Esp ch. 8: "Towards a Modal Grammar of English."]

Tagliamonte, Sali. "*Have to, gotta, must*: Grammaticalization, variation and specialization in English deontic modality." In *Corpus Approaches to Grammaticalization in English*, 33–55. Amsterdam: John Benjamins, 2004.

Traugott, Elizabeth. "On the rise of epistemic meanings in English: an example of subjectification in language change." *Language* 65 (1989): 31–55.

Visser, F.T. *An Historical Syntax of English*. Leiden: E.J. Brill, 1963–1973.

Warner, Antony. *The English Auxiliaries: Structure and History*. Cambridge: Cambridge University Press, 1993.

Van der Auwera, Johan, and Vladimir A. Plungian. "Modality's semantic map." *Linguistic Typology* 2 (1998): 79–124.

Wierzbicka, Anna. *Semantic Primitives*. Translated by Anna Wierzbicka and John Besemeres. Frankfurt: Athenäum Verlag, 1972.

———. *Semantics, Culture and Cognition: Universal Human Concepts in Culture-Specific Configurations*. New York: Oxford University Press, 1992.

———. *Semantics: Primes and Universals*. Oxford: Oxford University Press, 1996.

———. *Understanding Cultures Through their Key Words: English, Russian, Polish, German, and Japanese*. Oxford: Oxford University Press, 1997.

———. "German 'cultural scripts': public signs as a key to social attitudes and cultural values." *Discourse & Society* 9, no. 2 (1998): 241–282.

———. *Emotions Across Languages and Cultures. Diversity and Universals*. Cambridge: Cambridge University Press, 1999.

———. *English: Meaning and Culture*. New York: Oxford University Press, 2006a.

———. "Anglo scripts against 'putting pressure' on other people and their linguistic manifestations." In *Ethnopragmatics: Understanding Discourse in Cultural Context*, 65–98. Berlin: Mouton de Gruyter, 2006b.

———. "All people eat and drink: Does this mean that 'eat' and 'drink' are universal human concepts?" In *The Linguistics of Eating and Drinking*, 65–89. Amsterdam: John Benjamins, 2009a.

———. "Exploring English phraseology with two tools: NSM semantic methodology and Google." *Journal of English Linguistics*, 37, no. 2 (2009b): 101–129.

———. *Experience, Evidence, Sense: The Hidden Cultural Legacy of English*. New York: Oxford University Press, 2010.

CHAPTER 3

How 'Logical' are Logical Words?

Negation and its Descriptive vs. Metalinguistic Uses

Jacques Moeschler

1 Introduction

In this contribution, I would like to disentangle some issues about negation and its scope. The first question to address is whether linguistic negation is connected or not to truth-conditions, and consequently to veridicality. From an intuitive point of view, a negative utterance should have as its main property to negate or contradict an utterance rather than deny a state of affairs. For instance, what is the meaning of (1)?

(1) Mary is not happy.

Does the speaker contradict a previous utterance as (2) or does she claim that the world in which Mary is not happy bears the contradictory property of being happy?

(2) Mary is happy.

In this contribution, I will not focus on the logical meaning of negation but will mainly describe the type of contexts in which utterances such as (1) occur in a way that both interpretations—that is, a contradiction of an utterance and a negative description—arise.

Now, this short description does not say anything about the relation between negation and truth. Nor does it explain the scope issue, that is, the way contextual or linguistic information imposes or not a restriction on its semantic domain. From a purely logical point of view, (1) does not exhibit the same scope property as (3), (4), or (5):

(3) Mary is not happy; she is desperate.
(4) Mary is not happy; she is only sad.
(5) Mary is not happy; she is very happy.

 | DOI: 10.1163/9789004258174_004

As we shall see, in (3) there is a contrariety relation between *happy* and *desperate*; in (4), there is a contrast relation between being *happy* and *sad*, whereas in (5), being *very happy* explains why Mary is not only happy, but more than happy. From a logical point of view these examples will be described in terms of the entailments that the corrective sentence (COR) entertains with the negative sentence (NEG) or its positive counterpart (POS).

The scope issue has a long story, from syntax to semantics (Horn 1989), as well as from semantics to pragmatics (Carston 2002). This chapter will not investigate how negation scope can be computed at the syntax-semantics interface, nor at the semantics-pragmatics interface (see Moeschler 2010a for a general presentation). On the contrary, it will mainly concern the type of environment (linguistic and non-linguistic) that allows computing negation scope. Here, we assume that the scope issue is mainly resolved by means of discourse and contextual information, because structural or semantic information are not sufficient to compute the scope of negation.

More precisely, my contribution aims at answering the following questions:

a. What is the relation between the logical meaning of negation and its pragmatic meanings?
b. What is the meaning of a negative sentence?
c. Does linguistic negation have a default orientation?
d. What is the contribution of contexts in the computation of negation scope?
e. What is the relationship between negation and events?

2 The Logical Issue

Let us begin with the main issues concerning the semantics and pragmatics of negation. One way of tackling the pragmatics of negation is to address three questions relating to logic, semantics, and pragmatics. In a nutshell, the logical issue refers to the entailment relation between COR and NEG; the semantic issue refers to the scope of negation, or the scope of the semantic domain of negation; finally, the pragmatic issue concerns the discourse relationship between COR and NEG. The main hypothesis of this chapter is that negation is a three-sided operator in which all three properties converge. The main goal of the paper is thus to give a coherent picture of negation from a logical, semantic, and pragmatic point of view.

The logical issue is thus about the type of entailments between a negative sentence (NEG) and its corrective one (COR): in ordinary negation (6), the relation between COR and NEG is not the same as in non-ordinary negation, as in metalinguistic negations (7) and (8):

(6) Abi n'est pas belle (NEG), elle est quelconque (COR).
'Abi is not beautiful; she is ordinary'.

(7) Abi n'est pas belle (NEG), elle est extraordinaire (COR).
'Abi is not beautiful; she is gorgeous'.

(8) Abi ne regrette pas d'avoir échoué (NEG), elle a réussi (COR).
'Abi doesn't regret having failed; she passed'.

In other words, in ordinary negation, the corrective sentence (COR) entails the negative one (NEG), whereas with metalinguistic negation, two situations arise. With upward negation, mainly with scalar predicates, COR entails the corresponding positive sentence (POS), whereas with a presuppositional negation, COR entails NEG and other entailed propositions, as presuppositions (PP). (9) to (11) make these entailment relations explicit:

(9) COR → NEG
Abi is beautiful → Abi is not ugly[1]

(10) COR → POS
Abi is gorgeous → Abi is beautiful

(11) COR → NEG & NEG(PP)
Abi passed → Abi doesn't regret to have failed & not(Abi failed)

The entailment relations is a good test, because it gives a first semantic description of linguistic negation: apart descriptive negation, there are two metalinguistic negations (Moeschler 2006a, 2012a): (i) ordinary or descriptive negation is truth-conditional, which means it scopes over a proposition and is entailed by COR; (ii) metalinguistic negation 1, or *upward negation*, as well as

1 It is crucial here to assert that the reverse entailment is not valid: NEG does not entail COR: *Abi is not ugly* ↛ Abi is beautiful.
I will not address here the issue of the difference between positive and negative scalar predicates, which concerns their entailment.

metalinguistic negation 2, or *presuppositional negation*, are non-truth-conditional because they scope over more specific contents and not over the asserted proposition.

Table 1 gives a first illustration of these differences, which are only sketched here to make the difference between these three uses of negation clearer. The whole chapter aims not only to justify these observations, but also to predict them from discourse usages.

TABLE 1 *Three uses of negation*

	Assertion	Entailment	Presupposition	Implicature
Descriptive negation	not-P	Q or not-Q	Q	
Metalinguistic negation 1	not-P	not-Q	not-Q	
Metalinguistic negation 2	~~not-P~~	P & Q		~~not-Q~~

2.1 *Descriptive Negation*

First, the entailment of a descriptive negative sentence is either true or false: for instance, in (12), NEG, that is not-P, is compatible both with the entailment (Q) of POS (13) or its negation (not-Q), whereas its presupposition (Q) is safe:

(12) Nath did not buy a chow → Nath bought a dog or Nath did not buy a dog
not-P → Q or not-Q

(13) Nath bought a chow → Nath bought a dog
P → Q

(14) Abi regrets having failed → Abi failed
P → Q

In the previous description, I hypothesized that a negative descriptive sentence does not give a clear result as its entailment is concerned. This presumes that two situations are possible: either the entailment is preserved or it is cancelled, as illustrated by (15) and (16) (Moeschler 2013):

(15) a. Nath did not buy a Chow (not-P); he bought a Labrador (P').
b. P' → Q
c. not-P → Q

(16) a. Nath did not buy a chow (not-P); he bought a cat (P').
b. P' →not-Q
b. not-P → not-Q

In fact, as we will see, (15a), which yields a Correction Discourse Relation (cf. section 4), is the preferred reading of descriptive negation including concepts belonging to a hierarchy. Figure 1 explains why in (15a) the entailment relation (15b) is the case: a subordinate concept entails its hyperonyms. Figure 1 also explains why (15a) is the preferred reading, and Figure 2 explains why (16a) is not the preferred reading for descriptive negation. In that case, the change of category makes the correction less predictable.

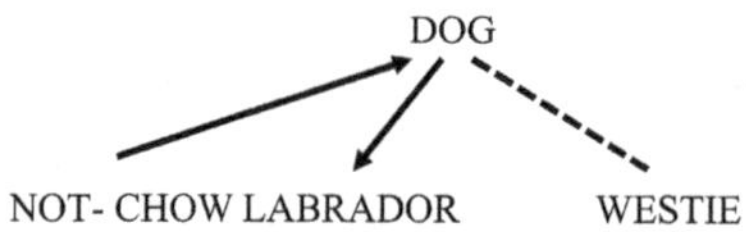

FIGURE 1 *A conceptual hierarchy for the entailment from NOT-CHOW (1)*

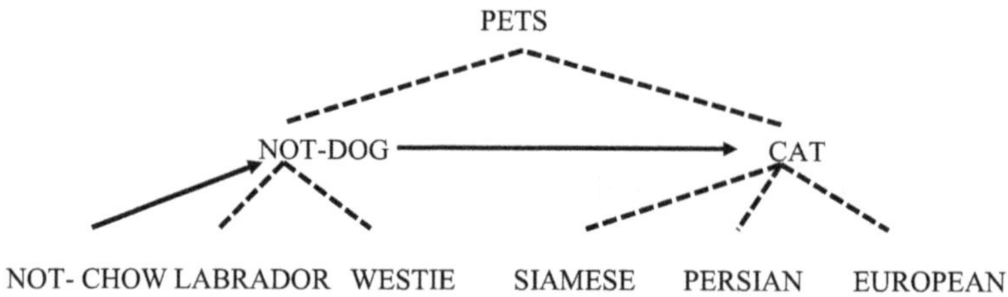

FIGURE 2 *A conceptual hierarchy for the entailment from NOT-CHOW (2)*

However, (16a) is not a case of metalinguistic negation, because the truth-functional properties of entailment are preserved. Moeschler (2013) argues that entailment is truth-functional and corresponds from a logical point of view to material implication:

TABLE 2 *Truth-conditions for entailment*

P	Q	P entails Q
1	1	1
1	0	0
0	1	1
0	0	1

Indeed, when P is false (0), its entailment Q can be either true (1) or false (0), preserving the truth of the entailment relation.

2.2 *Presuppositional Negation*

Secondly, within metalinguistic negation 1 (presuppositional negation), the presupposition is negated and belongs to the scope of negation, as shown in (8), repeated in (17):

(17) Abi ne regrette pas d'avoir échoué (NEG), elle a réussi (COR).
'Abi doesn't regret having failed; she passed'.

In that case, COR defeats POS and its presupposition, given in (18):

(18) Abi regrets having failed (P) PRESUPPOSES Abi failed (Q)

In this case, not-P entails and presupposes not-Q, because COR (Q') entails not-Q. So the logical relations in (17) can be made explicit in (19):

(19) a. Q' → not-P & not-Q
b. Abi passed → not (Abi failed)
c. Abi passed → not (Abi regrets having failed)

Presuppositional negation is one of the metalinguistic uses of negation. A main property of metalinguistic negation is that it does not defeat a proposition, but scopes over the act of utterance (*énonciation*). A metalinguistic analysis of (17) states that by uttering *Abi ne regrette pas d'avoir échoué*, the speaker does not negate the proposition *Abi regrets that Q*, but refuses to assert it: the reason why she refuses such an assertion is because its presupposition Q is false. In other words, the question under discussion is not whether Abi regrets or not that Q, but Q. Q, as a presupposition, is taken for granted and as such is seen as belonging to the context, that is, the common ground or mutual knowledge (respectively Sperber & Wilson 1995; Stalnaker 1977; Gazdar 1979). This analysis, as we shall see it later on, supposes that only COR defeats the presupposition of P. As such, a bare negative sentence preserves its presupposition Q:

(20) a. Abi ne regrette pas d'avoir échoué.
 'Abi does not regret having failed'.
 b. not-P → Q

2.3 *Upward Negation*

The third case, what I call metalinguistic negation 2, is more complex, because the negative proposition is not asserted. In fact, the positive proposition is not under the scope of negation, what is represented by ~~not-P~~. With scalar predicates, as in (21), the implicature of P (not-Q) is defeated, but P is not. So the corrective sentence Q is contradictory to the implicature of POS (not-Q), and entails POS, or P. So, as an effect, both P and Q are entailed by COR.

(21) a. Anne does not have three children; she has four.
 b. Anne has three children +> Anne does not have four children
 c. Anne has four children →Anne has three children

Metalinguistic negation 2 is a very special case of metalinguistic negation; its main purpose is to defeat an implicature and not the proposition that triggers it. In other words, it looks like a negation, but its effect is only to defeat one part of its pragmatic meaning, not one constituent of its semantic content.

As a metalinguistic use of negation, (21a) can be paraphrased in the same manner as presuppositional negation: the speaker cannot assert that Anne has three children, and the reason is that she has four. This use will be called *upward negation*.

Let us resume our description. So far, I have described three main uses of negation: one descriptive negation and two metalinguistic negations: in descriptive negation, COR entails NEG; in presuppositional negation, COR entails NEG and its presupposition PP; in upward negation, COR entails POS:

(22) a. descriptive negation: NEG, COR, where COR → NEG
 b. presuppositional negation: NEG, COR, where COR → NEG & PP
 c. upward negation: NEG, COR, where COR → POS

We have made a substantial progress by defining one criterion distinguishing three types of negation. But we need much more—namely, semantic and pragmatic criteria. COR bears some properties that must be discovered, because NEG, by itself, is not sufficient. Without COR, NEG, whatever its syntactic and semantic properties, always triggers a descriptive use of negation. So the main issue is how, through COR, the intended use of negation can be obtained.

3 The Semantic Issue

The semantic issue concerns what the negation scopes over. Descriptive and metalinguistic negations display an asymmetrical behaviour: whereas descriptive negation is downward oriented, metalinguistic negation 2 is upward oriented. This seems to be a basic fact. (23a) entails that Abi is less than beautiful, whereas (23b) says that she is more than beautiful:

(23) a. Abi n'est pas belle.
'Abi is not beautiful'.
b. Abi n'est pas belle, elle est extraordinaire.
'Abi is not beautiful; she is gorgeous'.

So the question is whether a downward orientation of descriptive negation is a semantic property or the result of a pragmatic process.

Ducrot (1980) gives a very precise analysis of French descriptive negation, but its downward orientation is for him the result of discourse laws (*lois de discours*), or pragmatic processes (see Moeschler 1991 and 2006b for a detailed description of Ducrot's analysis).

What I would like to argue here is that downward orientation of negation is the result of a semantic process, not a pragmatic one. Downward orientation of descriptive negation is a basic property of scalar predicates. Moreover, I will argue that downward orientation is a consequence of the convergence between its scopes and its entailments.

3.1 *Negation as a Propositional Operator*

Let us begin with what is required for the semantics of negation. From a logical point of view, negation is a *propositional operator*, whose function is to inverse the truth-value of the proposition. In a two-valued propositional logic, negation makes a true proposition false and a false proposition true. So from a logical point of view, the conditions under which a negative utterance is used represents a situation where the negated proposition is false. In other words, negation operating on a false proposition makes a true proposition. For instance, if a speaker asserts (24), it is because the proposition (25), negated in (24), is false. It is in effect a non-sense to negate a true proposition to yield a false assertion (26), because an assertion implicates (Searle 1979; Gazdar 1979) that the speaker believes the truth of the asserted proposition. So a negated proposition such as (24) is true,[2] not false; its semantic value is given in (27), not in (28), and negation applies to (25), not to (26):

(24) It is not raining.
(25) $[\![\text{it rains}]\!]^{M,g} = 0$
(26) $[\![\text{it rains}]\!]^{M,g} = 1$
(27) $[\![\text{not}]\!]^{M,g} [[\![\text{it rains}]\!]^{M,g}] = 1$
(28) $[\![\text{not}]\!]^{M,g} [[\![\text{it rains}]\!]^{M,g}] = 0$

The first assumption we must admit is that, from a linguistic point of view, negation has simple semantics. It makes a false proposition true, and does not make a true proposition false.

3.2 *Negation as a Constituent Negation*

The second property of linguistic negation is that it is a *constituent negation* (Klima 1964). It scopes over a specific semantic material. When no special construction is used, as with a cleft sentence for instance (29), linguistic negation scopes over the predicate of the sentence, whatever its linguistic category is (verb, adjective, preposition) (30):

(29) Ce n'est pas Paul qui écrit des poèmes, mais Pierre.
'It is not Paul who writes poems, but Peter'.

(30) a. Paul n'aime pas Marie.
'Paul does not like Mary'.
b. Abi n'est pas grande.
'Abi is not tall'.
c. Le livre n'est pas sur la table.
'The book is not on the table'.

2 By 'true', I do not mean necessary truth, but contingent truth.

(31) gives a simple logical analysis of these uses of negation:[3]

(31) a. NOT-LOVE[PAUL, MARIE]
b. NOT-TALL[ABI]
c. NOT-ON[THE BOOK, THE TABLE]

3.3 *The Semantic Domain of Negation*

The third issue concerning the scope of negation is its *semantic domain*. Let us take predicates belonging to a contrast set, where entailment relations are clearly defined by the meaning of the words. *Married*, *single* and *engaged* are in contrast relations. So if Abi is single, it entails that she is neither married nor engaged. Now, what is the actual meaning of NOT-MARRIED, as in (32)?

(32) Abi is not married.

If the contrast set includes *married*, *single*, and *engaged*, then (32) entails that Abi is single or engaged. This means that the meaning of a negated predicate is unspecified. The information entailed by (32) is thus loose and not sufficient to attribute to Abi a precise property relative to the contrast set she is included in. The only possible way to make a negative utterance more specific in meaning is to add what I call a corrective sentence, COR. The function of COR is to restrict and specify the actual property of the argument whose predicate is negated. So (33a) and (33b), which contain a correction, have precise meanings, which are consistent from a semantic or logical point of view, as COR entails NEG (34):

(33) a. Abi is not married; she is single.
b. Abi is not married; she is engaged.

(34) a. Abi is single → Abi is not married
b. Abi is engaged → Abi is not married

3 Even if the narrowing of logical scope of negation is crucial, because in logical form of (30) negation has wide scope—that is, it scopes over a complete proposition and not a predicate—it will not be addressed here for reason of space (see Moeschler 2010a):

a. NOT [LOVE [PAUL, MARIE]]
b. NOT [TALL [ABI]]
c. NOT [ON [THE BOOK, THE TABLE]]

Now we know more on the semantics of a negative sentence. A bare negative sentence has an unspecified meaning; the COR sentence's main function is to make the domain of negation more specific.

With scalar predicates, the domain of negation seems to be less unspecified. The question is whether it can be computed or not without any COR sentence. In effect, (35) is consistent with two orientations: a downward, as in (36a), and an upward, as in (36b):

(35) Abi n'est pas belle.
'Abi is not beautiful'.

(36) a. Abi n'est pas belle, elle est quelconque.
'Abi is not beautiful; she is ordinary'.
b. Abi n'est pas belle, elle est extraordinaire.
'Abi is not beautiful; she is gorgeous'.

The question is the following: as (35) can receive two orientations, given in (36), is a negative utterance neutral or oriented? I would argue that a negative utterance is not neutral and that negation is not symmetrical. The test is the following: what is the entailment of (35)? If negation were neutral with regards to its entailment, then (35) should have as an entailment a disjunction, given in (37):

(37) Abi is not beautiful → Abi is ugly OR Abi is ordinary OR Abi is gorgeous

So the set of entailments would correspond to all possible degrees in a scale of beauty: in that case, NOT-BEAUTIFUL should entail all positions (downward as well as upward) in the scale given in Figure 3:

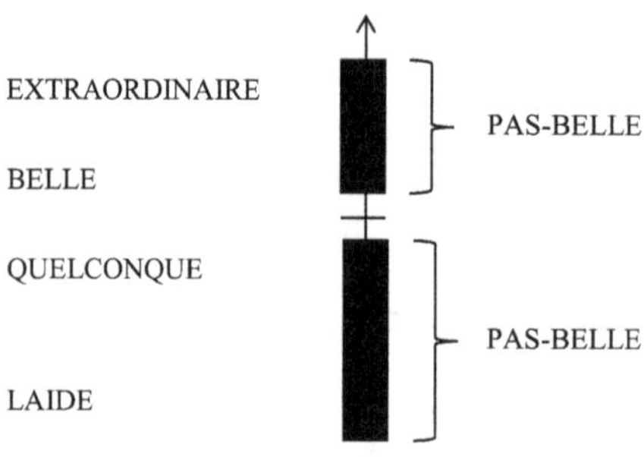

FIGURE 3 *The domain of PAS-BELLE*

But this is not a good description of scalar predicates, which are oriented and have a polarity. In that case, *belle*, as a positive predicate, is positively oriented and contrasts with its antonym *laide*, which is negatively oriented (Figure 4). The question is now the following: how can the negation of a positive predicate be consistent with a positive COR and a negative COR?

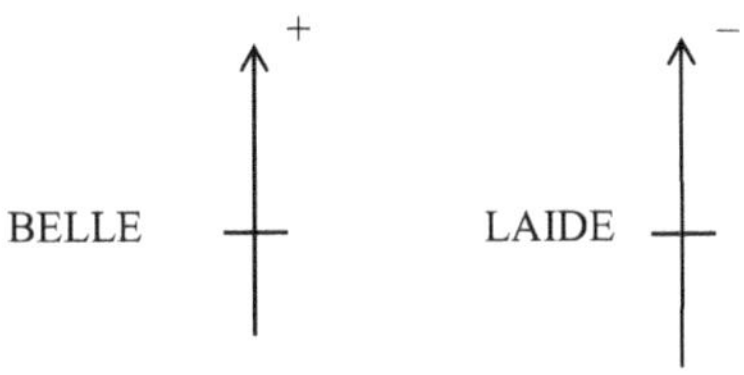

FIGURE 4 *Positive and negative scales*

Ducrot (1980) gives an argument for a two-scale description of descriptive negation in his theory of argumentation, asserting that all possible ranks in a scale are more or less strong arguments for a conclusion consistent with the orientation of the scale. It means that being more or less beautiful in that scale is positively oriented, as (38) shows. With a negative predicate, (39), it is the other way around.

(38) a. Abi is beautiful; she can play the role of the princess.
b. Abi is beautiful enough to play the role of the princess.

(39) Abi is ugly: she cannot play the role of the princess.

Now, what happens when positive and negative predicates are in negative sentences, as in (40) and (41)? Their orientation is simply reversed.

(40) a. Abi is not beautiful enough to play the role of the princess.
b. Abi is not beautiful; she cannot play the role of the princess.

(41) a. ?? Abi is not beautiful; she can play the role of the princess.
b. Abi is not ugly; she can play the role of the princess.

So it seems that the orientation of a negative predicate is the reverse of the orientation of the positive one. Ducrot (1980) describes this property of scalar predicates as the result of a discourse law of *argumentative inversion*: if an argument p' is stronger than an argument p for a positive conclusion r, then non-p is stronger than non-p' for the negative conclusion non-r (Moeschler 2006b).

Suppose now that predicate p' is stronger than p, and that p' is *très belle*, whereas p is *belle*. Then the prediction is that *pas très belle* will be a weaker argument for a negative conclusion than *pas belle*. Let us check this hypothesis by using the test of *même* (*even*) insertion, which introduces a stronger argument:

(42) a. Abi est belle et même très belle: elle fera une magnifique princesse.
'Abi is beautiful and even very beautiful; she will be a wonderful princess'.
b. ?? Abi est très belle et même belle: elle fera une magnifique princesse.
'Abi is very beautiful and even beautiful; she will be a wonderful princess'.

(43) a. Abi n'est pas très belle et même pas belle du tout: elle ne fera pas une magnifique princesse.
'Abi is not very beautiful and even not beautiful; she will be a wonderful princess'.
b. ?? Abi n'est pas belle et même pas très belle: elle ne fera pas une magnifique princesse.
'Abi is not beautiful and even not very beautiful; she will be a wonderful princess'.

Obviously, (42a) is more acceptable than (42b), as is (43a) relative to (43b).

So, what have we shown with this excursus? The negation of positive scalar predicates gives rise to a negative scale. So the prediction is that this property, which is strictly argumentative for Ducrot, is in fact a basic semantic fact: negation is downward oriented, and this explains why in ordinary usages of negation (that is, descriptive usages), negation is downward oriented. When an upward orientation is the case, negation is not descriptive, but metalinguistic.

Now the question 'why is a corrective sentence necessary only in the case of upward entailment?' can be addressed. If negation is intrinsically downward, no corrective sentence is necessary, whereas it is the other way around with upward negation—the COR sentence is necessary to make the COR to POS entailment available to the audience. More precisely, in descriptive negation, the scope of negation equals its entailments, whereas in upward negation, the entailments are distinct from its scope; negation scopes over a precise content, its scalar implicature. Figure 5 makes this difference explicit for examples (44) and (45):

(44) Anne does not have three children.
(45) Anne does not have three children; she has four of them.

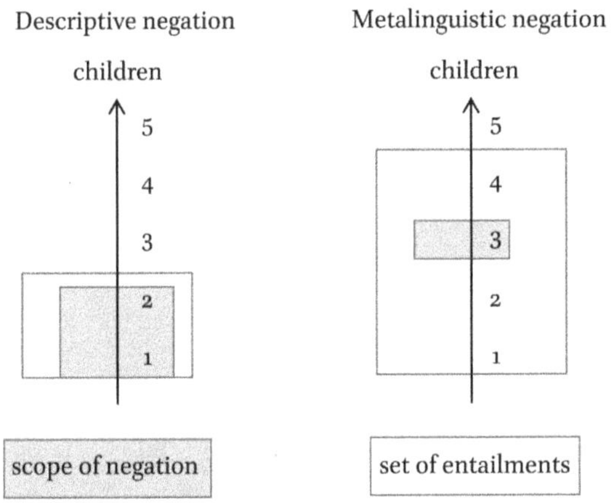

FIGURE 5 *Scope of negation and entailments*

Now we have a second property distinguishing descriptive and metalinguistic negation: descriptive negation is downward oriented, whereas metalinguistic negation is upward oriented.

4 The Pragmatic Issue

What I would like to discuss now is the pragmatic or discourse relation between NEG and COR. My hypothesis is that the three types of negation proposed in this chapter are not the same. The question is whether there are pragmatic evidences for distinguishing between these three types of negation. I wish to propose two criteria: discourse relations and connectives.

4.1 *Discourse Relations*

The hypothesis is that the discourse relations between NEG and COR are not of the same type.

4.1.1 Correction

In the case of descriptive negation, the discourse relation is a Correction one. Here is the definition of Correction:[4]

(46) 'not-α CORRECTION β' is the case between not-α et β if α is a false description of the world and β is a true description.

Let takes example (36a), repeated in (47):

(47) Abi n'est pas belle, elle est quelconque.
'Abi is not beautiful; she is ordinary'.

The following description is the case for example (47):

(48) a. $[\![$Abi is beautiful$]\!] = 0$
b. $[\![$Abi is ordinary$]\!] = 1$
c. Abi is ordinary → not [Abi is beautiful]

In other words, Correction is the case because α (ABI IS BEAUTIFUL) is false and β is true and β entails not-α. In this case, COR (β) entails not-α (NEG).

4.1.2 Contrast

What about metalinguistic negation? In the case of upward negation, the relation between NEG and COR is a Contrast relation. Here is a definition of Contrast:

(49) 'not-α CONTRAST β' is the case between non-α et β if not-α implicates not-β.

In (50), COR entails POS (51a) and NEG implicates the negation of COR (51b):

(50) Abi n'est pas belle, elle est extraordinaire.
'Abi is not beautiful; she is gorgeous'.

---

4 I will make a difference between Correction and Contrast. In Rhetorical Structure Theory, only Contrast seems to be relevant. Contrast belongs to the category of "Other relations" (Taboada 2012).

(51) a. Abi is gorgeous → Abi is beautiful
b. Abi is not beautiful +> Abi is not gorgeous

In the Contrast relation, the COR sentence contrasts with the NEG sentence in the sense they lead to different conclusions. The contrast can be simply explained by the semantic orientation of NEG and COR: NEG is negatively oriented, and COR positively oriented. This contrast is not a Correction; in Correction, the polarity of NEG and COR is identical. In the next section (4.2), we will make this difference explicit via different discourse connectives.

4.1.3 Explanation

Last but not least, the discourse relation between NEG and COR in presuppositional negation is Explanation. In that case, COR explains why NEG has been asserted. The definition of Explanation is the following:

(52) 'not-α Explanation β' is the case if β explains why α is false and β entails not-α and the negation of its entailments.

In (53), COR entails NEG and its presupposition, as made explicit in (54):

(53) Abi ne regrette pas d'avoir échoué, elle a réussi.
'Abi does not regret having failed; she passed'.

(54) a. Abi passed → Abi does not regret having failed
b. Abi passed → not (Abi failed)

What does it mean that COR is an Explanation of NEG? It means that COR gives a reason why NEG and its entailments are false.

So COR can have at least three functions: Correction, Contrast, and Explanation. These different discourse relations explain the differences in entailments between COR and NEG.

A second argument can strengthen such differences: connectives.

4.2 *Connectives*

These three types of discourse relations and negation are made explicit by different connectives. The Correction relation is made explicit by the French connective *au contraire* (on the contrary), the Contrast relation by *mais* (but), and the Explanation by *parce que* or *puisque* (because, since). (55) to (57) make these relations explicit by means of connectives:

(55) a. Abi n'est pas belle, **au contraire** elle est quelconque.
'Abi is not beautiful; on the contrary she is ordinary'.

(56) Abi n'est pas belle, **mais** extraordinaire.
'Abi is not beautiful but gorgeous'.

(57) Abi ne regrette pas d'avoir échoué, **parce que/puisqu**'elle a réussi.
'Abi does not regret having failed, because/since she passed'.

Moreover, these connectives are not substitutable; they are specific to these discourse relations, as shown the following examples:

(58) a. Abi n'est pas belle, au contraire elle est quelconque.
'Abi is not beautiful; on the contrary she is ordinary'.
b. Abi n'est pas belle $mais_{SN}$ quelconque.
'Abi is not beautiful but ordinary'.
c. Abi n'est pas belle, parce qu'elle est quelconque.
'Abi is not beautiful, because she is ordinary'.

In (58b), *mais* is not a contrastive *mais*, as in (56), but a corrective *mais*, what Anscombre and Ducrot (1977) call a $mais_{SN}$—the contrastive or argumentative $mais_{PA}$.[5] In (58c), *parce que* is possible, but the discourse relation is no more a corrective one. Rather, it is an Explanation, exactly what the connective requires to draw. The paraphrase of (58c) is given in (59):

(59) The reason why Abi cannot be said to be beautiful is that she is ordinary.

With the contrast relation, the possible connectives are restricted to $mais_{PA}$:

(60) a. Abi n'est pas belle, mais extraordinaire.
'Abi is not beautiful but gorgeous'.
b. ?? Abi n'est pas belle, au contraire elle est extraordinaire.
'Abi is not beautiful; on the contrary she is gorgeous'.
c. ? Abi n'est pas belle, parce qu'elle est extraordinaire.
'Abi is not beautiful, because she is gorgeous'.

5 SN is for *sondern* (German) and *sino* (Spanish), whereas PA stands for the German *aber* and the Spanish *pero*.

Finally, the Explanation case is clearer: no other connective than *parce que/puisque* is possible:

(61) a. Abi ne regrette pas d'avoir échoué, parce que/puisqu'elle a réussi.
'Abi does not regret having failed, because/since she passed'.
b. *Abi ne regrette pas d'avoir échoué, au contraire elle a réussi.
'Abi does not regret having failed; on the contrary she passed'.
c. *Abi ne regrette pas d'avoir échoué, mais elle a réussi.
'Abi does not regret having failed, but she passed'.

The last issue to be made explicit is to know whether the semantics of these three connectives is consistent with the entailments and the discourse relations implied within the three types of negation. I will give the following descriptions that make this hypothesis acceptable.

4.3 *The Semantics of* au contraire, mais *and* parce que

4.3.1 *Au contraire*

Au contraire has as a basic semantic, a contrary relation. The contrary relation can be expressed by the following truth-conditions, expressed in Table 3, and utterance (62):

(62) Abi n'est pas belle, au contraire elle est quelconque.
'Abi is not beautiful; on the contrary she is ordinary'.

TABLE 3 *Contrary relation*

P: Abi is beautiful	Q: Abi is ordinary	P IS CONTRARY TO Q
1	1	0
1	0	1
0	1	1
0	0	1

In other words, Abi cannot be *beautiful* and *ordinary* at the same time, but she can be beautiful or ordinary, or neither beautiful nor ordinary. So POS and COR in descriptive negation are in contrariety relation. This corresponds to the semantics of *au contraire*: *au contraire* can be used neither with contradictory predicates nor with sub-contrary ones. (63), which is an example of a contradiction, is unacceptable with *au contraire*; the same holds for sub-contrariety relations, exemplified in (64):

(63) *Abi n'est pas belle, au contraire elle est belle.
'Abi is not beautiful; on the contrary she is beautiful'.

(64) * Abi n'est pas quelconque, au contraire elle n'est pas belle.
'Abi is not ordinary; on the contrary she is not beautiful'.

So, it happens that if *belle* and *quelconque* are contrary predicates, *pas quelconque* and *pas belle* are sub-contrary predicates. Figure 6 makes these relations explicit (cf. Horn 2012a), and the examples in (65) make explicit all possible logical relations (entailment, contradiction, contrariety, and sub-contrariety in the logical square):

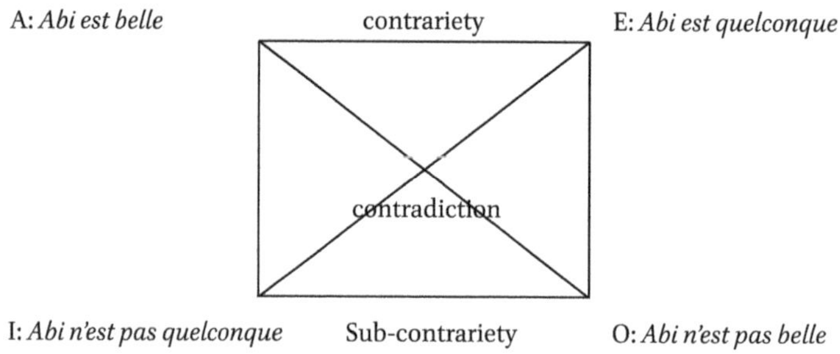

FIGURE 6 *Logical square and contrary predicates*[6]

(65) a. Abi est belle ENTAILS Abi n'est pas quelconque
b. Abi est quelconque ENTAILS Abi n'est pas belle
c. Abi est belle IS CONTADICTORY TO Abi n'est pas belle
d. Abi est quelconque IS CONTADICTORY TO Abi n'est pas quelconque
e. Abi est belle IS CONTRARY TO Abi est quelconque
f. Abi n'est pas quelconque IS SUB-CONTRARY TO Abi n'est pas belle

6 A and I stand for the positive corners of the logical square (AffIrmo), E and O for the negative ones (NegO). A and E are universals, I and O particular. See Horn (2004, 2012b) and Moeschler (2007) for an application of the logical square to pragmatics and the theory of scalar implicatures.

4.3.2 *Mais*

Mais has as its semantics the logical meaning of conjunction (∧), which corresponds linguistically to *et* (and) and has as its pragmatic meaning a contrast between the implicatures of its discourse segment. Moreover, whereas its semantics is symmetrical (*P and Q* is truth-conditionally equivalent to *Q and P*), its pragmatics is asymmetrical: *P mais Q* is not pragmatically equivalent to *Q mais P*.

Let us test the logical meaning of *mais* (conjunction):

(66) Abi n'est pas belle (not-P), mais extraordinaire (Q).
'Abi is not beautiful but gorgeous'.

TABLE 4 *Truth-conditions of conjunction relation*

P: ABI EST BELLE	Q: ABI EST EXTRAORDINAIRE	P and Q
1	1	1
1	0	0
0	1	0
0	0	0

POS and COR have to be true together: they cannot be false together nor false or true.

This is the case because negation is metalinguistic and not descriptive in (66). The conjunction relation is made explicit in (67):

(67) Abi est belle et extraordinaire.
'Abi is beautiful and gorgeous'.

So, what happens in (66) from a pragmatic point of view? If a contrast relation takes place, it means that NEG must trigger some implicature, which is not compatible with COR.

The point is that a contrast relation is the case if and only if NEG is first interpreted as a descriptive negation. In this interpretation, NEG implicates a negative conclusion, which is defeated by COR. So the paradox of the contrastive use of *mais* is that NEG must be taken descriptively, not interpretatively (Sperber & Wilson 1995). So (66) receives the following analysis:

(68) a. Abi n'est pas belle +> Abi cannot play the role of the princess
b. Abi est extraordinaire +> Abi can play the role of the princess
c. Abi est extraordinaire → Abi est belle
d. Abi n'est pas belle mais extraordinaire +> Abi can play the role of the princess

Remember that *mais* in a contrast relation is PA, not SN. When *mais* is used in a Correction relation, it is a $mais_{SN}$ and not a $mais_{PA}$:

(69) Abi n'est pas belle, mais laide.
'Abi is not beautiful but ugly'.

Remember also that *belle* and *laide* are contrary and that *laide* entails *pas belle*. So none of the entailments and implicatures made explicit in (68) are the case in (69).

I would like to make explicit that $mais_{PA}$ can be used when the first segment is not in a negative form. In this case, the contrast is not lexical but pragmatic. For instance, in the same semantic domain, the contrast should be the case between *belle* (beautiful) and *timide* (shy). The famous example contrasting being a Republican and being honest gives rise to the same analysis:

(70) Abi est belle, mais timide.
'Abi is beautiful but shy'.
+> there is a contrast between being beautiful and shy

(71) He is a Republican but honest.
+> there is contrast between being a Republican and honest

4.3.3 *Parce que*

Parce que and *puisque* are connectives introducing causal relations.[7] In Moeschler (to appear), *parce que* has as entailment a causal and a conjunction relation between its arguments. In other words, *P parce que Q* entails *Q CAUSE P* and *P and Q*. Is this analysis compatible with the presuppositional use of

7 Cf. Moeschler (2011) for a general description of *parce que* in French, Blochowiak (2010) for a formal analysis of *because* and its interactions with negation, Zufferey (2010, 2012) for revised analysis of *parce que, car, puisque* of the classical analysis by the Groupe λ-l (1975). Cf. Zufferey & Cartoni (2012) for a cross-linguistic analysis of causal connectives in French and English.

negation? In this case, it must be specified that the use of *parce que* is not causal, but speech act (Sweetser 1990). So the description of (72) is given in (73):

(72) Abi ne regrette pas d'avoir échoué, parce que/puisqu'elle a réussi.
'Abi does not regret having failed, because/since she passed'.

(73) a. Abi passed CAUSE TO SAY Abi does not regret having failed.
b. Abi does not regret having failed AND Abi passed.
c. Abi passed → not(Abi failed)

So (72) entails (74)—that is, what is predicted by the analysis of presuppositional negation:

(74) Abi does not regret having failed and not(Abi failed).

4.4 *A Synthesis*

We have discussed three issues about the scope of negation: the logical, semantic, and pragmatic issues. As a result, we have a convergence of properties and criteria distinguishing three types of negation: ordinary negation, upward negation, and presuppositional negation.

These criteria are resumed in Table 5:

TABLE 5 *Criteria distinguishing three types of negation*

	Entailments	Scopes	Discourse relations	Connectives
Descriptive negation	COR → NEG	Set of entailments	Correction	*au contraire*
Upward negation	COR → POS	Restricted	Contrast	*mais*
Presuppositional negation	COR → NEG (P & PP)	Wide	Explanation	*parce que, puisque*

5 Negative Utterances and Their Contexts

The crucial issue is how to infer negation scope. In this section, I will show that this issue is basically a contextual one, and the computation of negation depends on the type of contextual effects. Our hypothesis is that negative utterances are pragmatically processed against contexts in which some contextual assumptions and previous utterances are required. In order to yield the right interpretation of negative utterances, contextual information should not only be consistent with the four types of properties described (entailment, scope, discourse relation, and connective), but also predict logical, semantic, and pragmatic properties of the usages of negation. Our description predicts that the context for downward and upward negation should be the same, but their contextual effects should not. It also predicts that the contexts for presuppositional negation is more complex and differs from downward and upward negations.

5.1 *The Context of Ordinary Downward Negation*

In ordinary negation, the context must contain POS as a contextual assumption, even if POS is not necessarily made explicit. So POS can belong to the previous discourse context (75) or not (76). However, in this case, the presumption is that someone believes POS:

(75) A: Paul croit qu'Anne a trois enfants.
B: Non, Anne n'a pas trois enfants, elle en a deux.
'A: Paul believes that Anne has three children.
B: No, Anne does not have three children, she has two'.

(76) Sais-tu qu'Anne n'a pas trois enfants, mais seulement deux?
'Do you know that Anne does not have three children, but only two?'
Contextual assumption: Anne has three children.

Now, if the utterance is NEG + COR, what is its contextual effect? By contextual effect, I refer to positive cognitive effects, as defined in Relevance Theory (Wilson & Sperber 2004). A positive cognitive effect is either the addition of a new assumption (as a contextual implication, that is, the result of a contextual assumption and the explicature of the utterance), the strengthening of an old assumption (an assumption belonging to the mutual cognitive environment), or the suppression of an old assumption. In the case of a negative utterance, the cognitive effect distinguishing three types of negation is either the *strengthening* or the *suppression* of an assumption, not the addition of a new assumption.[8]

What is the function of COR? As COR entails NEG, COR has as a main effect the strengthening of NEG. As a result, the effect of COR + NEG is the eradication of POS. So the context of ordinary downward negation is the following:

(77) a. Contextual assumption: POS
b. Utterance: NEG + COR
c. Contextual effect: ~~POS~~[9]

With scalar and presuppositional predicates, the same analysis holds:

(78) A: Je trouve qu'Abi est belle.
B: Non, elle n'est pas belle, elle juste quelconque.
'A: I think Abi is beautiful.
B: No, she is not beautiful, she is just ordinary'.

(79) A: Abi regrette d'avoir échoué.
B: Non, elle ne regrette pas d'avoir échoué: elle se moque de ses études.
'A: Abi regrets having failed.
B: No, she doesn't regret having failed: she doesn't care about her studies'.

In each case, POS belongs to the context and is suppressed as a contextual effect:

(80) Contextual assumption: Abi is beautiful
Contextual effect: ~~Abi is beautiful~~

(81) Contextual assumption: Abi regrets Q
Contextual effect: ~~Abi regrets Q~~

What has been stressed here is the difference between the meaning of a negative utterance (*Abi is not beautiful, Abi doesn't regret having failed*) and the eradication or suppression of its positive counterpart from the context. In effect, a negative sentence is not sufficient, which is why COR is crucial for the

8 See Moeschler (1997) for a description allowing as a contextual effect a contextual implication, *via* an invited inference *à la* Geis & Zwicky (1971).

9 ~~POS~~ means 'suppress POS'.

computation of the contextual effect. Without COR, a contradictory exchange can be pursued without ending (Moeschler 1982 for an analysis of these cases).

(82) A: Je trouve qu'Abi est belle.
B: Non, elle n'est pas belle.
A: Si, elle est belle.
B: Non!
A: Si!
B: Non!
…
'A: I think Abi is beautiful.
B: No, she is not beautiful.
A: Yes, she is.
B: No, she is not!
A: Yes!
B: No!'

Last but not least, POS can be extracted from a discourse context in which it is not said explicitly. For instance, it can be extracted, not as a presupposition, but as a presumed belief, as in question (81):

(83) A: Combien Anne a-t-elle d'enfants?
B: Elle n'a pas trois enfants.
'A: How many children does Anne have?
B: She does not have three children'.

Its context and contextual effects are given in (82):

(84) a. Contextual assumption: Anne has three children
b. Contextual effect: ~~Anne has three children~~

5.2 *The Context of Upward Negation*

Within upward negation, the context is different. POS belongs to the context, as in downward negation. But POS is maintained and NEG+COR strengthens it. So the contextual effect is POS+:

(85) a. Contextual assumption: POS
b. Utterance: NEG + COR
c. Contextual effect: POS+

In (86), contextual assumption and contextual effect are given in (87):

(86) A: Abi est belle, tu ne trouves pas?
B: Non, elle n'est pas belle, elle est extraordinaire.
'A: Abi is beautiful, isn't she?
B: No, she is not beautiful, she is gorgeous'.

(87) a. Contextual assumption: Abi is beautiful
b. Contextual effect: Abi is more than beautiful.

In this analysis, the entailment COR→POS is now consistent. The contextual effect POS+ explains why negation is not truth-conditional, but metalinguistic. Its scope is restricted to a specific degree on a scale, the one described by POS. So the pragmatic analysis makes explicit the following assumptions:

(88) The assertion of a degree D_i on a scale S implicates the limitation of the degree to D_i. D_i is incompatible with D_{i+1}, and entails D_{i-1}.

The counterpart of (88) is given in (89):

(89) The negation of a degree D_i on a scale S entails D_{i-1}.

(89) explains why a bare negative utterance conveys a descriptive negation or, in other words, a downward entailment.

5.3 *The Context of Presuppositional Negation*

In presuppositional negation, the context contains either NEG or POS, with a presupposition PP. Both NEG + COR defeat POS+PP or NEG+PP. (90) is a positive context, whereas (91) is a negative one:

(90) A: J'ai vu Abi. Apparemment, elle regrette d'avoir échoué.
B: Non, elle ne regrette pas d'avoir échoué, parce qu'elle a réussi.
'A: I met Abi. Apparently, she regrets having failed.
B: No, she doesn't regret having failed, since she passed'.

(91) A: J'ai vu Abi. Apparemment, elle ne regrette pas d'avoir échoué.
B: En effet, elle ne regrette pas d'avoir échoué, parce qu'elle a réussi.
'A: I met Abi. Apparently, she does not regret having failed.
B: In effect, she doesn't regret having failed, since she passed'.

(90) is a more expected context that (91), because the negative utterance, from a formal point of view, is opposed to a positive one. Generally, when the context is negative, a denial takes the form of the positive one:

(92) A: Abi n'est pas belle.
B: Si, elle est belle.
'A: Abi is not beautiful.
B: No, she is beautiful'.

However, the negative context in (91) gives rise some pragmatic effects, which are not propositional, that is, not representational. The effect is a kind of irony. This is due to the echoic nature of an ironical utterance (Wilson & Sperber 1981; Sperber & Wilson 1995; Carston 2002; Wilson 2006; Sperber & Wilson 2012). In Relevance Theory, irony is indeed defined as an interpretative use of language, implying an echo to a previous utterance or to a thought belonging to the context.

However, the ironical effect does not occur within a positive context, when the positive echo mimics ironically the positive utterance:

(93) A: J'ai vu Abi. Apparemment, elle regrette d'avoir échoué.
B: ?? En effet, elle regrette d'avoir échoué, parce qu'elle a réussi.
'A: I met Abi. Apparently, she regrets having failed.
B: In effect, she regrets having failed, since she passed'.

(93B) is not ironical because it is not negative, and POS is inconsistent with COR.[10]

So the context for presuppositional negation is double, positive and negative.

(94) Positive context
a. Contextual assumption: POS & PP
b. Contextual effect: ~~POS~~ & ~~PP~~

10 Ducrot (1984) gives a very interesting analysis of negative ironical utterance. His approach combines his analysis of negative utterance: negation implies two points of view (*énonciateur*), and the speaker assimilates only the point of view that denies the positive one; on the other hand, ironical utterances imply a mention to a previous utterance, or to a thought, without any assimilation to this point of view. Hence, a negative ironical utterance implies two points of view, the second being an echo of the first positive one, but without assimilation. See Moeschler (1991) and Moeschler & Reboul (1994) for a detailed discussion.

(95) Negative context
   a. Contextual assumption: NEG & PP
   b. Contextual effect: ~~NEG~~ & ~~PP~~

5.4 *Summary*

If we combine Table 5 and the results of section 3, we obtain the following result:

TABLE 6 *Criteria distinguishing three types of negation (é)*

	Entailments	Scopes	Discourse relations	Connectives	Contextual assumption	Contextual effect
Descriptive negation	COR → NEG	Set of entailments	Correction	*au contraire*	POS	~~POS~~
Upward negation	COR → POS	Restricted	Contrast	*mais*	POS	POS+
Presuppositional negation	COR → NEG (P & PP)	Wide	Explanation	*parce que, puisque*	a. POS & PP b. NEG & PP	a. ~~POS~~ & ~~PP~~ b. ~~NEG~~ & ~~PP~~

Do we obtain is a consistent picture? The new pragmatic criteria (contextual assumption and effect) are consistent with the logical, semantic, and classical pragmatic criteria. But one of the issues is to know what the basic criteria are. On a classical account of negation, pragmatic criteria are the results of logical or semantic properties (Moeschler 2010a). In the proposed framework, on the contrary, the scope of negation is the result of contextual assumptions and logical entailments.

(i) In downward negation, the eradication of POS from the current context yields as a result a set of entailments.
(ii) In upward negation, the strengthening of POS implies a restricted scope.
(iii) In presuppositional negation, the suppression of POS or NEG and their presupposition has as an effect a wide scope.

Moreover, discourse relations and connectives do not trigger the right contextual effect: they are the results of an interpretation process that can be made explicit by one specific connective and discourse relation.[11]

6 Conclusion

In this chapter, I gave descriptive and theoretical arguments in favour of a three-sided analysis of negation. Logical, semantic, and pragmatic properties converge to give rise to a consistent picture of the meaning of negative utterances.

However, a lot of empirical and theoretical issues are still open to questions and should be answered within such a pragmatic framework. I would like to close this chapter by mentioning two issues for further investigations. The first one deals with negative events and the second one with morphological negation.

6.1 *Negative Events*

First of all, the topic of negative events is very intriguing. Negative events are descriptions of events under negation, which have as a main property the change of their aspectual class.[12] For instance, (96a), whose positive description is an event (96b), becomes a state under negation:

(96) a. Jacques did not run today STATE
b. Jacques ran today EVENT

So the first research question is to explain how such a shift in aspectual class is made possible. The second research question is the precise meaning of such an utterance. If we adopt the same type of analysis as before, that is, inferring a specific meaning from a corrective sentence, then (96a) can mean a very large set of descriptions, given in (97). Such meanings are easily explainable, since negation scopes over a specific sub-semantic constituent, given in (98) and formalized in (99):

11 See Wilson & Matsui (2000), who argue on the bridging case that discourse relations are the results of a more high-level interpretation process, contra Asher & Lascarides (2003). See also Reboul & Moeschler (1998) for a general argument and Moeschler (2010b) for an updated version.

12 See Blochowiak (2009) for a pragmatic analysis of the relationship between causal relations and negative descriptions of events.

(97) $\neg\exists e$ [run(e) $\wedge$ agent(Jacques, e) $\wedge$ happen(e, today)][13]

(98) a. Jacques did not run today; he ran yesterday.
b. Jacques did not run today; Peter did.
c. Jacques did not run today; he biked.

(99) a. $\exists e$ [run(e) $\wedge$ agent (Jacques, e) $\wedge$ $\neg$happen (e, today) $\wedge$ happen (e, yesterday)]
b. $\exists e$ [run(e) $\wedge$ $\neg$agent (Jacques, e) $\wedge$ happen (e, today) $\wedge$ agent (Peter, e)]
c. $\exists e$ [$\neg$run (e) $\wedge$ agent (Jacques, e) $\wedge$ happen (e, today) $\wedge$ bike (e)]

In all interpretations of (98), the semantic analysis predicts that the description does not give rise to a state, but to an event. Negation then receives a narrow scope, exactly in the same way it applies to downward negation. However, here the scope of negation is not a degree on a scale but a semantic constituent (*happen, agent, run*). It can also be a more abstract property, which is not directly connected to a predicate of the logical form of POS but to a sub-constituent of the predicate RUN, as in (100):

(100) a. Jacques did not run today; he walked. MANNER OF MOVING
b. Jacques did not run today; he rested. TYPE OF ACTIVITY
c. Jacques did not run today; he worked all day. TYPE OF ACTIVITY

In this perspective, the question is the effect of scope on a negative event. First of all, in (97), wide scope is responsible for the aspectual shift. Secondly, the question is whether an event can be under metalinguistic negation. (101) is a good argument in favour of metalinguistic negation scoping over events:

(101) Jacques did not stop at the gas station; he did not take his car.

Last but not least, a negative event can have the same pragmatic effect as a real event; namely, it can trigger a temporal order effect (Moeschler 2000a, 2000b): (102a) receives the interpretation (102b), which makes temporal order explicit:

(102) a. Jacques did not stop at the gas station; he took the highway.
b. Jacques did not stop at the gas station, and then he took the highway.

13 This is a typical neo-Davidsonian description of an event. See Parsons (1990).

In this case, the best hypothesis is that negation does not have a wide scope but a narrow scope, and it does not scope over the property of being an event. So the representation of NEG in (102a) must provide as a result the description of an event, such as an inferred event from a negative description:

(103) Jacques did not stop to the gas station → Jacques went on driving.

6.2 *Morphological Negation*

The second issue is the relationship between syntactic negation and morphological negation. It is well known that morphological negation does not generally introduce a contradiction, but another semantic relation, for instance a contrary one. So, what could be the relationship between *malheureux* (unhappy) and *pas heureux* (not happy)? One way of describing these differences is to follow Horn (2012a) and to use the logical square. In this case, (104a) does not mean (104b), because only (104b) entails (104c), which is contradictory to *Il est heureux* (he is happy) and subcontradictory to *il n'est pas malheureux* (he is not unhappy), as is made explicit in Figure 7:

(104) a. Il est heureux.
'He is happy'
b. Il est malheureux.
'He is unhappy'
c. Il n'est pas heureux.
'He is not happy'
d. Il n'est pas malheureux.
'He is not unhappy'

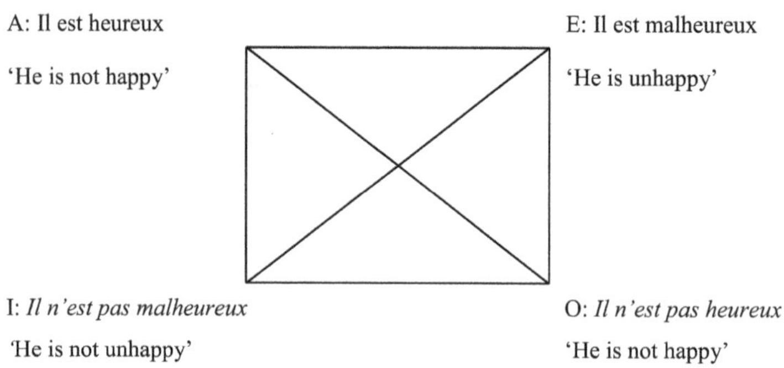

FIGURE 7 *Logical square and contrary predicates*

Now, the last issue, as the relation between contrary predicates can be explained by the logical square, is to explain why I (*il n'est pas malheureux*) does not implicate the negation of A (*il est heureux*) and O (*il n'est pas heureux*) does not implicate the negation of E (*il est malheureux*). In this case, the relationship between a syntactic negation and a morphological one short-cuts the classical semantic-pragmatic interplays as described with quantifiers (Horn 2004), where particulars (*some, some ... not*) implicate the negation of their corresponding universals (*all, none*), as illustrated in (105). In effect, the particulars in Figure 7, which are negative, have as pragmatic effects the implicature of their respective universals, which correspond to a *litotes* in classical rhetoric (106):

(105) a. Some students passed IMPLICATES not all students passed
b. Some students did not pass IMPLICATES it is false that no students passed

(106) a. Il n'est pas malheureux IMPLICATES il est heureux
b. Il n'est pas heureux IMPLICATES il est malheureux

All French readers remind the famous reply by Chimène to Rodrigue in Le Cid (Corneille):

(107) Va, je ne te hais point.
'Leave, I don't hate you'.

These two issues will give rise to further empirical and theoretical works.[14]

In terms of the general theme of the volume, we would add that the interpretation of negation, as a nonveridical phenomenon (nonveridicality as defined by Giannakidiou, this volume) presents an interesting challenge, since its interaction with evaluation needs to take into account pragmatic and contextual effects. As Gros and Stede (this volume) show, accurate negation interpretation is crucial in many Natural Language Processing tasks.

14 This further research will be pursued in the SNSF project LogPrag (*The semantics and pragmatics of logical words: Negation and logical connectives*), project no. 100012_146093.

References

Asher N., A. "Lascarides. Lexical disambiguation in a discourse context." *Journal of Semantics* 12 (1993): 69–108.

Anscombre, J.-C., and O. Ducrot. "Deux *mais* en français?" *Lingua* 43 (1977): 23–40.

Blochowiak, J. "La relation causale, ses relata et la négation." *Nouveaux cahiers de linguistique française* 29 (2009): 153–175.

———. "Some formal properties of causal and inferential 'because' in different embedding contexts." *Generative Grammar in Geneva* 6 (2010): 191–202.

Carston, R. *Utterances and Thoughts. The Pragmatics of Explicit Communication*. Oxford: Blackwell, 2002.

Ducrot, O. *Les échelles argumentatives*. Paris: Minuit, 1980.

———. *Le Dire et le dit*. Paris: Minuit, 1984.

Gazdar, G. *Pragmatics. Implicature, Presupposition and Logical Form*. New York: Academic Press, 1979.

Geis, M., and A. Zwicky. "On invited inference." *Linguistic Inquiry* 2 (1971): 561–566.

Groupe λ-l. *Car, parce que, puisque. Revue Romane* 10 (1975): 248–280.

Horn, L.R. *A Natural History of Negation*. Chicago: The University of Chicago Press, 1989.

———. "Implicature." In *The Handbook of Pragmatics*, 3–28. Oxford: Blackwell, 2004.

———. "On the Contrary: Pragmatic strengthening revisited." Lecture given at AMPRA 1, University of Northern Carolina, Charlotte, October 2012a.

———. "Histoire d'*O: Lexical pragmatics and the geometry of opposition." In *New Perspectives on the Square of Opposition*, 393–426. Bern: Peter Lang, 2012b.

Klima, E.S. "Negation in English." In *The Structure of Language. Readings in the Philosophy of Language*, 246–323. Englewood Cliffs: Prentice Hall, 1964.

Moeschler, J. *Dire et contredire. Pragmatique de la négation et acte de refutation dans la conversation*. Bern, Peter Lang, 1982.

———. "The pragmatic aspects of linguistic negation: Speech acts, argumentation and pragmatic inference." *Argumentation* 6 (1991): 51–75.

———. "La négation comme expression procédurale." In *Negation and Polarity. Syntax and Semantics*, 231–249. Amsterdam: John Benjamins, 1997.

———. "Representing events in language and discourse." In *Triani augusti vestigia pressa sequamur. Studia linguistica in honorem Liliane Tasmowski*, 461–479. Padova: Unipress, 2000a.

———. "Le Modèle des Inférences Directionnelles." *Cahiers de linguistique française* 22 (2000b): 57–100.

———. "Négation, polarité, asymétrie et événements." *Langages* 162 (2006a): 90–106.

———. "The French tradition in pragmatics: From structuralism to cognitivism." *Intercultural Pragmatics* 3–4 (2006b): 381–407.

———. "Why are there no negative particulars? Horn's conjecture revisited." *Generative Grammar in Geneva* 5 (2007): 1–13.

———. "Negation, scope and the descriptive/metalinguistic distinction." *Generative Grammar in Geneva* 6 (2010a): 29–48.

———. "Is pragmatics of discourse possible?" In *Perspectives on Language, Use, Pragmatics*, 217–241. Munich: Lincom Europa, 2010b.

———. "Causal, inferential and temporal connectives: Why *parce que* is the only causal connective in French?" In *Marqueurs discursifs et subjectivité*, 97–114. Rouen: Presses Universitaires de Rouen et du Havre, 2011.

———. "Pourquoi le sens est-il structuré? Une approche vériconditionnelle de la signification linguistique et du sens pragmatique." *Nouveaux cahiers de linguistique française* 30 (2012a): 53–71.

———. "Conversational and conventional implicatures." In *Cognitive Pragmatics*, 407–434. Berlin: Mouton de Gruyter, 2012b, 407–434.

———. "Is a speaker-based pragmatics possible? Or how can a hearer infer a speaker's commitment?" *Journal of Pragmatics* 48 (2013): 84–97.

———. "Argumentation, Connectives, and Explicature. How Do Discourse Connectives Constrain Argumentations and Utterances Interpretations." In *Perspectives on Pragmatics and Philosophy*. Wien: Springer Verlag (to appear).

Moeschler, J., and A. Reboul. *Dictionnaire encyclopédique de pragmatique*. Paris: Seuil, 1994.

Parsons, T. *Events in the Semantics of English*. Cambridge: The MIT Press, 1990.

Reboul, A., and J. Moeschler. *Pragmatique du discours. De l'interprétation de l'énoncé à l'interprétation du discours*. Paris: Armand Colin, 1998.

Searle, J.R. *Speech Acts: An Essay in the Philosophy of Language*. Cambridge: Cambridge University Press, 1969.

———. *Expression and Meaning. Studies in the Theory of Speech Acts*. Cambridge: Cambridge University Press, 1979.

Sperber, D, and D. Wilson. "Irony and the use-mention distinction." In *Radical Pragmatics*, 295–318. New York: Academic Press, 1981.

———. *Relevance: Communication and Cognition*. Oxford: Basil Blackwell, 1995.

———. *Meaning and Interpretation*. Cambridge: Cambridge University Press, 2012.

Stalnaker, R. "Pragmatic presuppositions." In *Proceedings of the Texas Conference on Performatives, Presuppositions and Implicatures*, 135–147. Arlington, Center for Applied Linguistics, 1977.

Sweetser, E. *From Etymology to Pragmatics: Metaphorical and Cultural Aspects of Semantic Structure*. Cambridge: Cambridge University Press, 1990.

Taboada, M. "Implicit and explicit coherence relations." Lecture given at L'empirie en linguistique: variété et complexité des approaches. 7e Journées de linguistique Suisse (SSL/SSG), Università della Svizzera Italiana, Lugano, September 2012.

Wilson, D. "The pragmatics of verbal irony: Echo or pretence?" *Lingua* 116, no. 10 (2006): 1722–1743.

Wilson, D., and T. Matsui. "Approches récentes du pontage inférentiel: Vérité, coherence et pertinence." In *Référence temporelle et nominale*, 7–40. Bern: Peter Lang, 2000.

Wilson, D., and D. Sperber. "Relevance Theory." In *The Handbook of Pragmatics*, 607–632. Oxford: Blackwell, 2004.

Zufferey, S. *Lexical Pragmatics and Theory of Mind*. Amsterdam: John Benjamins, 2010.

———. "'Car, Parce Que, Puisque' Revisited: Three empirical studies on French causal connectives." *Journal of Pragmatics* 44, no. 2 (2012): 138–153.

Zufferey S., and B. Cartoni. "English and French causal connectives in contrast." *Languages in Contrast* 12, no. 2 (2012): 232–250.

PART 2

Evaluation, Nonveridicality and Coherence in Computation Modelling

CHAPTER 4

Determining Negation Scope in German and English Medical Diagnoses

Oliver Gros and Manfred Stede

1 Introduction

One aspect of analyzing subjectivity in text is the detection of *negation*. On the one hand, it is of theoretical interest from the perspective of semantics, and on the other hand, many language technology applications rely on it. Consider the case of opinion mining, where the difference between an author giving a positive or a negative judgement is of utmost importance, and this difference is often coded by means of explicit negation (for example, *I did not like that Cheeseburger very much*).

Another application, which is the focus of this chapter, concerns particular diagnoses in medical reports. In such reports, the doctor states what he or she has observed and possibly some consequence of such observations. Often, however, the doctor points out what is *not* being observed, since the absence of a certain symptom can be just as important for judging the case as the presence of another. Further, in medical reports as well as in other genres, negation can be employed in forms of hedging. With an expression like *There is no sign of X*, the author states that X is probably not the case/not present, but she does not firmly exclude the possibility of X. All in all, we therefore see the handling of negation as one subproblem of analyzing evaluation in text, and it is especially relevant to the notion of nonveridicality and its linguistic counterparts, as they are discussed in this volume by Goddard, Moeschler, and others.

Focusing now on medical diagnoses, one specific application for their automatic analysis targets the so-called *coding* step: the annotation of portions of text with a standard code from a terminology such as ICD-10.[1] Coding is the basis, *inter alia*, for the billing procedure, where the actions of the doctor have to be recorded precisely and according to such a terminological schema. Obviously, then, detecting negation is just as vital as in the above-mentioned example of opinion mining. Whether the doctor did or did not

1 http://www.who.int/classifications/icd/en/.

 | DOI: 10.1163/9789004258174_005

perform some examination, whether a certain symptom has been observed or not observed—these distinctions must be known. And the relevance of negation identification for the overall coding task was demonstrated by Farkas and Szarvas (2008), who found that the performance of their automatic coding system decreased by 10.66 % when the negation component was disabled.

In the work reported here, we built a system for finding negations in English and German text. Our primary target is medical diagnoses, but for testing the generality of our approach we also look at a very different genre, viz. political commentary so that we can compare the performance. The language in medical diagnoses, as is well known, can be very dense (a series of noun phrases rather than full sentences), so developing a computational approach is in the danger of being tailored to a rather specialized sublanguage (Kittredge & Lehrberger 1982).

"Finding negations" means identifying a negation *operator* and deciding on its *scope*, or the words representing the material that is being negated. Here are a few examples, with the operator underlined and the scope in square brackets:

(1) The patient <u>denied</u> [any knee problems].
(2) There is <u>no</u> [sign of pneumonia].
(3) You should <u>never</u> [breathe too quickly].

While these are relatively straightforward cases, negation can become tricky, as we will see later on. The remainder of the paper is structured as follows: section 2 briefly mentions some related work; section 3 introduces the negation annotation guidelines that we devised and the corpus we have built up so far; and section 4 describes *Negtopus*, our implementation. In addition, we take a brief look at the prospects of using off-the-shelf syntax parsers for the task of negation detection. Section 5 evaluates our approach and compares its performance to *NegEx*, a prominent competitor. Finally, Section 6 summarizes the paper and offers some conclusions.

2 Related Work

In Computational Linguistics, the issue of processing negation is just beginning to attract wider attention; the first workshop on this topic at a major conference was held in 2010 (Morante & Sporleder 2010). In the medical domain, as noted above, detecting negation is a very important step of text analysis. A highly influential approach, the NegEx algorithm (Chapman et al. 2001) was made publicly available in the early 2000s; today, several implementations can be chosen from.[2] NegEx operates with regular expressions over surface words, somehat similar to our own approach. Slightly different systems are *NegExpander* (Aronow, Feng & Croft 1999), which makes use of part-of-speech tagging, and *NegFinder* (Mutalik, Deshpande, & Nadkarni 2001), which proceeds to the next step and employs full syntactic parsing. We will mention these programs again later when explaining our own approach and its performance. More recently, corpora of medical text annotated with negation as well as uncertainty markers have become available; notably the BioScope corpus (Vincze et al. 2008).

3 The Corpus

In order to demarcate the problem of identifying negations, our first step consisted in collecting a corpus and drafting guidelines for human annotators. The annotation step allows for empirically determining the range of expressions the languages used in expressing negation, and to assess the overall difficulty of the task.

3.1 *Annotation Guidelines*

In designing our annotation guidelines, we took inspiration from (Vincze et al. 2008) but extended their approach so that it covers both German and English. We added several constructions that were not relevant in the medical texts but that played a role in the newspaper commentary texts we also considered. Also, some of our decisions on scope marking differ from those of Vincze et al.

As for the negation operators, our guidelines ask for annotating verbs (*to deny, to exclude*, etc.), nouns (*absence*), pronouns (*no one*), adverbs (*never, not*), coordinating conjunctions (*neither, nor*), subordinating conjunctions (*instead of*), determiners (*no*), prepositions (*without*), and morphemes (*un-, in-*). Operators can occasionally be composed of non-adjacent words, as in the split conjunction *neither, nor* and in support verb constructions.

The decision on operator identification is usually not hard (except for a grey area of certain verbs and nouns). Giving clear directions for marking the scope, however, can be tricky. Our first rule of thumb is that the scope correspond to a syntactic constituent where possible. Second, from the semantic viewpoint,

2 http://code.google.com/p/negex/.

we ask annotators to prefer narrow scopes but make sure that all semantically dependent material is included. For instance, in the case of determiners, the extent of the noun phrase needs to be specified; we define it as the noun plus any restrictive modifiers. Examples 4 and 5 below illustrate the distinction. We add paraphrases that serve to make the scope more explicit. Similarly, for adverbs we use the verb plus the constituents that are subcategorized for, thus excluding other adverbial phrases (see example 6).

(4) There are no [cars with electrical engines] to be seen.
What is not to be seen is [cars with electrical engines].

(5) Paul tolerates no [animals] in his apartment.
What Paul does not tolerate in his apartment is [animals].

(6) [Paul] never [reads newspapers] in the morning.
In the morning, what never happens is [Paul reading newspapers].

Notice that there may very well be ambiguity in determining the scope, which relates to focus marking. In example 5, when *apartment* receives stress, the better paraphrase is *What Paul does not tolerate is [animals in his apartment]*. Likewise, if *morning* in example 6 is in focus, the scope is to be extended: *What never happens is [Paul reading newspapers in the morning]*. In the absence of focus marking in written text, the annotation is guided by syntactic factors such as the distinction between restrictive and non-restrictive modification and between arguments and adjuncts.

It is well-known that a negation can be embedded in another so that due to cancellation, an overall non-negated proposition results. Our annotation thus allows for recursion, where operators and scopes are co-indexed:

(7) It is not$_1$ [im$_2$[possible]$_2$ that the patient will develop arterial disease]$_1$.

3.2 *Data*

The specific medical domains we target in our work are radiology and cardiology. This guided the selection of our texts, and thus our overall corpus, consists of five subcorpora:

- GER-CARD: 12 German reports from a cardiologist, comprising 7,449 words in total (on average, 745 words per text)
- ENG-RAD1: 6 radiology reports from a corpus collected at Carnegie Mellon University, 6,300 words in total (on average, 1,050 words per text)

- ENG-RAD2: 12 texts consisting of radiology reports from *The Computational Medicine Center*'s NLP Challenge[3] (Pestian et al. 2007), 11,188 words in total, (on average, 932 words per text)
- GER-COMM: 11 German newspaper commentaries from *Der Tagesspiegel*, 2,600 words in total (on average, 237 words per text)
- ENG-COMM: 10 English newspaper commentaries from *The New York Times*, 4,693 words in total (on average, 469 words per text)

For illustration, here are a few negation examples from the English radiology texts:

(8) No hydronephrosis.
(9) Social history: Positive smoker, nondrinker, no drug use.
(10) All other review of systems is negative.
(11) There is no focal, lobar consolidation to suggest bacterial pneumonia.
(12) The lack of interval growth in one month is not uncommon given differences in technique.

In the last two examples, we find scope ambiguity as discussed above. The purpose clause in example 11 could be inside or outside the scope; our guidelines urge the annotator to prefer the narrow scope in such cases. Likewise, the status of the two adverbial phrases in example 12 is semantically not clear, and thus we also resort to the narrow scope on merely syntactic grounds.

Considering the syntactic structure in our corpus, the distribution in examples 8 to 12 is not representative of the medical texts, since the verbless expressions in fact have a majority in German by a wider margin than in English. This might very well be specific to the genre of diagnosis reports, and could be different in related genres such as discharge summaries.

The annotation work is done with MMAX2,[4] a tool that can be used effectively for a variety of annotation purposes, including relations between spans of text, which is our scenario here. Since the set of negation operators is fairly small, we can detect the candidates automatically and present them to the human annotator for confirmation. She or he then marks the scope and finally establishes a link between the two. This allows for handling cases where operator and scope are not adjacent and for embedded negations as discussed above.

3 http://www.computationalmedicine.org/challenge.

4 http://mmax2.sourceforge.net.

MMAX2 generates standoff XML annotations, which is convenient for relating this type of annotation to others: When other layers of annotation, such as syntactic analyses or coreference links, are produced with different tools, the various standoff XML files can be merged and queried across layers: for this purpose, we use our linguistic database ANNIS (Chiarcos et al. 2008). With multiple layers in this vein, queries can check, for example, what types of syntactic constituents are in the scope of certain negation operators, or what the semantic scope of an operator is in case the syntactic scope contains a pronoun (whose antecedent is to be retrieved from the coreference layer).

Is negation a frequent phenomenon in medical text? Huang and Lowe (2007) found in their corpus of cardiology reports that 20% of the sentences contain a negation. Since "sentence" is a difficult notion in our texts (as explained above), we prefer to measure the ratio of negation operators over words (tokens) and find that one in 40 to 50 words in our medical texts is a negation operator. In the English commentaries, the frequency is considerably lower, while in the German commentary, it is in the same range. Table 1 shows the numbers for the various types of operators.

TABLE 1 *Distribution of negation operators in our corpus*

Operator	ENG-RAD1	ENG-RAD2	GER-CARD	ENG-COMM	GER-COMM	Σ ENG	Σ GER
Adverb	11 / 20%	40 / 18%	20 / 12%	34 / 50%	26 / 49%	105 / 23%	46 / 20%
Determ.	81 / 51%	127 / 56%	86 / 50%	9 / 14%	10 / 19%	217 / 48%	96 / 43%
Pronoun	5 / 3%	0	3 / 2%	4 / 6%	1 / 2%	9 / 2%	4 / 2%
Co conj	0	2 / 1%	0	2 / 3%	0	4 / 1%	0
Sub conj	0	0	0	0	1 / 2%	0	1 / 1%
Prep	4 / 3%	18 / 8%	9 / 5%	2 / 3%	1 / 2%	24 / 5%	10 / 4%
Verb	11 / 7%	8 / 3%	5 / 3%	2 / 3%	6 / 11%	21 / 5%	11 / 4%
Noun	0	5 / 2%	1 / 1%	0	0	5 / 1%	1 / 1%
Morph	26 / 16%	26 / 12%	48 / 28%	14 / 21%	8 / 15%	66 / 15%	56 / 25%
Σ	158	226	172	67	53	451	225
Words / neg op.	40	50	43	70	49		

4 Automatically Finding Negations and Their Scopes

4.1 *Our Approach:* Negtopus

Negtopus is a modular, multilingual text analysis tool for negation operators and their scope. It automatically tags negation operators and relates them to their scope. The algorithm works in several steps, and each module can be individually configured, or it could be replaced by some external module. The pipeline (to be explained below) consists of a tokenizer, a word class tagger, a named-entity recognizer, a scope finder, and an output generator. Negtopus can be used as a stand-alone module, but to enable interoperability with other text analysis tasks, we also integrated Negtopus into our workbench for text document analysis, MOTS (Stede & Bieler 2012).

4.1.1 Lexicon Construction

An important resource within Negtopus is a human-readable (and editable) lexicon file, which contains a list of words and their domain-specific (or task-specific) class labels. Most prominently, negation operators are assigned to the class **neg**, which includes all above-mentioned part-of-speech types of negations. Further, for determining scope boundaries, a list of connectives is maintained. These are syntactically also heterogeneous (conjunctions, adverbs); for our purposes here, they are bundled, together with some prepositions, into the class **conn**. Finally, nouns are given the label **noun**, and various other words are bundled into the class **attribute**.

neg and **conn** thus are sets of closed-class words that are to be manually assembled for the target language. For the open-class sets **noun** and **attibute**, we have implemented a lexicon construction procedure that extracts the relevant words from a suitable corpus. Our choice is to use the ICD-10 coding guide, which gives one or more natural language equivalents for each code. Table 2 shows a small excerpt. For extracting the words, we use a set of patterns (regular expressions) that define the contexts in which words of an "interesting" class (i.e., **noun** or **attribute**) occur. To give just one simple example, patterns operating on certain prepositions (e.g., *of*) will interpret unknown words immediately preceding and following them as **noun**. Since the identification of a new word can in turn provide evidence for the types of its neighbours, the rules are applied iteratively until no further type is induced. In this way, the coding guide is being mapped to the lexicon that we can subsequently use for analysing diagnoses.

TABLE 2 *Excerpt from ICD-10 coding guide*

Code	English text
ICD-10:C00	Malignant neoplasm of lip
ICD-10:C00.0	External upper lip
ICD-10:C00.1	External lower lip
ICD-10:C00.2	External lip, unspecified
ICD-10:C00.3	Upper lip, inner aspect
ICD-10:C00.4	Lower lip, inner aspect
ICD-10:C00.5	Lip, unspecified, inner aspect
ICD-10:C00.6	Commissure of lip
ICD-10:C00.8	Overlapping lesion of lip
ICD-10:C00.9	Lip, unspecified
ICD-10:C01	Malignant neoplasm of base of tongue
ICD-10:C02	Malignant neoplasm of other and unspecified parts of tongue

While the list of negation expressions and a small set of the main connectives and prepositions of the analyzed language (hence: a list of closed-class lexical items) is necessary for Negtopus to operate, the open-class items are in principle optional. If a resource for building such a lexicon is not available, the program will employ the same pattern rules in order to guess the class of unknown words in the text.

4.1.2 Algorithm

When Negtopus is given a plain text file, it performs tokenization and tags the words according to the four classes. Alternatively, this pre-processing information can already be part of the input, as separate annotation layers in our stand-off XML architecture, for example (PAULA format/MOTS workbench, see Stede & Bieler 2012). In this case, standard part-of-speech tags such as those produced by an off-the-shelf tagger are being mapped to our four abstract classes.

In the next and central step, the scope finder relates the negation operators to their scope using generic pre-defined patterns consisting of class labels, surface words, and punctuation symbols. We first identify a narrow, syntactically motivated scope, and afterwards a second set of patterns determines whether the narrow scope can be extended to a wider, semantically motivated one. For instance, given the phrase *no evidence of arterial disease*, the first pattern set would mark only *evidence*, since *of* in this syntactic step is a boundary marker.

The second pattern set detects (*inter alia*) such combinations of specific nouns as *evidence, indication* and prepositions that precede the noun phrase, which in these cases contains the crucial information. The second pattern set will thus identify *arterial disease* as the semantic scope of *no*. As a second example, consider the sentence *A malign neoplasm is not seen*. Here, the word *seen* is the direct/syntactic scope, whereas *malign neoplasm* is the semantic or indirect scope, which is likely to be the expression the doctor intended to negate. Patterns thus look for the scope extension not just in adjacency to the narrow scope but also in other parts of the phrase.

4.1.3 Results/Output

Negtopus writes its result in various formats according to the input:

- XML files in PAULA format (Dipper 2005), with annotation of negation operator, syntactic scope, and semantic scope
- XML files in MMAX2 format, with markables for negation operator and negation scope (the combination of syntactic and semantic scope)
- Plain text files with human-readable annotations like *Negation X at position N negates expression Y at position M*

The first option allows for easy post-processing, integration with other annotations (as in MOTS), or transfer into our linguistic database ANNIS (Chiarcos et al. 2008). The second option enables convenient viewing of this annotation layer (and others, if also annotated with MMAX2), and the third is a summary of the results for quick inspection without the need to start a software tool.

4.2 *Exploiting Syntactic Parsing—an Alternative?*

Since the scope of a negation is largely determined by the syntactic structure, ideally one would not employ heuristic token-based methods but find the scope on a full parse tree. Huang and Lowe (2007) tried this for English radiology reports, using the Stanford parser.[5] The authors manually wrote grammatical patterns that were matched against the parse tree. The main advantage is that long-distance dependencies between operator and scope can be handled, as long as the parse is good enough. Morphological negation was not considered, and some phrases like *several blood cultures, six in all, had been negative*

5 http://nlp.stanford.edu/software/lex-parser.shtml.

are also ignored.[6] The approach leads to a recall of 92.6% and a precision of 98.6%, but the authors point out that input sentences have to be "grammatical" for a useful parse tree to be constructed.

Given our own corpus, two central problems for syntactic parsing of medical texts are the abundance of medical terms and acronyms, on the one hand, and abridged language, on the other. We conducted several experiments with the Stanford parser and found that precisely the combination of missing verbs and unknown words causes great problems, since the parser is likely to interpret the unknown word as the missing verb, which leads to wrong analyses. To illustrate, we show an example in Table 3. As verbless phrases are so frequent in our data (slightly more than half of the "sentences"), we conclude that a POS-tag-pattern-based approach is more robust for this application. (An obvious alternative would be to train a statistical parser on our particular sublanguage, but we are not aware of any available training data.)

TABLE 3 *Sample output of Stanford parser*

```
No prior EKG to compare to.
(S
  (NP (DT No) (JJ prior))
  (VP (VBZ EKG)
    (S
      (VP (TO to)
        (VP (VB compare)
          (PP (TO to)))))) (. .))
```

5 Evaluation

5.1 *Medical Texts*

In Table 4 we show the results of evaluaing Negtopus on our annotated medical texts (with the two English radiology subcorpora combined into one). Negation operators—at least in this data—have no alternative readings, and therefore they are being recognized with perfect precision. The recall figures are lower, which is clearly due to a number of morphological operators that are not yet

6 This example is taken from Mutalik, Deshpande, and Nadkarni (2001).

built into Negtopus. For judging the scope, we distinguish between exact match and Negtopus suggesting a scope that is too narrow or too wide, respectively.[7] For different applications, either one or the other may be less problematic. The general tendency is for Negtopus to be somewhat "too careful", as the sum of exact and too-narrow scopes is 91% for English and 88% for German.

The NexEx algorithm (Chapman et al. 2001) also uses regular expressions to identify negation operators and, depending on the operator, marks the scope to the left or to the right of the operator. However, the extent of the scope is a fixed-size window of six elements, where "elements" are phrases replaced by UMLS[8] concepts or words. The authors report a recall of 77.8%, a precision of 84.5%, and a specificity (not-found non-relevant instances in all non-relevant instances) of 94.5%. Other authors (Mitchell et al. 2004) achieved a higher recall (80%) with almost identical precision (84%). Yet another approach is to replace the fixed-size window by a search for the nearest punctuation symbol and to take that as the borderline (Farkas & Szarvas 2008), which more closely resembles our approach (but we consider additional boundary signals besides punctuation). Farkas and Szarvas do not provide results for their negation detection but evaluate their system on the overall ICD-10 coding task, where negation recognition proved valuable, as we stated in the introduction.

TABLE 4 *Negtopus performance on medical text*

	ENG-RAD	GER-CARD
Op precision	1	1
Op recall	0.85	0.72
Non-morph op precision	1	1
Non-morph op recall	0.98	0.98
Exact scope	229 / 68%	68 / 54%
Scope too wide	32 / 9%	15 / 12%
Scope too narrow	78 / 23%	43 / 34%
Σ	339	126

7 The scope detection results where computed on the data containing correctly-recognized operators.

8 Unified Medical Language System: http://www.nlm.nih.gov/research/umls/.

5.2 *Commentary Texts*

Obviously, our appoach is clearly geared towards the sublanguage of diagnosis reports and cannot be expected to perform equally well with less restricted language. We wanted, however, to assess the difference quantitatively so that the amount of work needed for a more generic solution can be estimated. That is why we also applied our annotation guidelines to a number of English and German newspaper commentaries and then evaluated Negtopus on that data. Some examples from the *New York Times* data demonstrate that, as a result of complex sentence structures, scopes are typically much longer and often ambiguous (for instance, is a *because*-clause part of the scope?), and that embedding can create complicatons:

(13) [We will never know just how much better the fight in Afghanistan might be going if it had been managed more competently over the years.]
(14) CARE had decided to stop [selling subsidized American farm products in poor African countries] because the program was inefficient and undercut local farmers.
(15) The problem is that [it won't$_1$ stay so good without$_2$ [more government help]$_2$]$_1$.

The results in Table 5 show that precision of operator identification is quite high, indicating that there is also little ambiguity in negation operators in "general" language. Operator recall is somewhat lower in English, but in German it is just as good as with the medical texts; thus the set of operators we obtained from the medical texts seems to be representative for language in general (recall that our commentary corpus is fairly small, so we have to be somewhat cautious with conclusions on recall performance). Also, we find the same tendency as in the medical texts: recall problems are largely due to morphological operators that we don't account for. Operator scope, as can be expected, is generally too small: syntactic structures are considerably more complex, and our boundary detection heuristics fire too early when searching outward from the negation operator.

6 Summary

We presented Negtopus, a system for recognizing negation operators and their scopes in English and German text. Its principal target is medical diagnoses, but we also tested it on newspaper commentaries for comparison. Earlier research on negation detection in medical texts used similar approaches based

TABLE 5 *Negtopus performance on commentary text*

	ENG-COMM	GER-COMM
Op precision	0.95	0.96
Op recall	0.7	0.74
Non-morph op precision	0.97	1
Non-morph op recall	0.86	0.87
Exact scope	5 / 10%	5 / 12%
Scope too wide	14 / 27%	3 / 8%
Scope too narrow	32 / 63%	32 / 80%
Σ	51	40

on regular expressions but addressed slightly different tasks so that the results are not directly comparable. Furthermore, our approach uses heuristics based on abstract word classes and accounting for more scope boundary features.

Negtopus relies on a lexical resource: a relatively short list of closed-class items that have to be manually compiled for the target language and a long list of domain-specific, open-class content words. We suggest learning these words from standard textual resources (code books) on the basis of extraction patterns. Since these code books exist for many languages, we expect that our approach can quite easily be applied to other languages that structurally behave in similar ways (so that the scope detection heuristics apply).

An alternative to surface patterns, which quickly comes to mind, is to employ full-scale syntactic parsing. We argued, however, that current parsers (which are generally trained on newspaper language) have problems with the combination of medical terms and abbreviations and a very dense language (lack of verbs). One way to alleviate the problem could be to employ a domain-specific named-entity recognition and submit its results to the parser, but most parsers nowadays do not accept pre-tagged input.

References

Aronow, D.B., F. Feng, and W.B. Croft. "Ad hoc classification of radiology reports." *Journal of the American Medical Informatics Association* 6, no. 6 (1999): 393–411.

Chapman, W.W., W. Bridewell, P. Hanbury, G.F. Cooper, and B.G. Buchanan. "A simple algorithm for identifying negated findings and diseases in discharge summaries." *Journal of Biomedical Informatics* 34 (2001): 301–310.

Chiarcos, Christian, Stefanie Dipper, Michael Götze, U. Leser, A. Lüdeling, Julia Ritz, and Manfred Stede. "A flexible framework for integrating annotations from different tools and tagsets." *Traitement Automatique des Langues* 49 (2008): 217–246.

Dipper, Stefanie. "XML-based stand-off representation and exploitation of multi-level linguistic annotation." In *Proceedings of Berliner XML Tage*, 39–50, 2005.

Farkas, R., and G. Szarvas. "Automatic construction of rule-based ICD-9-CM coding systems." *BMC bioinformatics* 9, Suppl 3 (2008): S10.

Huang, Y., and H. Lowe. "A novel hybrid approach to automated negation detection in clinical radiology reports." *Journal of the American Medical Informatics Association* 14 (2007): 304–311.

Kittredge, Richard, and John Lehrberger. *Sublanguage: studies of language in restricted semantic domains*. Berlin: Walter de Gruyter, 1982.

Mitchell, K., M. Becich, J. Berman, W. Chapman, J. Gilbertson, D. Gupta, J. Harrison, E. Legowski, and R. Crowley. "Implementation and evaluation of a negation tagger in a pipeline-based system for information extraction from pathology reports." *Medinfo* 11, Pt. 1 (2004): 663–667.

Morante, Roser, and Caroline Sporleder, eds. *Proceedings of the Workshop on Negation and Speculation in Natural Language Processing* (*NeSp-NLP 2010*). Antwerp: University of Antwerp, B-Antwerp, 2010.

Mutalik, Pradeep G., Aniruddha Deshpande, and Prakash M. Nadkarni. "Use of general-purpose negation detection to augment concept indexing of medical documents." *Journal of the American Medical Informatics Association* 8, no. 6 (2001): 598–609.

Pestian, John P., Christopher Brew, Pawel Matykiewicz, D.J. Hovermale, Neil Johnson, K. Bretonnel Cohen, and Wlodzislaw Duch. "A shared task involving multi-label classification of clinical free text." In *Proceedings of the Workshop on BioNLP 2007: Biological, Translational, and Clinical Language Processing*, BioNLP '07, 97–104. Association for Computational Linguistics, 2007.

Stede, Manfred, and Heike Bieler. "The MOTS workbench." In *Modeling, Learning, and Processing of Text Technological Data Structures*. Berlin/Heidelberg: Springer, 2012.

Vincze, V., G. Szarvas, R. Farkas, G. Móra, and J. Csirik. "The bioscope corpus: biomedical texts annotated for uncertainty, negation and their scopes." *BMC Bioinformatics* 9, Suppl 11 (2008): S9.

CHAPTER 5

Assessing Opinions in Texts:
Does Discourse Really Matter?

Farah Benamara, Vladimir Popescu, Baptiste Chardon, Nicholas Asher and Yannick Mathieu

In this paper, we focus on measuring the effect of discourse structure on sentiment analysis. Using Segmented Discourse Representation Theory (SDRT) as our formal framework, we investigate how rhetorical relations interact with opinions and to what extent these interactions depend on the corpus genre. We propose a two-level annotation scheme: first at the segment level, where each elementary discourse unit is annotated according to the opinion it conveys, and then at the document level, where the discourse structure of the document is built. We conduct our annotation campaign on two French corpus genres: movie reviews and news reactions. We discuss our results and comment our observations.

1 Introduction

Discourse structure is essential in determining the content conveyed by a text. It affects for example, the temporal structure of a text, the interpretation of anaphoric expressions and presuppositions. It can also be used in word sense disambiguation (such as verb phrase ellipsis, and quantification scope) and in the identification of the conversational implicatures of agents in dialogue (Asher and Lascarides 2003). Discourse structure has been shown to be useful in many NLP applications, such as automatic text summarization (Marcu 2000) and textual entailment (Mirkin et al. 2010). In this paper, we focus on measuring the effect of discourse structure on sentiment analysis.

Few research efforts to date have used discourse for opinion analysis. Pang and Lee (2004) assume that subjective and objective sentences are more likely to appear together. Asher et al. (2008) propose a shallow semantic representation using a feature structure and five types of SDRT-like rhetorical relations (such as Contrast and Result). They manually annotate lexically marked opinion expressions and analyzed how the clauses involving these expressions are related to each other within a discourse. Taboada et al. (2008) as well as Heerschop et al. (2011) have used a Rhetorical Structure Theory discourse parser in

 | DOI: 10.1163/9789004258174_006

order to calculate semantic orientation at the document level by weighting the nuclei more heavily. Somasundaran (2010) proposes the notion of opinion frames as a representation of documents at the discourse level in order to improve sentence-based polarity classification and to recognize the overall stance. Two sets of 'home-made' relations are used: relations between targets ('same' and 'alternative' relations) and relations between opinion expressions ('reinforcing' and 'non-reinforcing' relations). The frames are used to annotate a multi-party meeting corpus. Zhou et al. (2011) use the semantic sequential representations (SSRs) and an unsupervised method to recognize RST-based discourse relations for eliminating intra-sentence polarity ambiguities. More recently, Trnavac and Taboada (2010) examine how nonveridical markers and rhetorical relations contribute to the expression of Appraisal in movie and book reviews. They focus on two different types of lexically marked rhetorical relations, conditional and concessive, as defined in RST. They show that these two relations affect polarity, as well as the intensity of opinion expressions. Finally, Polanyi and van den Berg (2011) discuss the application of the Linguistic Discourse Model theory (LDM) (Polanyi et al. 2004) to sentiment analysis at the discourse level in movie reviews. In this paper, we aim to go further by investigating how different types of rhetorical relations interact with opinions and by analyzing to what extent these interactions depend on the corpus genre. We attempt to do this by using Segmented Discourse Representation Theory (SDRT) (Asher & Lascarides 2003) as our formal framework.

Discourse structure can be a good indicator of the subjectivity and/or the polarity orientation of elementary discourse units (EDUs). It can also be used to recognize implicit opinions and to enhance the recognition of the overall stance of texts. The following examples extracted from our corpus of French movie reviews illustrate this (the reviews are translated in English, and EDUs are between square brackets). We show, for each example, how segments are discursively related:

(1) [The movie is not bad,]$_a$ [although some persons left the auditorium]$_b$. *Contrast*(*a*, *b*)

(2) [Mary liked the movie.]$_a$ [Her husband too.]$_b$ *Parallel*(*a*, *b*)

(3) [Laborious]$_a$ [and copy/paste of the first part.]$_b$ *Continuation*(*a*, *b*)

(4) [Very bad movie.]$_a$ [I do not recommend it.]$_b$ *Result*(*a*, *b*)

(5a) [The movie was excellent.]$_a$ [The actors were great]$_b$. *Elaboration*(*a*, *b*)

(5b) [It is an action movie with two superb actors.]$_a$ [It stars Angelina Jolie and Brad Pitt as a bored married couple]$_b$ [who are contracted to kill each other]$_c$. *Elaboration*(*a*, *Elaboration*(*b*,*c*))

(6) [If you want to waste your time,]$_a$ [go see the movie]$_b$. *Conditional(a, b)*
(7) [I suppose]$_a$ [that the employment policy will be a disaster]$_b$. *Attribution(a, b)*

We observe in our corpus that segments related by a *Contrast, Parallel* or a *Continuation* relation often share the same subjective orientation. This allows us to detect the implicit opinions conveyed in segments (1)b, (2)b, and (3)b, since no explicit opinion expressions are lexically marked. Polarity is reversed in case of *Contrast* and usually preserved in case of *Parallel* and *Continuation*. We also notice that *Result* does not have a strong effect on subjectivity and that polarity is not preserved. For instance, in: "[Your life is miserable?] [You don't have a girlfriend?] [Go see this movie]", the prior positive polarity of the recommendation follows negative opinions. Hence, *Result* can help to determine the contextual polarity of opinionated segments. In the case of *Elaboration*, subjectivity is usually not preserved (see examples (5a) and (5b)), in contrast to polarity. (One cannot say: "[The movie was excellent.] [The actors were bad]".) Finally, *Attribution* plays a role only when its second argument is subjective. In this case, depending on the reported speech act used to introduce the opinion, *Attribution* affects the degree of commitment of the author and the holder (Asher 1993).

This seems very nice, but we have to deal with three main problems: (i) relatively few discourse relations are lexically marked, (ii) some discourse markers can introduce several rhetorical relations, and finally (iii) segments can be part of complex discourse units (CDUs).[1] Having the complexity of the task in mind, the key questions are:

- How may a discourse-based approach be used to enhance standard approach? To answer this question, we propose a two-level annotation scheme: first at the EDU level, where each segment has to be annotated according to the opinion it conveys, and then at the document level, where each EDU has to be discursively related to other EDUs or CDUs.
- Is this dependent on the corpus genre? To study the impact of genre constraints, we conduct our annotation campaign on two French corpus genres: movie reviews and news reactions.

1 In "[This movie is poignant,]$_a$ [and the actors excellent.]$_b$ [It will remain in your DVD closet.]$_c$", we have *Continuation*(a, b) and *Result*$([a, b], c)$ where $[a, b]$ is a complex segment. Therefore, the subjectivity of c depends on $[a, b]$.

The paper is organized as follows. We first present our annotation scheme and then describe our corpus. Section 3 presents our data, Section 4 describes the annotation campaign and finally, Section 5 gives the results of our annotation campaign along with our observations. We conclude this paper by suggesting some answers to the previously asked questions.

2 Annotation Scheme

The sentence level is not appropriate for analyzing opinions in discourse since, in addition to objective clauses, a single sentence may contain several opinion clauses that can be connected by rhetorical relations. Moving to the clause level is also not appropriate, since several opinion expressions can be discursively related as in "The movie is great but too long", where we have a *Contrast* relation, or "Mr. Dupont, a rich business man, has been savagely killed", where we have an *Elaboration* because the appositive gives further information about the eventuality introduced in the main clause. Therefore, we need to move to a finer-grained analysis, at the segment level. Somasundaran et al. (2007) have used a similar level to detect the presence of sentiment and arguing in dialogues. They show that adding dialogue structure annotations (where dialogue acts are linked via adjacency pair relations) at the segment level improved their results over the sentence level. However, segment annotations were provided by their corpus, whereas in our case segments are defined according to the Segmented Discourse Representation Theory (SDRT) (Asher & Lascarides 2003) and are automatically detected (see section 4).

EDUs are our basic annotation units. Hence, the first step is discourse segmentation. EDUs typically correspond to verbal clauses, but also to other syntactic units describing eventualities, adjuncts (like appositions or frame adverbials), non-restrictive relatives, and appositions (for embedded EDUs). In addition to this standard definition, we observe that several opinion expressions (often conjoined NP or AP clauses) can be linked by discourse relations. We resegment such EDUs into separate clauses—for instance "the film is beautiful and powerful" is taken to express two segments: "[the film is beautiful] [and powerful]". For segment annotation, we rely on an already existing annotation guide (Afantenos et al. 2012) that we refine in order to take into account the particulars of opinion texts. To avoid errors in determining the basic units (which would thus make the inter-annotator agreement study tedious), we have decided to discard the segmentation from the annotation campaign. Instead, we chose to automatically identify EDUs and then manually correct the segmentation if necessary. Our segmenter yields an average F-measure of 72.80%. A detailed description of our discourse segmenter is presented in Benamara et al. (2011). We elaborate two annotation guides: one at the EDU level and the other at the document level as described below.

2.1 *EDU Annotation Level*

For each EDU in a document, annotators were first asked to annotate its subjectivity orientation as well as its polarity and strength. Then, within each EDU, annotators had to identify a set of specific lexical units that interact locally with opinion expressions, including negations and modalities.

2.1.1 Annotating Subjective Orientation of an EDU

An EDU has three properties:

- a category that can be any of the following:
  - **explicit segments (SE)**—segments that contain explicitly lexicalized *subjective and evaluative expressions*, as segment *a* in the examples (1) to (5) and segment *b* in (7) (cf. examples in the introduction).
  - **objective segments (O)**—segments that contain neither a lexicalized subjective term nor an implied opinion. They are purely factual, as in "[I went to the cinema yesterday]".
  - **subjective, but non-evaluative segments (SN)**—segments that are used to introduce opinions. In general, these segments contain verbs that report the speech and opinions of others, as in segment *a* in the example (7). The opinion polarity (positive, negative, or neutral) is given by the verbs' complements. It is important to note that the *SN* category does not cover the cases of neutral opinion.
  - **SE and SI**—segments that contain both explicit and implicit evaluations of the same topic or different topics. For instance, "[Fantastic pub!]$_a$ [The pretty waitresses will not hesitate to drink with you]$_b$", segment *b* contains two opinions: one explicit, towards the waitress, and the other positive implicit, towards the pub.
- a polarity that can be of five different values: **positive**; **negative**; **neutral**, in the sense that the positivity/negativity of the segment depends on the context (as in "[This movie is poignant]"); **both** positive and negative, which indicates a mixed polarity, as in "[this stupid president made a wonderful talk]"; and **no polarity**, which indicates that the segment does not convey any evaluation (for segments of category *O* and *SN*).
- a strength that has to be stated on a three-level scale [1, 3] where 1 indicates a weak strength.

Wiebe et al. (2005) have already proposed an expression-level annotation scheme that distinguishes between explicit mentions of private states, speech events expressing private states, and expressive subjective elements. Liu (2012) has also observed that subjective sentences and opinionated sentences (which are objective or subjective sentences that express implicit positive or negative opinions) are not the same, even though opinionated sentences are often a subset of subjective sentences. Finally, Toprak et al. (2010) distinguish in their annotation scheme between explicit opinions and facts that imply opinions. We follow the same observations and propose, in addition to studying the correlations between our segment types and the overall opinion, on the one hand, and between segment types and rhetorical relations, on the other hand (see section 5).

2.1.2 Annotating Opinions with an EDU

Once each EDU is annotated, annotators have to look inside each EDU to annotate the following:

- the topic of the opinion. It can be of three types: the main topic of the document, such as "the movie"; a part-of topic, in the case of features related to the main topic such as "the actors"; "the music"; and finally another topic that has no ontological relation with the main topic, such as "theater" in "The movie was great. Shame that the theater was dirty".
- the holder. We distinguish between two types of holders: main and other (as in "my mother loved the movie").
- the opinion expression spans. Annotators have to specify their polarity, strength, and semantic category and subcategory (a detailed description of these categories is given in Asher et al. (2008)). No opinion expressions have to be annotated in case of *SI* and *O* segments.
- the operators that interact locally with opinion expressions. We deal with four types of operators: (i) negations that may affect the polarity and the strength of an expression; (ii) modals that are used to express the degree of belief of the holder; (iii) intensifiers that are used to strengthen (we use the operator **Int+**) or weaken (**Int-**) the prior polarity of a word or an expression; and, finally, (iv) restrictors that narrow the scope of the opinion in the sense that the positivity and/or negativity of the expression can be evaluated only under certain conditions, as in "the restaurant is very good for children".

The annotation at the EDU level is very similar to state-of-the-art opinion annotation schemes. However, our treatment of valence shifter terms is novel in three ways: (i) it deals with different kinds of operators, (ii) operators are not a part of the opinion expression annotation (as is the case in MPQA (Wiebe et al. 2005), for example), and finally, (iii) every operator has to be linked to the expression it modifies by using a specific *Scope* relation.

2.2 *Document Annotation Level*

The next step is to annotate opinions at the document level. First, annotators have to give the overall opinion orientation of the document (the initial star ratings in MR corpus were removed) by using a six-level scale, going from −3 to −1 for negative opinion documents and from +1 to +3 for positive ones. Then, annotators have to build the discourse structure of the document following the principles of SDRT. The global rating is an important step in the annotation process since it is used to evaluate the contribution of implicit opinion segments to the author's global opinion on the main topic of the document (cf. section 5.2.1). Before detailing our second annotation level, we first motivate the choice of SDRT as our formal framework.

2.2.1 Why SDRT?

There are a number of reasons why SDRT is an attractive choice for opinion analysis. First, SDRT segmentation is more fine-grained than in Wolf and Gibson (2006) or annotation schemes for RST (Carlson et al. 2003) or the PDTB (Prasad et al. 2006). Indeed, in RST, EDUs can be simple sentences or clauses in a complex sentence that typically correspond to verbal clauses. EDUs can also correspond to other syntactic units describing eventualities, such as prepositional and noun phrases. RST does not allow for nested EDUs. On the contrary, SDRT allows for embedded segments in order to encode adjuncts such as appositions or cleft constructions with discursive long-range effects such as frame adverbials, non-restrictive relatives, and appositions. Second, most discourse theories define hierarchical structures by constructing complex segments (CDUs) from EDUs in recursive fashion. In RST, a document is represented as a rooted tree where adjacent EDUs are grouped together. PDTB also focuses on adjacent EDUs, but, unlike RST, it does not focus on structure; rather it focuses on discourse relations and the explicit or implicit discourse markers that can trigger those relations. The GraphBank model (Wolf & Gibson 2006) and SDRT, in contrast, go beyond adjacent discourse units allowing for the creation of full discourse graphs that capture complex discourse phenomena, such as long-distance attachments and long-distance discourse pop-ups, as well as crossed dependencies. The discourse structure is a graph and not a tree, which allows us to adequately represent discourse structure (Danlos 2007). Finally, SDRT aims to model the semantics/pragmatics interface using discourse relations that describe the rhetorical roles that utterances play in context, on the basis of truth conditional content alone. So the taxonomy of SDRT relations is smaller than for RST.

2.2.2 Building the Discourse Structure

We recall that our goal is to evaluate how discourse can help in opinion analysis and not to build a discourse bank that examines how well SDRT predicts the intuition of subjects, regardless of their knowledge of discourse theories. Therefore, in addition to a precise definition of the meaning of discourse relations, our annotation manual clearly details the constraints that annotators should respect according to the structural principles of SDRT (such as the right frontier principle (Asher & Lascarides 2003), structural constraints including accessibility, complex segments, no cycles, etc.).

During the elaboration of the second annotation manual, we were faced to a dilemma:

(1) Should we annotate opinion texts using a small set of discourse relations, as already done by Asher et al. (2008), Somasundaran (2010), and Trnavac and Taboada (2010), or (2) should we use a larger set of discourse relations? Of course, the first solution is more convenient since the annotation task is simpler. However, we chose the second solution because our aim here is to answer several questions:

- What are the most frequent relations that occur in opinion texts?
- Does this frequency depend on the corpus genre?
- What are the effects of these relations on both polarity and subjectivity of EDUs?
- What is the impact of discourse structure when assessing of the overall opinion of a document?

We used 17 oriented and mostly backward-looking relations grouped into coordinating relations (*Contrast, Continuation, Conditional, Narration, Alternation, Goal, Result, Parallel, Flashback*) and subordinating relations (*Elaboration, E-Elab, Correction, Frame, Explanation, Background, Commentary, Attribution*). A coordinating relation links arguments of equal importance, whereas a subordinating relation links an important argument to a less important one. Annotators were asked to link constituents (EDUs or CDUs) through whichever discourse relation they felt appropriate from our list above. They were also told that they could group constituents together whenever they felt the constituents jointly formed an argument of a discourse relation. In addition to this set of 17 relations, we also added the relation *Unknown* in case annotators were not able to decide which relation is more appropriate to link two constituents. This set of relations was already used to annotate French news documents in the ANNODIS project,[2] which aims at building a discourse bank that examines how well SDRT predicts the intuition of subjects, regardless of their knowledge of discourse theories. For a detailed description of non-expert annotations using SDRT as well as the obtained results in terms of inter-annotator agreements, see Afantenos et al. (2012).

3 Data

In order to better capture the dependencies between discourse structure and corpus genre, we conducted our annotation campaign on two different types of on-line corpora, each with a distinctive style and audience: movie reviews (*MR*) and news reactions (*NR*), both in French. *MR* were taken from *AlloCiné.fr*, while *NR* were taken from *Lemonde.fr*. In *MR*, the writing style is simple and brief (generally one paragraph that goes from one line to a dozen lines), and opinion expressions are mainly adjectives and nouns. Reviewers often summarize their overall opinion (for example, by using stars), give an opinion on a different feature such as actors or screenplay, conclude their review with expressions of recommendation (as in "go see this movie") and sometimes expressions of suggestion ("this movie should win an Oscar"). We also notice that opinions in movie reviews are mostly lexically marked.

In order to guarantee that the discourse structure is informative enough, we only selected those topics that are associated with more than 10 reviews/reactions. We also filtered out documents containing fewer than three sentences. In addition, for *MR*, we balanced the number of positive and negative reviews according to their corresponding general evaluation. We have selected articles from the politics and economy section of the *Le Monde* newspaper. This selection yielded a total of 180 documents for *MR* and 131 documents for *NR*.

2 http://w3.erss.univ-tlse2.fr/annodis.

4 Annotation Campaign

Annotators used the GLOZZ platform,[3] which is a new, state-of-the-art tool for linguistic annotation. Since documents are already segmented, annotators first have to click on each EDU; specify its category, polarity, and strength (see section 2.1.1), and then isolate, within each EDU, spans of text corresponding to the annotation scheme described in section 2.1.2. Discourse annotation is performed by inserting relations between selected constituents using the mouse. When appropriate, EDUs can be grouped to form CDUs using GLOZZ schemata. GLOZZ also provides a discourse graph as part of its graphical user interface, which helps the annotator to better capture the discourse structure while linking constituents.

Each document of our corpus was doubly annotated by three undergraduate linguistic students who benefited from a complete and revised annotation manual as well as an annotation guide that explains the inner workings of GLOZZ. The annotation proceeded in two stages: first the annotation of the movie reviews and then the annotation of news reactions. For each stage, we performed a two-step annotation where an intermediate analysis of agreement and disagreement between the three annotators was carried out. Annotators were first trained on 12 movie reviews, and then they were asked to annotate separately 168 documents from *MR*. Then, they were trained on 10 news reactions. Afterwards, they continued to annotate separately 121 documents from *NR*. The training phase for *MR* was longer than for *NR* since annotators had to learn about the annotation guide and the annotation tool. Each corpus genre took around three months to annotate. The time needed to annotate one text at both the EDU and the document level was about one hour.[4] Table 1 presents the total number of common documents (as well as common segments) doubly annotated by each annotator. A_i stands for annotator number $i = \{1, 2, 3\}$.

In order to get consistent annotations according to the instructions given in the manual, we designed a tool to automatically detect some annotation errors, both at the EDU and the discourse level. Some of the EDU-level errors include opinionated segments (*SE*, and *SEandSI*) with no opinion expression inside, *O* or *SI* segments with an opinion expression inside, *O* and *SN* segments with a prior polarity and/or strength, opinion expressions with no associated semantic category, and so on. Some of the discourse-level errors include violation of

3 www.glozz.org.

4 The number of segments in a document varies from 8 to 30 EDUs.

the right frontier constraint, cycles, overlapping CDUs, and so on. Among all the provided annotations, 15 % of the documents contained errors at the opinion level, whereas just a few documents were ill-formed at the discourse level. Our tool provided each annotator with a list of their errors. Annotators were then asked to correct them before annotating new documents.

TABLE 1 *Characteristics of the annotated data*

		A1–A2	A1–A3	A2–A3
MR	Number of common documents	47	58	50
	Number of common segments	496	612	598
NR	Number of common documents	44	40	40
	Number of common segments	341	386	333

5 Analysis of Our Results

Since our goal is to measure the impact of discourse on opinion analysis, in this section we give an overview of our results focusing only on the evaluation of:

- our annotation scheme at the EDU level. We give a quantitative description of the annotated data as well as the inter-annotator agreements on segment types and polarities.
- our annotation scheme at the document level. More specifically, we analyze:
  - the impact of implicit opinions on the document-level subjective stance.
  - the frequency of discourse relations per corpus genre.
  - the impact of discourse relations on both the subjectivity and the polarity of EDUs.

5.1 *Results at the EDU Level*

Table 2 gives a quantitative overview of the annotations provided by our three annotators.

TABLE 2 *Quantitative overview of the annotated data (percentage, frequency)*

	Movie reviews (*MR*)	News reactions (*NR*)
Total number of segments	3825	2071
SE	50.17 % (1919)	27.57 % (571)
SN	2.98 % (114)	5.74 % (119)
SI	26.54 % (1015)	43.47 % (900)
O	13.57 % (519)	17.91 % (371)
SEandSI	6.75 % (258)	5.31 % (110)
Positive	45.67 % (1747)	23.13 % (479)
Negative	33.65 % (1287)	52.73 % (1092)
Neutral	0.84 % (32)	0.82 % (17)
Both	3.32 % (127)	2.90 % (60)
No polarity	16.52 % (632)	20.42 % (423)
Segments with one opinion expression	96.77 % (2271)	93.82 % (689)
Subjective segments with at least one operator	40 %	32 %

We observe that the weight of the segments containing implicit opinions (*SI*) depends on the corpus genre: indeed, for the *MR* this weight is less important (26.57 %) than for the *NR* (43.47 %). Moreover, in both corpora, the purely objective segments are not very widespread (less than 18 % of all segments). The same goes for segments that contain at the same time an explicit and an implicit opinion (*SEandSI*), with a yet lower frequency for *NR* than for *MR*. As for the subjective non-evaluative segments (*SN*), they are rather infrequent as well, especially in *MR*. However, they are slightly more numerous for *NR*, which shows that the reported speech constructions are more frequent in reactions to newspaper articles than in movie reviews.

Another interesting corpus genre bias concerns the polarity of the segments: whereas in movie reviews positive polarity segments are a majority in spite of balancing the corpus between overall positive and overall negative documents (in terms of their star counting), this is not the case for the reactions to newspaper articles, where negative polarity segments are a majority.

Lastly, we also notice the importance of opinion operators. At least one such operator is present in 40% of subjective segments in the *MR* and in 20% of those in *NR*. This also confirms the importance of valence shifter terms when assessing the contextual polarity of opinion expressions within an EDU.

In Tables 3 and 4 we show the inter-annotator agreements on segment type and segment polarity, respectively. These measures have been averaged over the three annotators. When computing these statistics, we have discarded the "neutral" category since we do not have any instance of it in our data. The "both" category has only been counted with the positive polarity opinions (so that we count it only once). On the subjectivity class side segments in the *SE* and *SI* class have only been counted with the *SE* segments.

TABLE 3 *Inter-annotator agreements on segment type per genre*

	SE + *SEandSI*	*SN*	*SI*	*O*	Average Kappa
Reviews (*MR*)	0.74	0.74	0.56	0.63	0.66
Reactions (*NR*)	0.56	0.58	0.48	0.40	0.50

TABLE 4 *Inter-annotator agreements on segment polarity per genre*

	Positive + Both	Negative	No Polarity	Average Kappa
Reviews (*MR*)	0.78	0.77	0.68	0.76
Reactions (*NR*)	0.47	0.56	0.43	0.49

For *MR*, we get very good kappa measures for both explicit opinion segments *SE* (0.74) and the polarity (positive and negative) of a segment (respectively 0.78 and 0.77). These results are consistent with state-of-the-art inter-annotator agreements obtained in contemporary annotation campaigns (see, for example, Wiebe et al. (2005)). The kappa for the *SN* class is also very good. We observe that this category often contains specific verbs that belong to our "reporting" category (such as "say", "affirm", "tell", "guess", and so on), or to the "advice" category (such as "recommend", "hope", "suggest") that do not have a prior polarity.

Within an *SN* segment, the arguments of these verbs are not in the EDUs. For instance, "[I think] [that the movie is not good]"—where the two segments are related through a relative pronoun—and "[I don't think] [the movie is good]"—where they are not. Finally, the agreement for the *SI* and *O* classes are moderate because annotators often fail to decide whether a segment is purely objective and thus if it conveys only facts or if a segment holds an implicit opinion. This can also explain the lower kappa measure we get for "no polarity". This figure is, we believe, an artifact of the length of the texts. Indeed, the longer a text is, the higher difficulty for human subjects is in detecting discourse context in longer texts. However, the study of this hypothesis falls out of the scope of this paper and is therefore left for future work. Nonetheless, these figures are well in the range of state-of-the-art research reports in distinguishing between explicit and implicit opinions. For instance, Toprak et al. (2010) obtained a kappa of 0.56 for polar fact sentences, which is close to our *SI* category.

5.2 *Results at the Discourse Level*

5.2.1 Implicit Opinions and Overall Ratings

We have also computed statistics (in terms of Pearson's correlations—similarity measure between vectors, going from −1 for maximum distance to +1 for perfect matching) on the link between the global opinion score of the documents (viz. movie reviews or newspaper article reactions) and the weight of the segments, which contain explicit and implicit opinions. The segments have also been split according to their polarity. Through these statistics, we have investigated whether there is a contribution of implicit opinion segments to the author's global opinion on the main topic of the document.

We thus have computed the Pearson's correlation between the global opinion score (on a scale going from 0 for a strongly negative opinion to 4 for a strongly positive opinion) and the subjectivity class and polarity of the segments. More specifically, for each of the two corpora, we have constructed a vector with the global opinion scores for all the annotated document instances.[5] Then, another set of four vectors has been built for each corpus, with the counts of segments of a given subjectivity class and polarity: Expl_Pos for explicit positive opinion segments (*SE* class with polarity +); Expl_Neg for explicit negative opinion segments (*SE* class with polarity −); Impl_Pos for implicit negative

5 If one input document has been doubly annotated, we obtained two document annotation instances.

opinion segments (*SI* class with polarity +); and Impl_Neg for implicit negative opinion segments (*SI* class with polarity –). The results are shown in Figure 1.

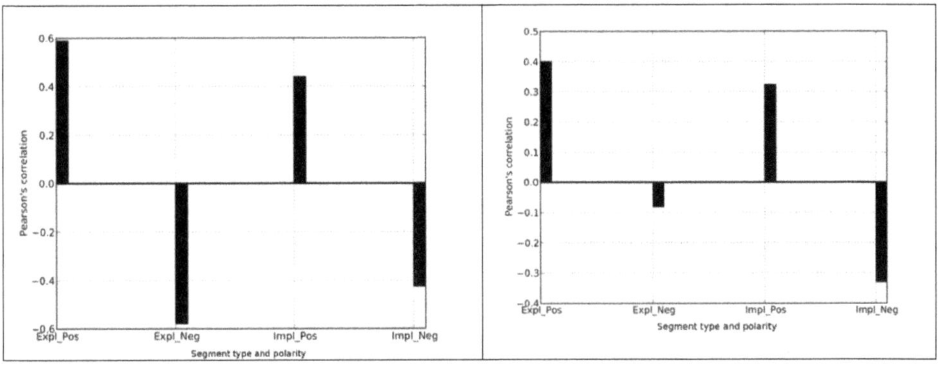

FIGURE 1 *Global opinion scores vs. segment type and polarity counts, for the "Reviews" and "Le Monde" corpora*

We observe that for *MR* there is a better correlation between global opinion score and explicit subjective segment counts (of both positive and negative polarities—for negative polarities, a good correlation means a negative Pearson's correlation of high absolute value) than between global opinion score and implicit subjective segment counts. For *NR*, a different behavior is observed: for positive polarities, the correlation with the global score is better for explicit subjective segments, whereas for negative polarities, the correlation is better for segments that contain implicit opinions. This brings us to the conclusion that the importance of implicit opinions varies depending on the corpus genre. For movie review, more direct and sometimes terse explicit opinions are better correlated to the global opinion score, whereas for news reactions, implicit opinions are more important when negative opinions are concerned. This could indicate a tendency to "conceal" negative opinions as apparently objective statements, which can be related to social conventions (politeness in particular).

5.2.2 Distribution of Discourse Relations in Opinion Text

In Table 5 we show the frequency of discourse relations per corpus genre.

TABLE 5 *Frequency of discourse relations per genre*

	MR	*NR*
Unknown	2.06	0.69
Explanation	4.58	5.57
Goal	1.07	3.33
Result	7.12	5.18
Parallel	0.81	1.09
Contrast	9.30	6.67
Continuation	29.92	24.83
Conditional	0.67	1.90
Alternative	0.64	1.95
Attribution	3.42	3.62
Background	0.78	0.63
Narration	1.04	0.86
Flashback	0.12	0.06
Frame	1.94	2.41
Elaboration	12.25	12.99
E-Elab	8.46	10.17
Commentary	14.57	17.59
Correction	1.25	0.46

We observe that the *Continuation* relations are the most frequent ones. However, *Explanation, Elaboration, E–Elab,*[6] *Comment, Contrast, Result* and *Goal* also have non-negligible frequencies. These results are essentially stable from one corpus to the other, except for the *Unknown* relation, more frequent in *MR*. Perhaps this difference could be explained by the fact that for *NR* the annotators were more experienced with respect to the "Reviews" corpus

6 *E–Elab*(a, b) (entity elaboration) holds when the second argument (b) gives more details about an entity introduced in a. A frequent case is when the segment b is an apposition or a relative.

annotated first), thus being less inclined to place this relation between discourse units.

Also, *Conditional* is more frequent in *NR* than in *MR*, which is consistent with a logically more structured discourse for news reactions than for movie reviews. The same goes for the *Attribution* relation, which denotes that in *NR* people tend to reference others' stances more often ("The president thinks that ...") or even tend to be more reserved when stating opinions, ("I guess that this is a good measure"), unlike in the reviews, where people might tend to be more categorical ("This movie is great") without modalizing the statement.

5.2.3 Discourse Relations and Opinions

5.2.3.1 *Importance of Complex Discourse Units*

We have also analyzed the ratio of complex segments to the total number of rhetorical relation arguments in our annotations (see Table 6).

TABLE 6 *Frequency of CDUs, for each type of rhetorical relation*

	MR			*NR*		
	EDU-EDU	EDU-CDU	CDU-CDU	EDU-EDU	EDU-CDU	CDU-CDU
Explanation	64.33	23.57	12.10	58.76	18.56	22.68
Goal	81.08	16.22	2.70	81.03	18.97	0.00
Result	47.25	31.75	21.00	43.68	35.63	20.69
Parallel	53.57	17.86	28.57	68.42	15.79	15.79
Contrast	45.17	27.11	27.73	39.66	25.86	34.48
Continuation	73.76	10.75	15.49	80.32	10.42	9.26
Conditional	73.91	17.39	8.70	63.64	18.18	18.18
Alternative	81.82	13.64	4.54	70.59	17.65	11.76
Attribution	78.81	20.34	0.85	60.32	36.51	3.17
Background	70.37	18.52	11.11	45.45	54.55	0.00
Narration	61.11	27.78	11.11	40.00	26.67	33.33
Flashback	75.00	25.00	0.00	0.00	100.00	0.00
Frame	46.27	46.27	7.46	59.53	35.71	4.76
Elaboration	29.80	42.31	27.90	29.64	40.71	29.60
E-Elab	77.74	20.21	2.05	74.01	22.60	3.39
Commentary	41.15	33.20	25.65	26.47	34.64	38.89
Correction	56.61	28.30	15.09	50.00	25.00	25.00

We first see that, for both corpus genres, rhetorical relation instances between EDUs only are a minority. This underscores the importance of CDUs for our task. CDUs are yet more numerous in NR (56%) than for MR (53%), perhaps because newspaper reactions tend to be more elaborate than movie reviews. For certain relations, very important to our task, this trend is salient; for both corpora, less than 35% of the *Contrast* instances link EDUs only. The same goes for *Result, Elaboration* and *Commentary*. This trend is not stable from one corpus to the other for *Parallel* relations: in *NR*, most of the *Parallels* link EDUs only. It remains to be seen why it is so. Given the higher complexity of the news reactions, perhaps the annotators have a harder time finding *Parallels* involving CDUs.

5.2.3.2 *Impact on Subjectivity*

In our task, we assume that we start from discourse structure to predict the subjective stance of the EDUs, especially of those containing implicit opinions. We assess, for each of the 10 most frequent relations, linking EDUs only, whether they preserve the subjectivity or not. That is, we compute statistics on the stability of the subjectivity class (for the (*SE, SE*), (*SI, SI*) and (*SI, SE*) couples) or the variation of the stability class (for the (*O*, other) couples, where "other" spans the set of subjectivity classes other than *O*). Table 7 summarizes our results.

TABLE 7 *Discourse relations and subjectivity preservation/non-preservation frequencies*

	MR		*NR*	
Subjectivity	**Preserved**	**Not preserved**	**Preserved**	**Not preserved**
Continuation	91.00	9.00	79.00	21.00
Commentary	72.46	27.54	80.25	19.75
Elaboration	71.43	28.57	71.64	28.36
Contrast	86.11	13.89	93.48	6.52
E-Elab	64.76	35.24	73.28	26.72
Result	81.00	19.00	71.00	29.00
Attribution	20.00	80.00	50.00	50.00
Parallel	100.00	0.00	100.00	0.00
Explanation	73.27	26.73	80.70	19.30
Frame	41.94	58.06	43.00	57.00

5.2.3.3 *Impact on Polarity*

We finally computed similar statistics for the polarities, but only between subjective (*SN, SE, SEandSI, SI*) EDUs—the (+, +) and (–, –) for stability and (+, –) for polarity change. We assess in Table 8 the behavior of the 10 most frequent relations linking EDUs only with respect to polarity preservation and non-preservation.

TABLE 8 *Discourse relations and polarity preservation/non-preservation frequencies*

	MR		*NR*	
Polarity	**Preserved**	**Not preserved**	**Preserved**	**Not preserved**
Continuation	93.36	6.64	86.05	13.59
Commentary	78.23	21.77	75.81	24.19
Elaboration	85.37	14.63	73.68	26.32
Contrast	23.57	76.43	56.00	44.00
E-Elab	80.17	19.83	76.54	23.64
Result	82.35	17.65	81.00	19.00
Attribution	64.29	35.71	57.14	42.86
Parallel	72.00	28.00	83.33	16.67
Explanation	90.28	9.72	75.56	24.44
Frame	100.00	0.00	87.50	12.50

6 Does Discourse Really Matter?

In light of the results presented, the answer is yes. Here are the main conclusions of our annotation study:

- Segment-based opinion analysis is more appropriate to study opinions in discourse. Indeed, our results show that more than 90% of segments contain only one opinion expression. Hence, computing the opinion orientation at the local level is easier compared with sentence- or clause-based level approaches. In addition, our automatic discourse segmentation is feasible and yields very good results.
- Our subjectivity classification at the segment level is more appropriate for discourse-based sentiment analysis. Indeed, we have proposed to

distinguish between subjective non-evaluative and objective segments and between implicit and explicit opinions. Our results show that the frequency of each class is highly correlated to the corpus genre: *SE* segments are more frequent in movie reviews, whereas *SI* and *O* segments are more frequent in news reactions. In addition, we have shown that the manual annotation of these classes is reliable for movie reviews and more complex for news reactions. However, we believe that automatic subjectivity classification is feasible. In Benamara et al. (2011), we have proposed a method to distinguish between four types of discourse units in movie reviews by using both local and discursive features.

- Implicit opinions are important. Our results show that the importance of implicit opinions varies, depending on the corpus genre. For movie reviews, explicit opinions are better correlated to the global opinion score, whereas for news reactions, implicit opinions are more important when negative opinions are concerned.
- Among our set of 17 discourse relations, the distribution of the most frequent relations is essentially stable from one corpus genre to the other. Our results show that the most relevant relations for opinion analysis of movie reviews and news reactions are *Continuation, Explanation, Elaboration, E-Elab, Comment, Contrast, Result*, and *Goal*. In addition, *Conditional* and *Attribution* are important relations in the news reactions corpus.
- The effect of the most frequent relations on polarity and subjectivity of adjacent segments has been assessed. Our results show that each rhetorical relation type has a specific impact on both the subjectivity and polarity of EDUs.
- Complex discourse units (CDUs) are an important part of the discourse structure of a document. Our results show that the proportion of CDUs (compared with the relations between two EDUs) are about two-thirds of the total number of attachments in both corpus genres. Hence, CDUs are important for assessing the overall opinion of a document. Promising efforts in this direction have been undertaken by Chardon et al. (2012a), where we empirically measured the effect of discourse structure (and thus CDUs) on opinion analysis. We proposed two main strategies. The first one is based on a partial use of the discourse structure where the overall opinion is computed using a subset of relevant segments that have been chosen according to subjectivity and/or topic filters. The other strategy is based on the full use of discourse structure where a rule-based approach aggregates the opinion scores of all segments in a bottom-up fashion. Our results show that the discourse-based strategies lead to better scores in terms of accuracy and Pearson's correlation evaluation measures.

7 Conclusion

This paper focused on the interaction between evaluation and coherence relations. It extends our earlier work (Asher et al. 2009) where Segmented Discourse Representation Theory (SDRT) was used to obtain a deeper understanding of contextual polarity. The chapter described an annotation study that aims to measure the impact of discourse structure on opinion analysis. We proposed a two-level annotation scheme: first at the segment level, where each elementary discourse unit is annotated according to the opinion it conveys, and then at the document level, where the discourse structure of the document is built. We conducted our annotation campaign on two French corpus genres: movie reviews and news reactions. This work is a first step towards a larger effort to use SDRT in sentiment analysis in different languages. An English-language annotation campaign, following the same methodology, is currently under way.

The application of our results in practical sentiment analysis systems depends on two factors: the automatic identification of the opinion information of each segment (subjectivity type and score) and the building of the discourse structure. Determining segment's contextual score requires a sentiment composition process which consists of computing the sentiment orientation of an expression or a sentence (in terms of polarity and/or strength) on the basis of the sentiment orientation of its constituents. This process, similar to the principle of compositionality (Dowty et al. 1989), aims to capture how opinion expressions interact with each other and with specific linguistic operators such as intensifiers and nonveridical markers such as negations and modalities. For instance, the sentiment expressed in the sentence "This student is definitely not brilliant" is a combination of the prior sentiment orientation of the words *brilliant, student*, and the nonveridical markers *definitely* and *not*. Similarity, in "My wife confirms that this restaurant is not good enough", sentiment composition has to deal with the verb *confirm*, the adjective *good* and the adverbs *not* and *enough*. The analysis of the interactions between evaluation and nonveridical markers is a necessary step in a sentiment analysis system since each segment's scores have to be aggregated in order to determine the overall polarity orientation and/or the overall rating at the document level. We have already experimented with such interactions in Chardon et al. (2012b) by proposing a computational model that accounts for the effects of negation and modality on opinion expressions. Based on linguistic experiments informed by native speakers, we distill these effects according to the type of modality and negation. The model relies on a parabolic representation. It computes the opinion characteristics at the phrase level. The empirical evaluation of our model shows that it matches the way humans handle negation and modality in opinionated sentences. Additional studies on nonveridical markers and evaluation can be found in the first part of this book, in chapters by Giannakidou, Goddard and Moeschler, as well as the chapter by Gros and Stede, which more directly deals with the interaction of the nonveridical phenomenon of negation and evaluation, and the chapter by Zappavigna, which examines Engagement and a specific coherence relation, Condition.

Our analysis relies on manually annotated discourse information. This is a first and a necessary step before moving on to real scenarios that rely on automatic annotations (we recall that as far as we know the only existing powerful discourse parser based on SDRT theory is the one that has been developed for a dialogue corpus (Verbmobil corpus)). The next step is to test the reliability of our results when discourse structure is built automatically. We attempt to do this by adapting Muller et al.'s (2012) parser to opinion texts.

Acknowledgement

This work was supported by a DGA-RAPID project under grant number 0102906143.

References

Afantenos, Stergos, Nicholas Asher, Farah Benamara Myriam, Bras, Cecile Fabre, Mai Ho-Dac, Anne Le Draoulec, Philippe Muller, Marie-Paul Pery-Woodley, Laurent Prevot, Josette Rebeyrolles, Ludovic Tanguy, Marianne Vergez-Couret, and Laure Vieu. "An empirical resource for discovering cognitive principles of discourse organisation: The annodis corpus." In Proceedings of the Eighth International Conference on Language Resources and Evaluation (LREC), 2012.

Asher, Nicholas. *Reference to Abstract Objects in Discourse*. Dordrecht: Kluwer Academic Publishers, 1993.

Asher, Nicholas, Farah Benamara, and Yvette Yannick Mathieu. "Distilling opinion in discourse: A preliminary study." In Proceedings of Computational Linguistics (CoLing), 7–10. Manchester, UK: Association for Computational Linguistics, 2008.

———. "Appraisal of opinion expressions in discourse." *Linguisticae Investigationes*, 32, no. 2 (2009) 27992.

Asher, Nicholas, and Alex Lascarides. *Logics of Conversation*. Cambridge: Cambridge University Press, 2003.

Benamara, Farah, Baptiste Chardon, Yannick Mathieu, and Vladimir Popescu. "Towards context-based subjectivity analysis." In Proceedings of the International Joint Conference on Natural Language Processing (IJCNLP), 2011, 1180–1188.

Carlson, L., D. Marcu, and M.E. Okurowski. "Building a discourse-tagged corpus in the framework of rhetorical structure theory." In *Current Directions in Discourse and Dialogue*, 85–112. Dordrecht: Kluwer Academic Publishers, 2003.

Chardon, Baptiste, Farah Benamara, Yannick Mathieu, Vladimir Popescu, and Asher Nicholas. "Measuring the effect of discourse structure on sentiment analysis." In International Conference on Intelligent Text Processing and Computational Linguistics (CICLING), 2012a.

———. "Sentiment composition using a parabolic model." In International Conference on Computational Semantics (IWCS), 2012b.

Danlos, L. "Strong generative capacity of RST, SDRT and discourse dependency DAGs." In *Constraints in Discourse*. Amsterdam: John Benjamins, 2007.

Dowty, David R., Robert E. Wall, and Stanley Peters. *Introduction to Montague Semantics, Volume 11*. Dordrecht: D. Reidel, 1989.

Heerschop, Bas, Frank Goossen, Alexander Hogenboom, Flavius Frasincar, Uzay Kaymak, and Franciska de Jong. "Polarity analysis of texts using discourse structure." In Proceedings of the 20th ACM international conference on Information and knowledge management, 2011, 1061–1070.

Liu, Bing. Sentiment analysis and opinion mining. Morgan & Claypool, 2012.

Marcu, Daniel. *The Theory and Practice of Discourse Parsing and Summarization*. Cambridge, MA: MIT Press, 2000.

Mirkin, Shachar, Jonathan Berant, Ido Dagan, and Eyal Shnarch. "Recognising entailment within discourse." In Proceedings of the 23rd International Conference on Computational Linguistics (COLING), Stroudsburg, PA, USA. 2010, 770–778.

Muller, P., Afantenos S., P. Denis, and N. Asher. "Constrained decoding for text-level discourse parsing." In Proceedings of International Conference on Computational Linguistics (COLING), Mumbai, India, 2012.

Pang, Bo, and Lillian Lee. "A sentimental education: Sentiment analysis using subjectivity summarization based on minimum cuts." In Proceedings of the 42nd Annual Meeting on Association for Computational Linguistics, Stroudsburg, PA, USA. 2004, 271–278.

Polanyi, L., and M. van den Berg. "Discourse structure and sentiment." In Data Mining Workshops (ICDMW), IEEE 11th International Conference, 2011, 97–102.

Polanyi, L., C. Culy, M. van den Berg, G.L. Thione, and D. Ahn. "A rule based approach to discourse parsing." In Proceedings of the 5th SIGdial Workshop on Discourse and Dialogue, 2004, 108–117.

Prasad, A., R. Miltsakaki, E. Dinesh, N. Lee, A. Joshi, and B. Webber. Penn Discourse TreeBank 1.0 Annotation Manual, 2006. www.seas.upenn.edu/~pdtb/.

Somasundaran, Swapna. *Discourse-level relations for Opinion Analysis*. PhD Thesis, University of Pittsburgh, 2010.

Somasundaran, Swapna, Josef Ruppenhofer, and Janyce Wiebe. "Detecting arguing and sentiment in meetings." In Proceedings of the SIGdial Workshop on Discourse and Dialogue, 2007, 26–34.

Taboada, Maite, Kimberly Voll, and Julian Brooke. "Extracting sentiment as a function of discourse structure and topicality." In School of Computing Science Technical Report, 2008, 20.

Toprak, Cigdem, Niklas Jakob, and Iryna Gurevych. "Sentence and expression level annotation of opinions in user-generated discourse." In ACL '10: Proceedings of the 48th Annual Meeting of the Association for Computational Linguistics, Morristown, NJ, USA, 2012, 575–584.

Trnavac R., and M. Taboada. "The contribution of non-veridical rhetorical relations to evaluation in discourse." *Language Sciences* 34, no. 3 (2010): 301–318.

Wiebe, Janyce, Theresa Wilson, and Claire Cardie. "Annotating expressions of opinions and emotions in language." *Language Resources and Evaluation* 39, 2–3 (2005): 165–210.

Wolf, F., and E. Gibson. *Coherence in Natural Language: Data Structures and Applications*. Cambridge, MA: MIT Press, 2006.

Zhou, Lanjun, Binyang Li, Wei Gao, Zhongyu Wei, and Kam-Fai Wong. "Unsupervised discovery of discourse relations for eliminating intra-sentence polarity ambiguities." In Proceedings of EMNLP, Edinburgh, Scotland, UK, July 2011, 162–171.

PART 3

Corpus Studies on Evaluation and Coherence in Nonveridical Contexts

CHAPTER 6

Subjectivity and Prototype Structure in Causal Connective Use across Discourse Contexts

Ninke Stukker and Ted Sanders

1 Introduction

Causal connectives are linguistic markers of causal relations between discourse segments, typically clauses. Across theoretical frameworks, and across languages, analysts strongly agree that different connectives specialize in expressing different types of causal relations. Cross-linguistically, semantic contrasts between causal connectives have been characterized with reference to the concept of *subjectivity* (Pander Maat & Degand 2001; Pit 2006, 2007), proposing a distinction between subjective (or epistemic, as in Sweetser 1990), internal (Martin 1992) causal relations that are *construed* by the speaker in ongoing discourse, on the one hand, and objective (or content, as in Sweetser 1990), external (Martin 1992) causal relations that are merely *reported* by the speaker, on the other hand. The crucial difference between these two causal categories is whether the speaker or author, as a communicating subject, functions as the causal relation's *locus of effect* (cf. Talmy 1988) or not.

In written discourse,[1] for example, German *weil*, French *parce que*, and Dutch *omdat* are typically used for marking *objective* causal relations such as (1), in which the speaker *reports* a causal relation that holds between two events, "starting to rain" and "going home," taking place in the outside world. This causal relation's locus of effect is situated in the persons referred to by *they*, who interpret the fact that it started to rain as a reason for performing the action of "going home". German *denn*, French *car*, and Dutch *want*, on the other hand, are typically used for marking *subjective* causal relations such as (2), in which the author functions as the relation's locus of effect, *construing* the causal relation in ongoing discourse by presenting the fact that "the neighbors' car is not in the

1 Usage conventions for causal connectives vary across communication modalities. In spoken discourse, *denn* is being replaced by *weil*+V2 (cf. Wegener 1993; Pasch 1997; Keller 1995); French *car* is being replaced by *parce que* (cf. Degand & Fagard 2008).

 | DOI: 10.1163/9789004258174_007

driveway" as an argument for his conclusion that "the neighbors clearly left" (Stukker & Sanders 2012).

(1) They went home *weil/parce que/omdat* (because[2]) it started to rain.
(2) The neighbors clearly left *denn/car/want* (because) their car is not in the driveway.

The concept of subjectivity is inextricably related to the broader concept of evaluation. Subjectivity concerns evaluations of aspects of reality regarding truth, desirability, or quality, uttered by a given 'subject of conceptualization' (cf. section 2 below).

We focus on the system behind the diversity of ways in which language users may mark causal discourse relations. We start from a linguistic categorization hypothesis. That is, we assume that when language users systematically prefer one highly grammaticalized linguistic item over another (even highly similar) one to express a certain type of causal relationship, they assign the relation expressed to a specific conceptual type of (subjective or objective) causality. Thus, we assume that such linguistic choices provide a window on speakers' cognitive categorizations of causality (Talmy 1988; Verhagen & Kemmer 1997; Stukker, Sanders & Verhagen 2008, 2009; Sanders & Sweetser 2009). In doing so we adopt a basic assumption of cognitive linguistics—the branch of linguistic study that explores the link between linguistic structure and more general human cognitive structure—that a direct link holds between cognitive categories and the linguistic categories used to express them in communication.

A frequently noted problem in causal connective analysis, however, has been the fact that connective use can*not* always be characterized in a black-and-white fashion with reference to these categories of objective and subjective causality. *Denn, car,* and *want* also occur in objective relations (3); and *weil, parce que,* and *omdat* also occur in subjective relations (4).

2 Although the tendency to have connectives specializing in either objective or subjective causality is cross-linguistically widespread, it is not 'universal'. A telling example is the fact that English does not contain direct equivalents of the connectives *parce que/weil/omdat* vs. *car/denn/want* (see, for example, Knott & Sanders 1998); *because* covers both objective and subjective relations. Findings in typological research suggest that cross-linguistic convergence may take place on a more abstract level than the level of concrete linguistic categories (cf. Kortmann 1997; Haspelmath 1997; Croft 2001). For a discussion of how these cross-linguistic patterns relate to our categorization hypothesis, see Stukker & Sanders (2012).

(3) She went home late, *denn/car/want* (because) she had a lot of work to do.
(4) She won't be home yet (I think), *weil/parce que/omdat* (because) she had a lot of work to do.

Despite the fact that these usage types occur less frequently, their acceptability is beyond doubt. Why is it that the intuition that causal connectives have a fixed meaning is widespread, whereas corpus studies show that their use is flexible? This paradox has presented a major problem in connective analysis. The occurrence of 'counterexamples' such as (3) and (4) has been interpreted as a challenge to the categorization hypothesis discussed above (cf. Le Groupe λ-l 1975; Pander Maat & Degand 2001; Pit 2006; Taboada & Mann 2006).

In previous studies, we proposed that apparent counterexamples are in fact non-prototypical instantiations of the same category that the more conventional cases (1) and (2) belong to (Stukker et al. 2008, 2009). As an explanation of why language users sometimes use connectives in a non-prototypical way, we put forward a conceptual construal hypothesis, which is built on the cognitive semantic assumption that language users perform acts of (linguistic) categorization not only on the basis of objective reality, but also on the basis of their particular understanding of a situation and their rhetorical purposes (cf. Langacker 1990; Verhagen 2007). Thus, we did not view variation in connective use as a problem, but rather as a natural consequence of their categorization function.

So far, studies identifying the linguistic and cognitive mechanisms underlying causal connective use have mainly focused on characteristics of the discourse segments (denoting cause and effect) related by the connectives (cf. Pander Maat & Degand 2001; Stukker, Sanders & Verhagen 2009). Various studies have noted, however, that the interpretation and linguistic categorization of causal discourse relations seem to be co-determined by factors residing in the broader context of communication as well. Examples include the findings of Sanders (1997) that the conceptual interpretation of causal relations that are ambiguous for relation type is influenced by the reader's understanding of the overall discourse goal, and findings by Zufferey (2012), Spooren, Sanders, Huiskes, and Degand (2010) and by Sanders and Spooren (under review) suggesting that patterns of causal connective use are affected by modality (channel) of communication (spoken, written, or chat discourse). Both discourse goal and modality are situational factors known to co-determine conditions of use of a wide variety of linguistic phenomena (for an overview see Biber & Conrad 2009).

The present paper investigates the role of the situational factor of discourse goal as an independent factor co-determining language users' selection of connectives as linguistic markers of subjective and objective causal relations. Our aim is to explore discourse context as a new source of evidence for our hypothesis that deviant usage events of causal connectives are actually rhetorically motivated, peripheral members of the same category that their more conventional contexts of use belong to.

We analyze how subjectivity is expressed in causal relations using the causal connectives *dus* (roughly equivalent to English *so*) and *daarom* (roughly equivalent to *that's why*) in Dutch newspaper discourse. Previous studies have suggested that the general mechanisms underlying the linguistic expression of subjectivity using causal connectives have cross-linguistic validity (cf. Pander Maat & Degand 2001; Stukker & Sanders 2012), implying that many of the phenomena we describe in this paper may be generalized to other languages as well.

We proceed as follows. In the next section, we show that non-prototypical use of *dus* and *daarom* in three different Dutch newspaper genres—news report, opinion piece, and feature article (the Dutch newspaper genre 'reportage')—coincides with indications in the local, linguistic context of the causally related segments that the author is using for a specific rhetorical effect in terms of subjectivity present, corroborating previous findings (section 2). But at the same time, our results suggest that distributional patterns of *dus* and *daarom* are sensitive to the situational factor of discourse goal as well. Section 3 reports a corpus analysis confirming our expectation that discourse goal acts as a distinct factor determining selection of *dus* and *daarom* as markers of subjective and objective causal relations. Extending the scope of relevance of our findings, section 4 compares distributional patterns of *dus* and *daarom* across the newspaper genres under investigation, showing that patterns of relative frequency, including their status as indicator of prototype structure, are affected by the situational factor of discourse goal as well. Section 5 discusses how the results of this study contribute to our understanding of causal connectives as linguistic devices assigning causal discourse relations to the cognitively deeply entrenched conceptual categories of objective and subjective causality, reflecting the characteristics of prototype structure and the subjective assessment of reality associated with the human cognitive capacity of categorization.

2 Linguistic Indications of 'Subjective Causality' and 'Objective Causality' Category Membership in the Discourse Segments Related by *dus* and *daarom* across Genres

In this section, we first explain how the more general characteristics of the human conceptual and linguistic categorization capacities are reflected in acts of linguistic categorization of causal discourse relations using the Dutch causal connectives *dus* (prototypically associated with subjective causal relations) and *daarom* (prototypically associated with objective causal relations). We summarize the line of reasoning we put forward in previous studies (cf. Stukker et al. 2008, 2009; Stukker & Sanders 2012; Fagel, Stukker & Van Andel 2012). In the second part of the section, we report a study suggesting that the more general patterns regarding frequency of use and subjective category construal that we found in previous studies are not only determined by the subjectivity characteristics of the *segments*, but also display signs of sensitivity to the situational factor of discourse goal as well.

2.1 *Subjectivity and Prototype Structure in* dus *and* daarom*: Previous Findings*

Dus and *daarom* mark causal relations with a forward order of presentation (cause precedes effect). Consider fragments (5) and (6), examples of their prototypical contexts of use, taken from a corpus of newspaper texts.

(5) *Zo richtten de betrokken instellingen al in de jaren zeventig samen een internationale 'denktank' op—de Unico banking group. Maar dit bleef beperkt tot uitwisseling van ervaringen en ideeën.* [*Voor de Rabo was dit op den duur niet voldoende.*]$_{cause}$ [*Sinds het einde van de jaren tachtig startte de Nederlandse coöperatie daarom pogingen om de internationale samenwerking te intensiveren.*]$_{effect}$
As far back as the seventies, the institutions involved cooperated in establishing an international 'think tank'—Unico banking group. But this [*sic*] was restricted to exchanging experiences and ideas. [In the long the term, this was not sufficient for the Rabo.]$_{\text{cause}}$ [From the late eighties onward, the Dutch cooperative society "daarom" started attempting to intensify international cooperation.]$_{\text{effect}}$

(6) (Dutch soldiers who served in Bosnia relate the high incidence of leukemia among them to frequent exposure to impoverished uranium.) [*Maar de huidige hypothese wijt de leukemieën aan een virus*]$_{\text{cause}}$ (...). [*Het is* <u>*dus*</u> *denkbaar dat de soldaten die nu leukemie hebben gekregen, slachtoffer zijn van iets anders dan verarmd uranium.*]$_{\text{effect}}$
[But the current hypothesis attributes the leukemias to a virus]$_{\text{cause}}$ (...). [It is "dus" conceivable that the soldiers who suffer from leukemia now are victims of something other than impoverished uranium.]$_{\text{effect}}$

In (5) the author reports a causal relation between the situation that the 'Rabobank' (a Dutch cooperative banking society) perceives international cooperation within 'Unico banking group' as insufficient to its needs, and its consecutive action of "starting to intensify international cooperation". The locus of effect of this causal process, "The Dutch cooperative society", which is acting as an agent, does not coincide with the author of the text. Therefore, the causal relation in (5) is classified as an objective causal relation. In (6), by contrast, the author *does* function as the causal relation's locus of effect. In ongoing discourse, he relates the situation that "the current hypothesis attributes leukemias to a virus" as an argument to the conclusion stated in the next sentence. Subjectivity in causal relations is defined in accordance with the broader concept of linguistic subjectivity, which refers to utterances reflecting the speaker's attitude toward the proposition expressed (cf. Traugott 1995). Subjective causal relations typically concern evaluation of aspects of reality (cf. Pit 2003: 116–123; Pander Maat & Degand 2001: 221[3]) regarding truth (as in (5)), desirability (*You shouldn't stay up so late.*), or simply quality (*That was a fantastic concert.*). In line with this definition, (6) is classified as a subjective causal relation. (5) and (6) are representative examples of the prototypical contexts of use of *daarom* and *dus*, respectively.

Now consider (7), in which subjective *dus* is used in an objective causal relation.

(7) *Haar man, negentien jaar in dienst van de RVV, was eerder bij ruimingen betrokken geweest. Hij had tijdens de varkenspest mee helpen ruimen en was, in het kader van de MKZ-crisis, ingezet op een boerderij in de Achterhoek.* [*Met emoties kon hij wel omgaan, angst had hij nooit gevoeld.*]$_{cause}$

3 Sanders & Spooren (under review) report that propositional attitude is second in the ranking of factors affecting selection of either the Dutch backward causal connective *omdat* or *want*, after causal relation type.

> <u>Dus</u> [*ging hij op 7 april, de dag van de boerenrellen in Kootwijkerbroek, vol vertrouwen zijn taak tegemoet.*]$_{effect}$ *Hij stuitte op blokkades, op razende boeren, werd gegijzeld, geslagen, zijn auto werd in brand gestoken. Bijna drie weken later kan hij nog steeds niet vatten hoe het daar zo uit de hand heeft kunnen lopen.* (Reportage, D-Coi reference corpus)
> Her husband, on the payroll of the RVV for nineteen years, had been involved in sanitary slaughter of diseased cattle before. He had assisted in a sanitary slaughter during the swine fever crisis and during the foot and mouth disease crisis, had been stationed on a farm in the Achterhoek [region in the Netherlands]. [Emotions he could deal with quite well, fear he never had felt.]$_{\text{cause}}$ "<u>Dus</u>" [on the 7th of April, the day the 'farmers' riots' in Kootwijkerbroek took place, he set off to work confidently.]$_{\text{effect}}$ He ran into blockades, furious farmers, got taken hostage, was beaten, his car was set on fire. After nearly three weeks, he is still not able to understand why things got out of hand so badly.

As in (5), in (7) the author reports a causal relation that originated from an external source; taking place independently from any (communicative) action of the author himself. The causal process is developing between the fact that its locus of effect "he" "could deal with emotions quite well and never had felt fear", leading to "his" action of "setting to work confidently". Yet despite the fact that the causal relations in (5) and (7) belong to the same conceptual category of objective causality, (5) is marked accordingly with objective *daarom*, whereas the author of (7) assigns the causal relation expressed with *dus* to the conceptual category of *subjective* causality.

How do deviant usage events of causal connectives like (7) relate to the categorization hypothesis we presented in the introductory section? In previous studies, we proposed to analyze 'deviant' cases not as counterexamples, but rather as non-prototypical instantiations of the same causal category the connective used as a linguistic marker is typically associated with. A first argument in favor of this position is that usage contexts which *do* corroborate the categorization hypothesis (in the present case, *dus* in subjective causal relations) are more frequent than the apparent counterexamples (Stukker et al. 2009). This pattern has cross-linguistic validity (Stukker & Sanders 2012). An accumulating body of evidence suggests that highly frequent language use patterns have a privileged status in cognition. This assumption has been elaborated notably within what has become known as the usage-based approach to language (Langacker 1987, 2000; Bybee 2006, 2007; Goldberg 2006; for an overview see Barlow & Kemmer 2000 and contributions to that volume). The usage-based conception of language assumes that the more frequent, or the more entrenched, contexts of use are the more prototypical members of a category, indicating its 'prototypical use' (from now on: PU).

A second argument concerns linguistic and conceptual characteristics of the apparent counterexamples themselves. The argumentation above automatically entails the hypothesis that counterexamples, being less frequent, must be considered as less prototypical, or more peripheral members of the category. This second prototype structure hypothesis is corroborated by the fact that the 'non-prototypical use' contexts (from now on: NPU) are more or less systematically ambiguous for causality type. That is, they systematically contain elements that are congruent with both an objective *and* a subjective interpretation (Stukker et al. 2009; Stukker & Sanders 2009). When applied to (7), we see that the causal relation should be analyzed, from an analytical point of view, as a case of objective causality. But at the same time, the causally related segments, as well as the wider contexts, contain explicit linguistic signals that this objective causal relation is construed in a broader context of a subjective perspective—not of the author of the text, but of the person whose experiences are reported; see, for example, reference made to "emotions", "fear", and "feeling" in the cause segment and reference to the emotional state of being "confident" in the effect segment. In line with observations reported in a number of previous studies of causal connectives in various languages (cf. Le Groupe λ-l 1975; Pasch 1983; Van Belle 1989; Pander Maat & Sanders 2000; Pander Maat & Degand 2001), we assume that selection of subjective *dus* rather than objective *daarom* as a marker for this causal relation is motivated by the author's desire to foreground the elements of subjectivity present in its context of use.

This analysis is in accordance with theoretical accounts of categorization as an important cognitive function. Acts of categorization do not under all circumstances reflect some 'objective reality', but rather they are based on an individual's understanding of a particular situation (cf. Lakoff 1987; Taylor 1995). Not surprisingly, this subjective basis of categorization is reflected in linguistic communication. In cognitive semantics, this phenomenon has been analyzed under the heading of 'linguistic construal', which implies that an expression's meaning is not just an objective characterization of the situation described. Equally important for linguistic semantics is how the speaker chooses to construe the situation and portray it for expressive purposes (cf. Langacker 2002: 315, 1987; Verhagen 2007; for a more elaborate discussion of construal mechanisms from a usage-based perspective in relation to causal expressions, see Verhagen 2000, 2004; Stukker et al. 2009).

In addition, our analysis is in accordance with the theoretical assumption in subjectivity theory as well as a large body of empirical evidence suggesting that subjectivity is a transferable concept. That is, in human communication the deictic center of subjectivity may be shifted away from the speaker to another subject of conceptualization (cf. Langacker 1990; Sanders & Spooren 1997; Semino & Short 2004; on causal relations see Pit 2003, with reference to Sanders 1994). See also similar accounts in terms of intersubjectivity (Verhagen 2005) and mental spaces theory (Sanders, Sanders & Sweetser 2009).

The processes of subjective construal ultimately result in an interpretation of (7) in which it is suggested that its locus of effect is not only relevant as an agent performing an action in an external reality, but also as a subject of consciousness justifying the particular course of action chosen and whose subjective point of view is conflated with the author's (cf. Dancygier & Sweetser 2012; on causal connectives, se Sanders et al. 2009). In other words, *dus* foregrounds the internal processes of assessment and evaluation of the situation leading to the causal process and the ensuing process of decision making taking place in the relation's locus of effect "he". This analysis implies that despite the fact that its context of use is a less-prototypical reflection of the conceptual category of subjective causality, *dus* in (7) ultimately refers to the subjective causal category it is prototypically associated with in a way that is highly similar to (6). Under this analysis, we do not view deviant usage events as a problem, but rather as a natural consequence of the connectives' categorization function.

2.2 *Corpus Study 1: Linguistic Indications of 'Subjective Causality' and 'Objective Causality' Category Membership in the Discourse Segments Related by* dus *and* daarom *across Genres*

In the remainder of this section we report a study investigating the correlation between segmental characteristics and selection of *dus* or *daarom* as markers of objective and subjective causal relations in news reports, opinion pieces, and feature articles (reportage) in Dutch newspapers—differing with respect to the situational factor 'discourse goal'. Our findings will be interpreted as a first indication that the more general patterns regarding frequency of use and subjective category construal described above are not only determined by the subjectivity characteristics of the segments, but vary in relation to discourse goal as well.

2.2.1 Hypothesis

In this section, we test the following hypotheses:

- Segments of NPU subjective causal relations marked with *daarom* contain objective elements more often than the segments of PU subjective causal relations marked with *dus*;

- Segments of NPU objective causal relations marked with *dus* contain subjective elements more often than the segments of PU objective causal relations marked with *daarom*.

2.2.2 Method

In order to test the linguistic NPU hypothesis, we assessed subjectivity type of the effect segments of causal relations marked with *dus* or *daarom*. The local context element that is maximally closely associated with the locus of effect, which is the element crucial for categorization (cf. discussion in section 1), is the causal relation's effect segment (cf. Stukker & Sanders 2009). Subjectivity type of the effect segments was assessed by classifying their 'representation mode', characterizing different linguistic strategies for representing speech or thought of the author of the text or characters in the text (cf. Leech & Short 2007; Semino & Short 2004). Following Sanders's (1994), and Pit's (2003) adaptation of this concept to causal relations, we assessed the categories represented in the second and third column in Table 1. For the purposes of our present study, the categories representing a gradual decrease of author subjectivity combined with a gradual increase of character subjectivity were conflated into one category of character subjectivity.

TABLE 1 *Representation mode types distinguished in this study*

Subjectivity type	Representation mode type	Example
Author	Subjective author's discourse	My house is beautiful.
Character	Direct mode	She said/thought: "My house is beautiful".
	Free indirect mode	She wanted to go home, she said/thought.
	Indirect mode	She said/thought (that) she wanted to go home.
	Perspectivized report	She liked her house.
Neutral	Neutral discourse	She went home. My house has a green front door.

In accordance with previous studies (Sanders 1994; Pit 2003) we assume that the resulting subjectivity types may be ordered on a cline ranging from maximally (which we expect to be associated with *dus*) to minimally subjective (which we expect to be associated with *daarom*) as indicated in Table 2.

TABLE 2 *Relative degree of subjectivity in representation mode types*

Degree of subjectivity		
Author subjectivity >	Character subjectivity >	Neutral discourse

Categories of representation mode were determined on the basis of linguistic signals of subjectivity in the causal relation's segments, such as linguistic reference to the causal relation's locus of effect, deictic expressions, tense and aspect, etc.[4]

PU and NPU contexts of use were identified making use of a paraphrase test (Knott & Dale 1994; for Dutch causal relations, see Sanders 1997), determining causal relation type by replacing the connective with a paraphrase representing its relational meaning as closely as possible. Our analysis focuses on specific subtypes of objective and subjective causal relations.

As the occurrence of NPU *dus* in objective relation seems to be restricted to the specific subtype of so-called volitional objective causal relations (Pander Maat & Sanders 2000) concerning intentional actions performed by loci of effect that do not coincide with the speaker or author of the text (cf. Stukker et al., 2008), we restricted our analysis of objective causal relations to this type at the expense of the subtype of non-volitional objective causality concerning states and events occurring without interference of an intentionally acting locus of effect.[5] The paraphrases we used are presented in Table 3.[6]

4 For a detailed demonstration of our procedure of analysis, see Stukker & Sanders (2009).

5 Non-volitional causal relations turned out to take up no more than 5% of *daarom*'s contexts of use in the samples analyzed.

6 Both *dus* and *daarom* are used in functions other than marking of causal coherence relations, such as: marking information status or referential function. We did not take these functions into account in this paper.

TABLE 3 *Causal relation types distinguished in this study and their paraphrases*

Causal relation type	Paraphrases
Objective	The situation in S1[7] leads to the following observable non-speaker action: S2
Subjective	The situation in S1 leads to the following conclusion or speech act performed by the author as a communicating subject: S2

Fragments were classified by one of the authors and checked by the other. Cases leading to disagreement were discussed, resulting either in agreement on classification, or on classification as 'ambiguous'. We excluded the latter cases (taking up 13% of the sample) from analysis. By doing so, our hypotheses were tested in a maximally conservative way, ensuring that in each of the fragments in the analysis causal relation type plays a crucial role in the reader's interpretation of the whole causal relation and connective. Of course, this is essential specifically for the NPU hypotheses discussed in this section and in section 3, ruling out the possibility that the selection of a given connective is based on the fact that the causal relation *itself* (instead of its segmental of broader discourse context—the factors we are investigating in this paper) is ambiguous in terms of causality type.

2.2.3 Corpus and Sample

In view of our ambition to investigate the situational aspect of 'discourse goal' as a factor co-determining selection of *dus* or *daarom* as a marker of subjective or objective causal relations, we tested the hypotheses stated in 2.2.1 against patterns of use in three newspaper genres (news report, reportage, and opinion pieces) that differ in their discourse goals (see section 3).

The hypotheses were tested against samples of 77,000 words for each genre. News reports and opinion pieces were taken from the newspaper subsample

7 'S1' refers to the first segment of the causal relation, which is the cause-segment in relations marked with *dus* and *daarom*. 'S2' refers to the second segment of the causal relation, which is the effect-segment in relations marked with *dus* and *daarom*.

of a pilot version of the D-coi reference corpus for Dutch written discourse (Oostdijk 2007), containing a randomized sample of Dutch quality daily newspapers. Reportages were collected by Boon (2009). Subsamples of news reports, reportages, and opinion pieces were built in a hand-based manner, making use of an inventory of (non-linguistic) content characteristics based on Asbreuk and De Moor (2007) and Kussendrager and Van der Lugt (2007).

2.2.4 Statistical Analysis

All of our hypotheses concern contrasts. Contrasts in our data were assessed with contrast analysis (Van den Bergh 1990), a statistical method of analysis for non-parametric data. This analysis enables us to test hypotheses concerning contrasts within and between samples in a more specific way than is possible with, for example, chi square analysis. In contrast analysis specific distributions are predicted in terms of relative 'weight'; the data are evaluated against this prediction. As our hypotheses are one-sided, we set our level of acceptance to $Z = 1.685$ ($p = .05$).

2.2.5 Results

We found the following distribution of *dus* and *daarom* over relation types.

TABLE 4 *Distribution of* dus *and* daarom *across objective and subjective causal relations in news reports, reportages, and opinion pieces*

		Objective causal relations	**Subjective causal relations**	**Total**
Daarom	News report	13	7	20
	Reportage	13	12	25
	Opinion	11	17	28
Dus	News report	2	20	22
	Reportage	9	25	34
	Opinion	0	30	30

2.2.5.1 *NPU Subjective* dus *in Objective Relations*

Our first NPU hypothesis predicts that the segments of objective causal relations marked with *dus* contain subjective elements more often than the segments of objective causal relations marked with *daarom*. In news reports and reportages *dus* and *daarom* were distributed over representation mode types in objective relations as indicated in Table 5. *Dus* did not occur in objective relations in our sample of opinion pieces.

TABLE 5 *Distribution of* dus *and* daarom *over representation mode types in objective relations in news reports and reportages (bold type indicates an effect)*

		Neutral discourse	**Character subjectivity**	**Total**
News report	*Daarom*	11	2	13
	Dus	1	1	2
Reportage	*Daarom*	7	6	13
	Dus	2	7	9

On the basis of the linguistic NPU hypothesis stated in section 2.2.1, we expect that *dus*, when marking objective relations, is used in subjective mode more often than *daarom*. This expectation is not borne out of analyses in which distributions of *dus* and *daarom* over representation mode types per genre are directly contrasted (news report: Z = 1.06; p = .14; reportage: Z = 1.44; p = .07). Analysis per connective per genre, however, reveals that *daarom* has a clear preference for neutral representation mode (Z = 2.22; p = .01). The contrast we thus find in news reports is in accordance with our linguistic NPU hypothesis.

Reportages appear to show the reverse picture: *daarom* is distributed equally over objective and subjective representation modes, whereas *dus* has a trend towards subjective mode (Z = 1.56; p = .059), which reveals a strong trend in the expected direction. An example of NPU *dus* in an objective relation in newspaper reportage was discussed as example (7) in section 2.

2.2.5.2 *NPU Objective* daarom *in Subjective Relations*

Our first NPU hypothesis predicts that segments of subjective causal relations marked with *daarom* contain objective elements more often than the segments of subjective causal relations marked with *dus*. Table 6 summarizes the distribution of *dus* and *daarom* over representation mode types in subjective causal relations in news reports, reportage, and opinion pieces.

TABLE 6 *Distribution of* dus *and* daarom *over representation mode types in subjective relations in news reports, reportages, and opinion pieces (bold type indicates an effect)*

		Character subjectivity	Author subjectivity	Total
News report	*Daarom*	**6**	1	7
	Dus	9	11	20
Reportage	*Daarom*	10	2	12
	Dus	19	6	25
Opinion piece	*Daarom*	1	16	17
	Dus	6	23	29[8]

Author mode being more subjective than character mode, our NPU hypothesis predicts that NPU subjective *daarom* is used with character mode more often than *dus*. This hypothesis is borne out of news reports (Z = 1.70; p = .04). An example of subjective *daarom* with character mode (free indirect mode) in this genre is (8). By way of contrast, consider example (6), discussed in section 2, which is a case of subjective *dus* with author mode.

(8) [On the role of UNHCR in EU policy concerning refugees] *"Het gaat ons niet om een buffer voor mensenstromen naar de EU, maar om een buffer van bescherming voor de vluchtelingen", zegt Durieux. (…) Met name in het tweede project ligt daarom volgens hem een kans besloten die de EU niet zou mogen missen.* "We are not concerned with a buffer against a rush of refugees into the EU, but with a buffer of protection for refugees", Durieux states. (…) The second project in particular "daarom" is according to him likely to offer possibilities that the EU shouldn't miss.

In reportages, *dus* and *daarom* display an overall tendency towards character mode (*daarom* Z = 2.08; p = .02; *both dus* Z = -2.46; p = .007; the minus

8 One fragment turned out to be ambiguous for representation mode, and was discarded from analysis. This explains why total of epistemic relations for *dus* in opinion pieces is lower than in other tables.

sign indicates an effect opposite to the direction of the effect predicted in the hypothesis). In opinion pieces, *both dus* and *daarom* display an overall tendency towards author mode (*daarom* Z = 2.08; p = .02; *dus* Z = -2.46; p = .007).

2.2.6 Discussion

Our overall prototype structure hypothesis predicts that *dus* and *daarom*'s non-prototypical contexts of use are conceptually related to their respective prototypical contexts of use. In this section we investigated subjectivity indicators of the effect segments. The contrasts we found in objective relations largely corroborate our expectations. Table 7 summarizes our findings in relation to the scalarly ordered subjectivity categories we distinguished in this study (section 2.2.2).

TABLE 7 *Distribution of* dus *and* daarom *over subjectivity types in objective causal relations (NB: In opinion pieces, objective causal relations marked with* dus *did not occur)*

Degree of subjectivity	**Author subjectivity >**	**Character subjectivity >**		**Neutral discourse**
News report				*daarom*
			dus	
Reportage			*daarom*	
		(*dus*?)		

Distribution of *dus* and *daarom* over subjectivity types in news reports corroborate our linguistic NPU hypothesis. NPU subjective *daarom* is more objective than PU subjective *dus*. NPU objective *dus* does not have a preference for more subjective representation mode types, but as PU objective *daarom* prefers the more objective types, the overall difference between *dus* and *daarom* corroborates our expectations.

Reportages reveal a similar pattern with respect to objective relations. Whereas *daarom* does not have a preference for neutral or character representation modes, *dus* shows a strong tendency towards the more subjective character mode. The fact that we do not find an effect in this case is potentially due to the relatively small sample investigated. Investigation of a larger sample is needed in order to assess this pattern properly. NPU objective *dus* did not occur in opinion pieces; therefore, we could not test our linguistic NPU hypothesis with respect to this genre.

Table 8 summarizes our findings with respect to subjective causal relations.

TABLE 8 *Distribution of* dus *and* daarom *over subjectivity types in subjective causal relations*

Degree of subjectivity	**Author subjectivity >**	**Character subjectivity >**	**Neutral discourse**
News report	*dus*	*daarom*	
Reportage		*daarom* *dus*	
Opinion	*daarom* *dus*		

The distribution of *dus* and *daarom* in subjective relations in news reports corroborates our expectations. Subjective relations in opinion pieces and reportages, on the contrary, reveal an initially unexpected overall pattern. In opinion pieces, both NPU subjective *daarom* and PU subjective *dus* have a preference for author subjectivity. In reportages, however, both connectives display a skewing towards character subjectivity.

As a matter of principle, we could interpret these patterns as counterevidence against our overall prototype structure hypothesis, but this is not a very attractive option since it would contradict a large body of findings reported in previous studies, which have consistently reported systematic differences between subjective relations marked with *dus* or *daarom* (cf. Pander Maat & Sanders 2000; Pander Maat & Degand 2001; Stukker et al. 2009), or with the backward order causal connectives *omdat* and *want* (an overview is presented in Stukker & Sanders 2012). A meta-analysis of previous corpus analyses on backward order causal connectives in Dutch (*want* and *omdat*), French (*car* and *parce que*), and German (*denn* and *weil*) reported in Stukker and Sanders

(2012) suggests that the prototype characteristics identified for Dutch causal connectives have cross-linguistic validity.

A potential alternative explanation could be that linguistic patterns in opinion pieces and reportages *in general* are subject to an overall bias in terms of subjectivity type, due to genre characteristics. The specific characteristics of the subjective relations in our sample seem to corroborate this post-hoc hypothesis: subjective relations in opinion pieces (author subjective genre) have an overall preference for author subjectivity (over character subjectivity); in reportages (character subjective genre) the reverse holds true. If this is interpretation is correct, the subjectivity characteristics of the effect segments in reportages and opinion pieces reported in this paper are an artefact of the way our concept of representation mode was operationalized in this study.

In the following sections, therefore, we do not assume that our findings in the first corpus analysis falsify our overall prototype structure hypothesis, but instead follow an alternative option, which is to interpret our initially unexpected finding as a first indication that segmental characteristics favoring NPU of *dus* and *daarom* interact with rhetorical factors originating from the situational context of the discourse as a whole. As we will see in section 3, news reports, reportages, and opinion pieces differ with respect to their overall subjectivity characteristics. News reports present news events from a neutral perspective, whereas in reportages and opinion pieces, news events tend to be presented from a character subjective and author subjective viewpoint, respectively. These overall generic characteristics do not only converge with our findings for *dus* and *daarom* in subjective relations in reportages and opinion pieces, but they also coincide very nicely with the fact that the category of objective causal relations marked with *dus* or *daarom as a whole* is more subjective in reportages than in news reports. We will return to this issue in section 5.

3 Corpus Study 2: Contextual Indications of 'Subjective Causality' and 'Objective Causality' Category Membership in the Genres' Communicative Goals *dus* and *daarom* are Used With

In the remainder of this paper, we investigate to what extent the contextual factor of 'discourse goal' acts as a distinct factor determining selection of *dus* and *daarom* as markers of subjective and objective causal relations. Various studies have suggested that patterns of causal connective use are sensitive to context factors (cf. Van den Hoven 1997; Bekker 2006; Spooren et al. 2010). These findings may be explained with reference to the more general assumption in discourse studies that a systematic relation holds between communicative 'needs' induced by specific factors of discourse contexts (such as characteristics of the participants in the communication, the channel chosen, production circumstances, topic, etc.) and specific linguistic choices made by the speaker or the author—of which causal connective selection obviously is only one very specific example. This interrelation between context and language use has been studied extensively within the theoretical framework of systemic functional grammar (cf. Halliday 1985); register study (cf. Martin 1992; Biber 1988) and many other types of (applied) discourse studies. We will investigate the role of discourse goal of newspaper genres as a potential rhetorical factor inducing NPU events of causal connectives, potentially relating the connectives' NPU to their PU contexts. Discourse goal is assumed to be among the more influential context factors co-determining linguistic choices (cf. Swales 1990; Askehave & Swales 2000; Biber & Conrad 2009).

3.1 *Hypothesis*

We contrasted three well-known, frequently encountered Dutch newspaper genres, which share their context characteristics with respect to medium (printed newspaper), author characteristics (professional, highly trained writers), reader characteristics (the newspaper's general audience), production circumstances, setting, and topic (news events), but differ with respect to one specific factor: discourse goal. Since our hypothesis concerns the relationship between connective meaning, the contrast between the discourse goals should be characterized, making use of the same global concept the contrast between the connectives studied is associated with: subjectivity. Table 9 below presents an overview of relevant characteristics of the newspaper genres included in this study.

The overall goal of a news report is to report a news event in a neutral, objective way, leaving the author's personal opinion regarding the reported events unexpressed (cf. Kussendrager & Van der Lugt 2007: 195).[9] Therefore, we classified news reports as an objective genre. The overall goal of opinion pieces is to state the author's personal opinion with respect to a current topic and to persuade the reader that this claim holds true (cf. Kussendrager & Van der Lugt 2007: 334). Thus, opinion pieces are classified as inherently subjective. Reportages are somewhere 'in between' on a scale of subjectivity. Although they share with news reports the characteristic that they report news events, a

9 Obviously, this is a normative definition. Our sample consists of Dutch 'quality newspapers', which are believed to observe this norm.

definitional criterion of newspaper reportage is that news events are presented in such a way that the reader co-experiences the reported event and experiences the feeling that 'he was part of the events himself'. In order to create this experience, the author should present the events in the form of an eyewitness report, including perceptions and reflections of the person(s) involved in the event (cf. Kussendrager & Van der Lugt 2007: 304). Reportage shares this aspect of subjectivity with opinion pieces. An important difference with opinion pieces, however, is that the most important source of subjectivity here is the author, whereas in reportage the subjective viewpoint may be carried over to another 'subject of consciousness' (cf. section 2), typically a person playing a central role in the reported events.

TABLE 9 *Subjectivity characteristics of newspaper genres news report, reportage, and opinion piece (Kussendrager & Van der Lugt 2007; see also Asbreuk & De Moor 2007)*

	News report	**Reportage**	**Opinion piece**
Rhetorical goal	Objective	Character subjective	Author subjective
Participants:			
– author subjective	No	No	Yes
– character subjective	No	Yes	No[10]

If discourse goal plays a distinct role in determining selection of *dus* or *daarom* as a marker of a subjective or objective causal discourse relation, we expect to find the following patterns of distribution over newspaper genres:

– Frequency of NPU subjective *dus* in objective relations: reportages > news reports

10 We investigated signed opinion pieces. In theory, these may contain stretches of discourse presented from character perspective, especially if the author of the piece intends to engage in a discussion with previous contributions to the newspaper, summarizing the relevant contents including this author's perspective. In our corpus we did not find clear examples of this strategy.

- Frequency of NPU objective *daarom* in subjective relations: news reports > reportages, opinion pieces

In opinion pieces we only found objective causal relations marked with *daarom*. As we could not assess a contrast with *dus* in this case, we excluded opinion pieces from our analysis of distribution patterns in objective causal relations. Corpus, samples, and methods of analysis were the same as described in section 2.

3.2 *Results*

In order to test this hypothesis in a reliable way, we have to correct for overall frequency of relation type. Therefore, our second conceptual NPU hypothesis is tested not against absolute numbers of occurrence of NPU patterns, but against the proportions of their absolute frequency per genre and the total amount of relation types in the genres under study. Table 10 summarizes our findings.

TABLE 10 *Frequency of occurrence of NPU patterns as a proportion of total frequency of relation type (in %) in news reports, reportages, and opinion pieces (bold type indicates an effect)*

		Daarom	*Dus*	**Total**
Objective	News report	86	14	100
	Reportage	59	**41**	100
Subjective	News report	26	74	100
	Reportage	32	68	100
	Opinion	36	64	100

Our data for *dus* corroborate our second hypothesis, which predicted that frequency of NPU subjective *dus* in character subjective reportage would be higher than in news reports (being an overall objective genre) ($Z = 3.47$; $p < .001$[11]).

11 These effects cannot solely be attributed to the artificially 'larger' sample sizes (computing percentages instead of absolute frequencies of occurrence in our small pilot samples). If we

Our second conceptual NPU hypothesis is not borne out by our findings with respect to NPU objective *daarom* in subjective relations. We predicted that *daarom* would be used in subjective relations in news reports (being an objective genre describing news events) more often than in reportage (being a character subjective genre describing events) and opinion pieces (being an author subjective genre arguing in favour of a claim). Distribution of NPU subjective *daarom* turned out to be equal across genres (Z = .786; p = .23 and Z = -1.26; p = .10, respectively). We will return to this issue in section 5.

4 Corpus Study 3: Prototypical Use across Discourse Genres

A pivotal argument in favour of our prototype structure hypothesis has been that prototypical uses of *dus* and *daarom* are more frequent than their non-prototypical uses. Following a large body of studies conducted within the framework of the usage-based theory of language, we have assumed that frequency reflects cognitive entrenchment (cf. section 2): the more frequently a linguistic form is encountered in a given context of use, the stronger this usage type will be associated with the form—to the extent that it will be considered as its prototypical meaning or function. Our findings in sections 2 and 3, as well as a large body of work in register and genre studies suggesting that linguistic patterns may be context-sensitive, raise the question of how stable frequency patterns are across discourse contexts. To our knowledge, this issue has not been addressed from a usage-based theory perspective so far.

4.1 *Hypothesis*

In principle, we would expect that a causal category's prototypical status is reflected in any discourse context in its relative importance in terms of frequency of use. In this final part of our paper, we will test this hypothesis from two different perspectives, addressing different aspects of the relationship between connectives and conceptual relations of causality that we are investigating in this study. The first perspective concerns *meaning*, or the semasiological perspective, answering the question "given linguistic item y, what meaning does it express?" This is the perspective traditionally studied in connective analysis. The second perspective concerns *naming*, or the onomasiological

correct for sample size with a factor 4 (which approaches the actual samples we worked with), we find reportages vs. opinion pieces: Z = 2.2; p = .014. Reportages vs. news reports: 1.55; p = .06; the latter represents a strong tendency.

perspective, approaching the assumed relation between connectives and causal relations from the opposite perspective, answering the question: "given concept x, what linguistic items can it be expressed with?" (Geeraerts 1997: 17[12]). We believe that the onomasiological level of analysis is an essential complementary perspective with regard to corpus studies into linguistic categorization (Stukker et al. 2009: 159–160).

The following hypotheses are tested:

- Semasiological perspective: use of *dus* in subjective relations is more frequent than in objective relations; use of *daarom* in objective relations is more frequent than in subjective relations.
- Onomasiological perspective: subjective causal relations are more frequently expressed with *dus* than with *daarom*; objective causal relations are more frequently expressed with *daarom* than with *dus*.

Corpus, samples, and methods of analysis were the same as described in section 2.

4.2 *Results*

4.2.1 Semasiological Perspective

Table 11 summarizes our findings from a semasiological perspective, answering the question: what meanings do *dus* and *daarom* express?

Our PU hypothesis predicted that use of *dus* in subjective relations is more frequent than in relations; use of *daarom* in objective relations is more frequent than in relations. Across contexts, the usage of *dus* can correctly be accounted for with reference to the conceptual category of subjective causality (news report: $Z = 3.11$, $p < .001$; reportage: $Z = 2.63$, $p = .004$; opinion: $Z = 3.35$, $p < .001$). This finding corroborates our hypothesis with respect to *dus*. With respect to *daarom*, however, things turn out differently. In none of the contexts was *daarom* used in objective relations more often than in subjective relations (news report $Z = 1.32$, $p = .09$; opinion: $Z = -1.13$, $p = .13$; reportage: $Z = .2$, $p = .42$).

12 For an elaborate discussion of the nature, benefits, and origins of the distinction between the semasiological and onomasiological levels of analysis, see Grondelaers, Speelman & Geeraerts (2007).

TABLE 11 *Distribution of* dus *and* daarom *over relation types across genres (bold type indicates an effect)*

		Objective	Subjective	Total
Daarom	News report	13	7	20
	Reportage	13	12	25
	Opinion	11	17	28
Dus	News report	2	**20**	22
	Reportage	9	**25**	34
	Opinion	0	**30**	30

4.2.2 Onomasiological Perspective

Table 12 summarizes our findings from an onomasiological perspective, answering the question: what connective are objective and subjective causal relations prototypically expressed with in news reports, reportages, and opinion pieces?

TABLE 12 *Distribution of relation types over* dus *and* daarom *across genres (bold type indicates an effect)*

		Daarom	*Dus*	Total
Objective	News report	**13**	2	15
	Reportage	13	9	24
	Opinion	**11**	0	11
Subjective	News report	7	**20**	27
	Reportage	12	**25**	37
	Opinion	17	**30**	47

Results for *dus* confirm the findings in the semasiological analysis. We expected that subjective, causal relations are typically expressed with *dus*. This hypothesis is corroborated for all of the genres (news report: Z = 2.40, p = .008; reportage: Z = 2.10, p = .018; opinion: Z = 1.90, p = .029). The onomasiological perspective of analysis adds interesting information to the semasiological analysis discussed above. We hypothesized that objective causal relations are most frequently expressed with *daarom*. This hypothesis is corroborated by our findings in news reports ($Z= 2.46$, $p = .007$) and opinion pieces ($Z = 2.30$, $p = .01$). The onomasiological PU hypothesis, however, is not corroborated by our findings in reportages ($Z = .85$, $p = .20$). In section 3 we interpreted this pattern in relation to our second NPU hypothesis. We argued that this diverging pattern can be explained as a consequence of the large amount of objective relations marked with *dus* in reportages, which we interpret as cases of rhetorically motivated subjective construals.

5 Discussion

The intuition that causal connectives have a fixed meaning is widespread; yet at the same time, corpus studies show that patterns of connective *use* are flexible. How can this paradox be accounted for from a theoretical point of view? In previous papers, we analyzed usage events of connectives, which reflect the causal category the connective is prototypically associated with in a less straightforward way, as non-prototypical instantiations of the same category that the more typical usage types belong to (cf. Stukker, Sanders & Verhagen 2008, 2009).

So far, studies identifying the linguistic and cognitive mechanisms underlying causal connective use have mainly focused on characteristics of the discourse segments (denoting cause and effect) related by the connectives. In this paper, we investigated the role of the situational factor of *discourse goal* as an independent factor co-determining language users' selection of connectives as linguistic markers of subjective and objective causal relations. Our aim was to explore discourse context as a new source of evidence for our hypothesis that deviant usage events of causal connectives are actually rhetorically motivated, peripheral members of the same category that their more conventional contexts of use belong to.

Table 13 summarizes our results. We found a number of indications in favour of our main hypothesis, as well as a number of issues that call for closer analysis.

TABLE 13 *Summary of the results per hypothesis. +: corroborates hypothesis; –: falsifies hypothesis; o: neutral; n.a.: not applicable*

	News Reports: Objective		**Opinion Pieces: Subjective author**		**Reportages: Subjective character**	
Overall hypothesis CC x subjectivity type:	*Daarom* Obj	*Dus* Subj	*Daarom* Obj	*Dus* Subj	*Daarom* Obj	*Dus* Subj
PU Hypothesis						
1. Semasiological	–	+	–	+	–	+
2. Onomasiological	+	+	+	+	–	+
NPU Hypotheses						
1. Level of segments						
Objective causal	+	o	n.a.	n.a.	o	+?
Subjective causal	+	+	–	+	+	–
2. Level of context	-	+	n.a.	n.a.	-	+

Our overall prototype structure hypothesis predicts that *dus* and *daarom*'s NPU are conceptually related to their respective PU. In a first corpus analysis we tested this more general hypothesis with respect to the degree of subjectivity of the segments related by the connectives. Subjectivity was measured in terms of representation mode of the effect segment. The distribution patterns we found in news reports largely corroborated our first hypothesis. In reportages and in opinion pieces, however, segmental characteristics appeared to interact with the second source of rhetorical motivations: the genres' communicative goals. Although this is an unanticipated finding, it does not come as a complete surprise. Connectives are among the linguistic elements that actually 'construe' a genre, including its subjectivity profile. In fact, it is this assumption that this study's design is built on. At the same time, it is possible that subjectivity markers (a class that both causal connectives and representation mode are taken to belong to, cf. Vis 2011) differ with respect to their relative contribution to construing a given genre. We could assume, for example, that representation mode adds to construing the overall subjectivity characteristics of opinion pieces and reportages relatively more importantly than connectives do. In future work, we aim to assess this interaction of factors using more sophisticated statistical methods and model of analysis.

In a second corpus analysis, we tested our hypothesis that the situational factor of 'discourse goal' may function as a distinct factor determining selection of *dus* or *daarom* as linguistic markers of subjective and objective causal discourse relations. This hypothesis was borne out of NPU objective *dus*, which turned out to occur more often in reportages than in news reports. This is in accordance with reportages' overall communicative goal of reporting news events in a narrative way—that is, invoking empathy with the characters involved in the events, be they the author or other persons.

We did not find differences with respect to distribution over context types of NPU subjective *daarom*. In this study, we explored the role of 'discourse goal' as a situational factor co-determining selection of *dus* or *daarom* as a marker of an objective or subjective causal discourse relations. Our choice was motivated by the fact that various studies have suggested that it is the more dominant situational factor determining linguistic choices across genres (Swales 1990; Askehave & Swales 2000; Biber & Conrad 2009; cf. discussion in section 3 above). A qualitative post hoc analysis of our findings in corpus study 2 suggests, however, that 'discourse goal' interacts with other situational factors determining the selection of *dus* and *daarom*, especially the factor of the author's social role. Various authors have noted that "characteristics like the speaker's (author's) age, sex, level of education, occupation and social class can all be important determinants of linguistic variation" (Biber & Conrad 2009: 41; cf. Hymes 1974; Halliday 1978).

In feature articles (the Dutch genre 'reportage'), for example, the marking of subjective causal relations with either *dus* or with *daarom* seems to vary in accordance with the identity of the person acting as the relation's locus of effect. More specifically, marking appears to vary according to the question of whether the locus of effect is the story's main character, or just some other person playing a supporting role in the story.[13] In the first case, *dus* tends to be selected, in the other cases, while *daarom* dominates as a marker. This pattern is in accordance with the Dutch genre convention that reportages may have one or more 'main characters' whose experiences, emotions, and opinions are focused upon (Asbreuk & De Moor 2007: 215). Yet, other characters' conclusions and speech obviously may be reported in the reportage genre as well—a fact that could explain the relatively high level of *daarom*-marked subjective causal

13 For discussion of the various conventional subjectivity strategies applied in newspaper genres, see Sanders (2010).

relations in this genre. Additional analyses are required to determine whether this explanation holds. If it does, the *daarom*-marked subjective causal relations in reportages may be explained exactly along the lines sketched in this paper: as situationally motivated rhetorical construals.

A similar additional situational explanation seems to account for the unexpectedly high amount of *daarom*-marked subjective relations in opinion pieces. This, too, was an initially unexpected pattern, as both author loci of effect and subjective causal relations have been strongly associated with *dus* as a causal marker in previous studies (cf. discussion in section 2.1). In addition, one would expect that in the opinion genre, subjective causal relations may be overtly marked as such, the genre's conventional goal being to express the author's personal opinion on a current topic (cf. section 3.2). However, closer scrutiny of the *daarom*-marked subjective causal relations in opinion pieces suggest that here, too, a situation-based subdistinction is made—that is, between subjective conclusion causal relations constituting a major point in the overall argumentation of the piece, one of its main conclusions, or a conclusion that is part of the author's central message, and 'any other' part of the reasoning set up.

Fragment (9), taken from a letter to the editor written by a Dutch defense expert,[14,15] illustrates this conceptual distinction.

(9) [Author's text, paragraph 14 out of 17] *Tot 11 september vonden alle terreuraanslagen tegen Amerikaanse doelen buiten de VS plaats. Dus ook andere landen worden het slachtoffer van het terrorisme. Bovendien maakt onze betrokkenheid bij de strijd tegen het internationale terrorisme in welke vorm dan ook, ons ook tot doelwit. Alertheid en transatlantische samenwerking blijven daarom van levensbelang.*

Until September 11, all of the terrorist campaigns against American targets took place outside the United States. "Dus" other countries fall victim to terrorism, too. In addition, our involvement in the battle against international terrorism in whatever form makes us a target. Attentiveness in transatlantic cooperation stay "daarom" of vital importance.

14 D-coi newspaper corpus text 4304 (published in the Dutch daily newspaper *NRC Handelsblad* on February 16, 2002).

15 Half of the opinion corpus consisted of this type of letters to the editor, written by professional writers who are not part of the newspaper's editorial team but who act as publicists and experts on the subject at hand. The other half of the corpus consisted of editorial opinion pieces. The pattern illustrated in (9) is found in the editorial subgenre in a similar form.

This fragment contains two subjective causal conclusion relations. The second causal relation, marked with *daarom*, is closer to the author's central message than the first (marked with *dus*). That it is may be inferred not only by reconstructing the structure of the argumentation in this fragment, but also by the fact that it is closely related to the paraphrase of the author's central message as presented in the (editorial) introductory paragraph preceding the author's text—see (10):

(10) [Editorial introduction to the piece, paraphrase of the author's main point] *De Atlantische kloof wordt steeds breder. De Europeanen weigeren de onderlinge gelederen te sluiten en missen een wereldwijde visie. Maar de Verenigde Staten op hun beurt gaan op basis van een enkelvoudig wereldbeeld autonoom hun eigen weg, zonder rekening te houden met anderen. Rob de Wijk vindt het daarom hoog tijd dat ook de Amerikanen de hand in eigen boezem steken.*

The Atlantic gap is widening. The Europeans fail to close the ranks and lack a world-wide view. But the United States, for their part, basing themselves on a simple worldview, act autonomously, without consideration for other parties. Rob de Wijk therefore thinks it is time that the United States search their own conscience. (…)

An important additional characteristic of the conclusion presented in the second causal relation in (9), which turns out to be a characteristic shared by many *daarom*-marked subjective relations in the opinion genre and is shared by only a small number of the *dus*-marked cases, is that they are part of the author's 'expert knowledge'—which is normally not shared by the majority of the newspaper's audience, and which is the very reason why the expert is entitled to write the piece: she or he knows things we don't. These *daarom*-marked subjective causal relations share the characteristic that we readers are not capable of inferring ourselves; we simply lack the knowledge, even if we read and understood the text. In general, the subjective causal relations marked with *dus* do not share this characteristic. The *dus*-marked conclusion in (9), for example, may be inferred directly from the preceding text. A systematically occurring characteristic of *daarom*-marked subjective relations in opinion pieces, then, is that they seem to mark a different type of subjectivity. 'Evaluation', and inviting the reader to evaluate the claim presented, does not seem to be their primary function. Rather, these relations appear to *explain* an aspect of reality to the reader that has a factual basis in the expert knowledge of the author. If this explanation holds, we may again put forward that in these cases, objectivity-construing *daarom* may be explained exactly along the lines sketched in this paper: as situationally motivated rhetorical construals.[16]

Obviously, more detailed and more systematic research into the nature of *daarom*-marked subjective relations in reportages and in opinion pieces is needed to fully understand their function, but the examples discussed above illustrate one important issue in relation to the present study: in future research, we will have to refine our conception of 'genre', and include in our analysis, next to overall communicative goal, factors such as participant roles and other register conventions that appear to play an important role in construing genres (cf. Biber & Conrad 2009; Martin 1992; Steen 2011).

In a third corpus analysis, we compared distributional patterns of *dus* and *daarom* across the newspaper genres under investigation, showing that patterns of relative frequency, including their status as indicator of prototype structure, are affected by the situational factor of discourse goal as well. We hypothesized that the connectives' PU are invariable across contexts. This hypothesis was corroborated by *dus*. Results for *daarom* were less clear at first sight. From a semasiological perspective ("what types of causal relations does a given connective express?") it does not have a PU in any of the contexts under investigation. The onomasiological level of analysis ("what connective does the language user choose for expressing a given relation type?"), however, suggests that the semasiological 'result' is an artefact of overall high frequency of subjective relations across the genres under investigation. When correcting for this factor (which is what the onomasiological perspective does, as a side effect), *daarom* turns out to be prototypically associated with objective causality in news reports and in opinion pieces. In reportages, this relation does not hold; objective causal relations are marked with *dus* as often as they are marked with *daarom*.

Above, we interpreted this relatively high frequency of *dus* in objective relations in reportages as a conceptually based construal of the objective causal category motivated by overall communicative goal. A remaining question, however, is how must we interpret this apparent context-dependency of PU patterns in relation to our overall prototype structure hypothesis? Our findings with respect to segmental characteristics of objective relations marked with *dus* vs. those marked with *daarom* suggest that, in spite of lacking an unambiguous PU 'anchor' for *daarom*, the contexts of use differ along the lines

16 We found a similar pattern in editorial opinion pieces. In this subgenre, *daarom* marks subjective relations referring to knowledge of the journalist as an expert in interpreting news events.

predicted by our prototype structure hypothesis—suggesting that even in these contexts, *daarom* still functions as a marker of the conceptual category of objective causal relations.

In sum, we interpret our findings as initial, yet promising evidence that situational factors in the discourse context may serve as a new source of evidence for our overall hypothesis that deviant usage events of causal connectives are actually rhetorically motivated, peripheral members of the same category that their more conventional contexts of use belong to. In addition, the results reported in this paper challenge a number of well-established ideas regarding the interaction between the language system, the situational context of language use, and human cognition directing processes of linguistic communication. To our knowledge, the issue of the context-dependency of patterns of cognitive entrenchment has not yet been discussed in usage-based theory, but in our view, this is an urgent question. We hope to be able to contribute to unravelling this issue in future research, making use of more sophisticated methods of analysis along the lines sketched in this paper.

This work is a piece in the puzzle presented in the volume, trying to tease apart and at the same time integrate the contribution of coherence relations to the interpretation of evaluation and subjectivity. Research by, for instance, Benamara et al. (this volume) proposes that coherence relations need to be taken into account in the study of sentiment in text. Zappavigna shows how one particular relation, condition, plays an important role in the system of Engagement, which is also related to our concept of subjectivity. In all, we see that the connections between coherence relations, subjectivity and evaluation are multiple, and can be studied from multiple points of view.

Acknowledgements

We would like to thank the editors of this volume, Maite Taboada and Rada Trnavac, and an anonymous reviewer, for useful comments on an earlier version of this paper.

The authors acknowledge the support of NWO vici-grant 277-70-003, awarded to Ted Sanders, while preparing this paper.

References

Asbreuk, H., and A. de Moor. "Basisboek journalistiek schrijven: voor krant, tijdschrift en web." Groningen: Wolters Noordhoff, 2007.

Askehave, I., and J.M. Swales. "Genre identification and communicative purpose: A problem and possible solution." *Applied Linguistics* 22 (2000): 195–212.

Barlow, M., and S. Kemmer, eds. *Usage based models of language*. Stanford: CSLI Publications, 2000.

Bekker, Birgit. *De feiten verdraaid. Over tekstvolgorde, talige markering en sprekerbetrokkenheid.* ("Twisted Facts. Textual ordering, linguistic signals and speaker involvement"). PhD dissertation, Tilburg University, 2006.

Biber, D. *Variation across speech and writing*. Cambridge: Cambridge University Press, 1988.

Biber, D., and S. Conrad. *Register, genre, and style*. Cambridge: Cambridge University Press, 2009.

Boon, R. Biedt genreverschil perspectief? Een corpusonderzoek naar afwijkende gebruiksgevallen van de connectieven dus, daarom en daardoor. Unpublished MA thesis, Universiteit Utrecht, 2009.

Bybee, J. "From usage to grammar: The mind's response to repetition." *Language* 82 (2006): 711–733.

———. *Frequency of use and the organization of language*. Oxford: Oxford University Press, 2007.

Croft, W. *Radical construction grammar*. Oxford: Oxford University Press, 2001.

Dancygier, B., and E. Sweetser, eds. *Viewpoint in language: A multimodal perspective*. Cambridge: Cambridge University Press, 2012.

Degand, L., and B. Fagard. "Intersubjectification des connecteurs. Le cas de car et parce que." *Revista de Estudos Linguisticos da Universidade do Porto* 3 (2008): 119–136.

Fagel, S., N. Stukker, and L. van Andel. "Hoe telbaar is stijl? Een kwantitatieve analyse van observatie en participatie in de stijl van Arnon Grunberg." *Nederlandse Letterkunde* 17 (2012): 178–203.

Geeraerts, D. *Diachronic prototype semantics. A contribution to historical lexicology*. Oxford: Clarendon Press, 1997.

Goldberg, A. *Constructions at work. The nature of generalization in language*. Oxford: Oxford University Press, 2005.

Grondelaers, S., D. Speelman, and D. Geeraerts. "Lexical variation and change." In *Handbook of Cognitive Linguistics*, 988–1011. Oxford: Oxford University Press, 2007.

Halliday, M.A.K. *An introduction to functional grammar*. Edward Arnold Publishers: London, 1985.

Haspelmath, M. *Indefinite pronouns*. Oxford: Clarendon Press, 1997.

Hymes, Dell H. *Foundations of Sociolinguistics: An Ethnographic Approach*. Philadelphia: University of Pennsylvania Press, 1974.

Le Groupe λ-l. "Car, parce que, puisque." *Revue Romaine* 17 X. Université de Kopenhague (1975): 249–280.

Keller, R. "The epistemic weil." In *Subjectivity and subjectivisation*, 16–30. Cambridge: Cambridge University Press, 1995.

Knott, A., and R. Dale. "Using linguistic phenomena to motivate a set of coherence relations." *Discourse Processes* 18, no. 1 (1994): 35–62.

Kortmann, B. *Adverbial subordination. A typology and history of adverbial subordinators based on European languages*. Berlin: Mouton de Gruyter, 1997.

Kussendrager, N., and D. van der Lugt. *Basisboek journalistiek. Achtergronden, genres, vaardigheden*. Groningen: Wolters-Noordhoff, 2007.

Lakoff, G. *Women, fire and dangerous things. What categories reveal about the mind*. Chicago: University of Chicago Press, 1987.

Langacker, R.W. *Foundations of cognitive grammar. Vol. I, Theoretical prerequisites*. Stanford: Stanford University Press, 1987.

———. "Subjectification." *Cognitive Linguistics* 1 (1990): 5–38.

———. *Concept, image, and symbol. The cognitive basis of grammar*. Berlin, New York: Mouton de Gruyter, 2002 [1990].

Leech, Geoffrey and Mick Short. *Style in Fiction* (2nd edition). London: Longman, 2007.

Martin, J.R. *English text: System and structure*. Philadelphia, John Benjamins, 1992.

Oostdijk, N. "Dutch Language Corpus Initiative Pilot Corpus." Dutch Language Corpus Initiative: Technical report D-Coi-06-09, 2007.

Pander Maat, H., and L. Degand. "Scaling causal relations and connectives in terms of speaker involvement." *Cognitive linguistics* 12–3 (2001): 211–245.

Pasch, R. "Die Kausalkonjunktionen 'da', 'denn', und 'weil': drei Konjunktionen, drei Lexicale Klassen." *Deutsch als Fremdsprache* 20 (1983): 332–337.

Pit, M. *How to express yourself with a causal connective? Subjectivity and causal connectives in Dutch, German and French*. PhD dissertation, Utrecht University. Amsterdam: Rodopi, 2003.

———. "Determining subjectivity in text: The case of backward causal connectives in Dutch." *Discourse Processes* 41 (2006): 151–174.

———. "Cross-linguistic analyses of backward causal connectives in Dutch, German and French." *Languages in contrast* 7 (2007): 53–82.

Rosch, E., and C. Mervis. "Family resemblances: studies in the internal structure of categories." Cognitive Psychology 7 (1975): 573–605.

Sanders, J. "Perspective in narrative discourse." Dissertation Katholieke Universiteit Brabant, 1994.

Sanders, J., and W. Spooren. "Perspective, subjectivity, and modality from a cognitive linguistic point of view." In *Discourse and perspective in cognitive linguistics*, 85–112. Amsterdam, Philadelphia: John Benjamins, 1997.

Sanders, J., T. Sanders, and E. Sweetser. "Causality, cognition and communication: A mental space analysis of subjectivity in causal connectives." In *Causal categories in discourse and cognition*. Berlin: Mouton de Gruyter, 2009.

Sanders, T. "Semantic and pragmatic sources of coherence: On the categorization of coherence relations in context." *Discourse Processes* 24 (1997): 119–147.

Sanders, T.J.M. and E.E. Sweetser, eds. *Causal Categories in Discourse and Cognition*. Berlin: Mouton de Gruyter, 2009.

Sanders, T., and W. Spooren. "Causality and subjectivity in discourse: The meaning and use of causal connectives in spontaneous conversation, chat interactions and written text." Paper submitted for publication.

Semino, E., and M. Short. *Corpus stylistics. Speech, writing and thought presentation in a corpus of English writing*. London: Routledge, 2004.

Spooren, W., T. Sanders, M. Huiskes, and L. Degand. "Subjectivity and causality: A corpus study of spoken language." In *Conceptual structure in discourse and language*, 256–270. Stanford: CSLI, 2010.

Steen, Gerard. Genre between the humanities and the sciences. In *Bi-directionality in the Cognitive Sciences*, 21–42. Amsterdam/Philadelphia: John Benjamins, 2011.

Stukker, N., and T. Sanders. "Another('s) perspective on subjectivity in causal connectives: A usage-based analysis of volitional causal relations." *Discours* 4 (2009). http://discours.revues.org/index7260.html.

———. "Diverging frequency effects in causal connectives across discourse contexts: a usage-based interpretation." LAUD-Linguistic agency, Universität Duisburg-Essen, paper A761, 2010.

———. "Subjectivity and prototype structure in causal connectives: A cross-linguistic perspective." *Journal of Pragmatics* 44 (2012): 169–190.

Stukker, N., T. Sanders, and A. Verhagen. "Causality in verbs and in discourse connectives. Converging evidence of cross-level parallels in Dutch linguistic categorization." *Journal of Pragmatics* 40 (2008): 1296–1322.

———. "Categories of subjectivity in Dutch causal connectives: a usage-based analysis." In *Causal categories in discourse and cognition*, 119–171. Berlin: Mouton de Gruyter, 2009.

Swales, J. *Genre analysis. English in academic and research settings*. Cambridge: Cambridge University Press, 1990.

Sweetser, E.E. *From etymology to pragmatics. Metaphorical and cultural aspects of semantic structure*. Cambridge: Cambridge University Press, 1990.

Taboada, M., and W.C. Mann. "Rhetorical structure theory: Looking back and moving ahead." *Discourse Studies* 8 (2006): 423–459.

Talmy, L. "Force dynamics in language and cognition." *Cognitive Science* 12 (1988): 49–100.

Taylor, J.R. *Linguistic categorization. Prototypes in linguistic theory*. Oxford: Clarendon Press, 1995.

Traugott, E.C. "Subjectification in grammaticalisation." In *Subjectivity and subjectivisation: linguistic perspectives*, 31–54. Cambridge: Cambridge University Press, 1995.

Van Belle, W. "Want, omdat en aangezien: een argumentatieve analyse." *Leuvense Bijdragen* 78 (1989): 435–556.

Van den Bergh, H. "On the construct validity of multiple-choice items for reading comprehension." *Applied psychological measurement* 14 (1990): 1–12.

Van den Hoven, P. "Niet wij doen het, maar het recht!" *Tijdschrift voor Taalbeheersing* 9 (1997): 207–214.

Verhagen, A. "Interpreting usage: Construing the history of Dutch causal verbs." In *Usage based models of language*, 261–286. Stanford: CSLI Publications, 2000.

Verhagen, A. "Language, culture, nature: Exploring new perspectives." In *Linguagem, Cultura Cognição: estudos de linguística cognitive*, 165–187. Almedina, Coimbra, 2004.

———. *Constructions of intersubjectivity. Discourse, syntax, and cognition*. Oxford: Oxford University Press, 2005.

———. "Construal and perspectivisation." In *Handbook of Cognitive Linguistics*, 48–81. Oxford: Oxford University Press, 2007.

Verhagen, A., and S. Kemmer. "Interaction and causation: Causative constructions in modern standard Dutch." *Journal of Pragmatics* 27 (1997): 61–82.

Vis, K. *Subjectivity in news discourse. A corpus linguistic analysis of informalization*. Dissertation Vrije Universiteit, 2011.

Wegener, H. "Weil—das hat schon seinen Grund: Zur Verbstellung in Kausalsätzen mit weil im gegenwärtigen Deutsch." *Deutsche Sprache* 21 (1993): 289–305.

Zufferey, S. "'*Car, parce que, puisque*' revisited: Three empirical studies on French causal connectives." *Journal of Pragmatics* 44, no. 2 (2012): 138–153.

CHAPTER 7

'If You Do It too Then RT and Say #idoit2'

The Co-patterning of Contingency and Evaluation in Microblogging

Michele Zappavigna

Introduction

Proposing an interpersonal bond in discourse involves offering a coupling of interpersonal and ideational meaning for negotiation. In making this offer we must adopt some kind of orientation toward the proposed bond. One resource that is used in interactive digital contexts such as social media is the *if-then* contingency, a coherence relation realising the social relation, 'if you agree with the coupling I am presenting, then share this bond with others', or, put more generally, 'if you like X, do Y'. Contingency is a consequential relation of condition (*then, if, provided that*) or purpose (*to, so that, in order to*) (Martin 1992: 195). The present chapter explores contingency and coupling patterns in microblogging, a form of social media whereby users post character-constrained messages (microposts) to the Internet. I employ a 100-million-word corpus of Twitter microposts (HERMES), to investigate how bonds are proposed in two very different domains of experience: celebration of a celebrity, Justin Bieber, and communal complaint about minor quotidian concerns. For example, consider the following microposts:

> RT @User: RT if you think justin bieber is gorgeous #BieberLove #BieberBeMine

> RT @IDoThat2: RT if you hate it when you move out the way for someone and they move the same way. #idothat2

The first post shares a positive appreciation of a celebrity, whereas the second invites us to share in negative affect regarding a common complaint. As we will see, these tweets invite other users to repost the message, contingent upon accepting the coupling of ideation and evaluation presented.

 | DOI: 10.1163/9789004258174_008

1 The Function of 'Retweeting'

Developed in 2006, Twitter allows users to post messages of 140 characters or less to the general Internet or to a set of users who subscribe to a user's message 'stream',[1] known collectively as followers. These microposts are referred to as tweets and are presented to the user in reverse chronological order as an unfolding feed of content. The content is public and searchable unless the user actively makes their account private. Tweets may be accessed, sent, and received via a variety of methods such the web, email, SMS, and third-party clients, often running on mobile devices. A tweet may also incorporate links to micromedia, small-scale multimedia, and shortened aliases of longer hyperlinks (Tiny URLs) intended to conserve characters within the constrained textual environment. An example of a tweet is the following:

> RT if you think haters need to get a life! #BelieberLove <3

This post invites other users to republish the tweet by retweeting the post so that it will be visible to a new set of followers. In this way retweeting "allows members to relay or forward a tweet through their network" (Nagarajan et al., 2010: 295).

Retweets are usually marked by the initialism *RT*, to indicate that the body of the tweet is quoted text. In other words, RT can mark grammatical projection, economically standing for 'User X has posted the following'. In most instances RT will be followed by the @ character to attribute the retweeted text to its initial author. The following tweet uses this structure to indicate that @iDoit2 is the source of the original post (shown underlined):

> **RT @iDoit2:** If #iDoit2 is trending by Friday, will do some big #followfriday shoutouts for the top retweeters whilst trending!! :)

Retweets may also append commentary (shown in bold) to the original text:

> RT @User: If assholes could fly this gym would be an airport.---- **Tee hee hee hee hee!!!!!!**

> RT@bgardner Probably the best night of the Olympics tonight—Shaun White, Apollo Ohno and Lindsey Vonn all going for Gold! <– **I agree!**

---

1 The metaphor of a 'stream' is commonly applied to Internet data feeds that unfold in time.

This appendage is often evaluative and a conversational reply to the original author (for example, the implicit positive evaluation seen in the exclamation of concurrence appended to the second example shown above).

Retweeting can significantly amplify the reach of a tweet, particularly when a user with a large body of followers, such as a celebrity, chooses to retweet something. Beyond rebroadcasting, retweeting "contributes to a conversational ecology in which conversations are composed of a public interplay of voices that give rise to an emotional sense of shared conversational context" (Boyd et al., 2010: 1). Page (2011), approaching media from the perspective of narrative, has suggested the role of retweeting in new "co-tellership practices" and noted the tendency of celebrities to attach evaluative assessment to their retweets as a means of aligning with their audience. The convention marks a tweet as worthy of attention within this conversational context.

Tweets also contain metadata (data about data, such as information about the author of a tweet) for managing interaction with others. For instance, @ indicates address (or reference) and a hashtag (#) labels a topic. Hashtags are a form of "conversational tagging" (Huang et al., 2010) related to other forms of collaborative tagging or 'folksonomy'. They may derive from Internet Relay Chat (IRC) conventions for naming channels (*#channelname*), where a channel is the essential mechanism that people use to communicate with each other during an IRC session. The # character is commonly used to mark a label that the user has assigned to a tweet. For example, *#justinbieber* in the following indicates that the tweet is about this celebrity:

> @User RT[2] if you LOVE the new video! http://thepopmonster.tumblr.com/ #justinbieber #baby #myworld2.0 #ilovebaby

The label means that other fans of Bieber can find the tweet even though the lexis 'Justin Bieber' does not occur in the body of the tweet. They may do this by searching for the tag via the search interface that Twitter provides, or, if they are likely to have an on-going interest in the tag, they may elect to subscribe to a feed of tweets containing this tag, a process known as 'following' the tag. This functionality allows a community of interested followers to accumulate around a tag. There is also considerable space for semiotic play with hashtags, with some users employing them to inscribe value positions directly (for example,

2 In this instance RT is being used as an imperative (asking another user to retweet something) rather than to mark a retweeted text.

#ihatejustinbieber) or create humorous references that are unlikely to be candidates as search terms.

2 Sharing Evaluation in Microblogging

Microblogging is rarely about presenting bald facts or narrating activity. While it can be an immediate way to deliver information to an audience, this is not undertaken in an interpersonal void. We use social media in the service of sharing values as a way of communicating our experience of the world and affiliating with others. Microblogging services such as Twitter are often parodied as the domain of the self-obsessed or compulsive, the kind of user who would post: *I had toast for breakfast*, *Just finished breakfast*, and *About to leave for work*. While amusing, this kind of characterisation does not reflect the complex ways in which microblogging is integrating itself into social life and its rapid growth as a technology for sharing social bonds. Some commentators, however, have begun to appreciate the importance of interpersonal meaning, observing that valued (and thus highly retweeted) tweets "tend to make an observation, take a stance, or crack a joke—none of which fall under the umbrella of using Twitter to tell the world what you're doing" (McCracken, 2009).

To date the field that has most thoroughly explored microblogging as a resource for understanding evaluative language is sentiment analysis, a subdomain of computational linguistics. This area, sometimes also referred to as opinion mining, aims to automatically[3] detect emotional language in text, such as film reviews (Whitelaw et al., 2005). These studies often use datasets derived from social media streams in the form of public reaction to major events such as the Olympics (Gruzd et al., 2011). Bollen et al. (2009) regard an individual tweet as "temporally-authentic microscopic instantiations of public mood state", suggesting that modelling this kind of data can reveal collective emotive trends. Applications of sentiment detection using social media include prediction of the stock market based on 'Twitter mood' (Bollen et al., in press). Interestingly, one study found evidence of an association between response to important events on Twitter and an increase in average negative sentiment strength (Thelwall et al., 2011).

3 Sometimes, given the difficulty of automatically analysing evaluative language, studies will incorporate some form of crowdsourcing.

3 Coupling and Evaluative Meaning

The perspective on ambient bonding applied in this chapter relies upon a social semiotic perspective on language as it is used in its functional contexts (Halliday, 1978). The discourse analysis undertaken is informed by Systemic Functional Linguistics (SFL), which acknowledges that language is itself "full of resources for negotiating community—both across metafunctions (ideational resources such as technical and specialized lexis, interpersonal resources such as naming and vocatives) and across strata (accents in phonology, grammatical variation and discourse semantic style)" (Martin, 2010: 24). The theory refers to the domain of meaning making associated with negotiating social bonds as *interpersonal meaning*. It is interpersonal meaning that sustains online social networks. The language used in social media, particularly microblogging, is also under significant interpersonal pressure. On the one hand, the language is deployed in a modality where interpersonal meanings that might otherwise be expressed paralinguistically must be expressed via other means.[4] On the other hand, it is bound by the need for linguistic economies arising from the character constraints imposed on microposts.

In adopting a social semiotic approach I look both qualitatively and quantitatively at the ways interpersonal meaning co-patterns with ideational meaning in texts. The theoretical basis of this approach is the concept of 'coupling' introduced by Martin (2000) and taken up by Zhao (2010, 2011) and Zappavigna et al. (2008b) for looking at textual relations:

> **Coupling** concerns the temporal relation of '*with*': variable *x* comes with variable *y*. To put it another way, it is the relation formed between two semiotic elements at one given point in time within the logogenetic timeframe. Coupling can be formed between metafunctional variables (e.g. ideational and interpersonal), between different semiotic resources (e.g. image and verbiage) and across strata (e.g. semantics and phonology).
>
> ZHAO, 2011: 144

This perspective is adopted in tandem with concepts drawn from corpus linguistics of collocation and clustering (in particular n-grams, or word level sequences) as means of exploring syntagmatic relationships in texts.

---

4 However, as we will see, the medium does afford new meaning potential not possible in face-to-face communication, and it is possibly not very productive to continue thinking of online communication as the poor cousin of spoken discourse.

Zhao (2011) argues that cultures incline toward stable coupling patterns when viewed from the perspective of a particular timeframe (for instances, a historical perspective) and that a set of stable coupling patterns can theoretically be described, noting that coupling is a process and that cultures change over time. This modelling perspective is akin to Bakhtin's (1986) work on speech genres as stable patterns of utterance. In a similar vein Knight's (2010) model of affiliation, developed through analysis of conversational humour, describes "communal identity as discursively negotiated in text" in terms of coupling (Knight, 2010: 43). The model considers how communities form as people rally around, defer, or reject different values construed in language (Knight, 2008). According to Knight, social bonds are negotiated via couplings of ideational and interpersonal meaning in discourse, and "we discursively negotiate our communal identities through bonds that we can share, and these bonds make up the value sets of our communities and culture, but they are not stable and fixed" (Knight, 2010: 43). This chapter will consider one such strategy for negotiation of couplings in terms of contingency relations, which I introduce in the following section.

4 Contingency Relations and Veridicality

Trnavac and Taboada (2010) have noted an interaction between evaluation and rhetorical relations in terms of (non)veridicality. For example, consider the following concordance lines showing examples of nonveridicality taken from HERMES. These examples employ contingency to qualify the evaluation made:

> This is definately someting I would not be watching **if it was not the #olympics**

> @User And **if it had been one of my guy friends** it would have just been funny.

> @User It does say alot about Zune HD that people say **if it had phone capabilities** they'd buy it in a heartbeat.

> So, the new We Are The World is really good, but I bet it would be much better **if it had Demi in it**. :I

> @User ewww lol, **if it was chocolate milk from coco puffs** that wudda been decent tho

The evaluations made are tempered by a nonveridical element realized as a hypotactic if-clause (shown in bold). These serve to place constraints on the scope of the evaluation realized as a dependent clause. Resources for tempering evaluation are usually involved in prosodies of dissipation (rather than propagation) whereby evaluative meanings are diffused rather that accumulated (Zappavigna et al., 2008a, Hood, 2010).

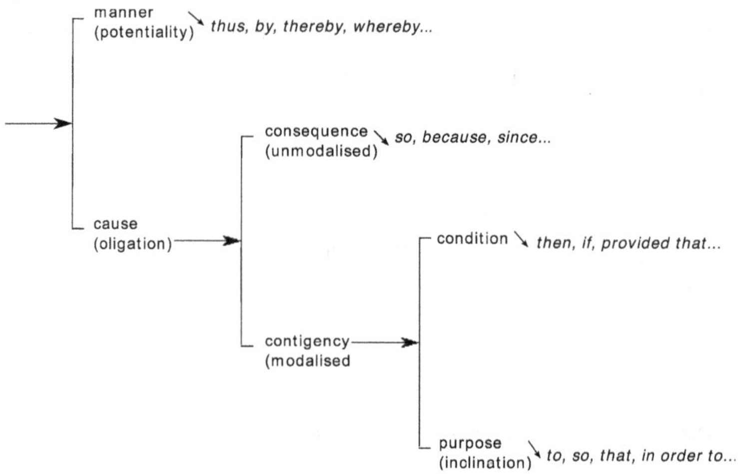

FIGURE 1 *The system of consequential relations*
MARTIN 1992: 195

Martin (1992) classifies the kind of logico-semantic relation involved in if-then structures as a causal relation of contingency (Figure 1). As this figure indicates, the logical relation of *condition* can be interpreted in terms of the interpersonal dimensions of modulation (obligation) and modalisation (probability): "With both condition and purpose the relation between Cause and Effect is a contingent one; and in both cases the Effect is irrealis—there is a possibility, a probability or a certainty that is will be determined by the Cause, but as the meanings are made it has not yet ensued" (Martin, 1992 p. 193). While the if-then contingencies shown in the examples presented earlier are the typical pattern, sometimes the Effect will be presented in a hashtag (shown in bold in the example below):

> if you tell everybody u the biggest freak but u don't even eat it **#youshouldbeashamed**

Condensing the Effect into a hashtag serves to interpersonally foreground the negative evaluation targeted at the ideation in the body of the tweet since it presents this as a higher order of abstraction (as is the function of metadata).

Contingency is a frequent feature in HERMES tweets, signaled by the position of IF[5] in the word frequency list (n = 46, 296, 645 instances). Interestingly, the fifth most common collocate[6] of IF is RT, suggesting a relation between contingency and retweeting that warrants further exploration.

TABLE 1 *Most common collocates of IF and RT in HERMES*

	IF		RT	
N	Word	Total	Word	Total
1	YOU	113,600	THE	181,812
2	I	74,017	HTTP	146,174
3	THE	57,680	TO	108,605
4	TO	55,913	I	106,331
5	**RT**	**49,252**	LY	88,132
6	A	42,667	BIT	78,706
7	IT	35,440	YOU	77,999
8	U	29,755	A	76,391
9	AND	26,786	IS	73,100
10	ME	24,676	COM	55,551
… 14			**IF**	**49,252**

The most common clusters for IF are shown in Table 2. Again RT is in a prominent position, with RT IF YOU being the second most common n-gram[7] and RT THIS IF being the tenth most common.

5 Collocates and n-grams are shown in caps throughout this chapter.

6 The default setting (five words to the left and the right of the search word) was used in Wordsmith to create the collocate list.

7 These were computed automatically by Wordsmith.

TABLE 2 *The 10 most common n-grams for IF in HERMES*

N	Cluster	Freq.
1	IF YOU WANT	8,617
2	**RT IF YOU**	**7,985**
3	IF YOU ARE	6,379
4	IF YOU HAVE	6,009
5	IF YOU DON'T	4,133
6	I WONDER IF	3,795
7	YOU WANT TO	3,540
8	IF YOU WANT TO	3,448
9	IF YOU THINK	3,138
10	**RT THIS IF**	**3,108**

TABLE 3 *Five most common 3-grams for RT*

N	Cluster	Freq.	Example
1	**RT IF YOU**	**14,263**	**RT @iDoit2: RT if you find it hard to keep a straight face when your getting told off #iDoit2**
2	THANKS FOR THE	5,545	@User thanks for the rt!
3	**RT THIS IF**	**5,434**	**RT @User: RT this if JUSTIN BIEBER ROCKS!**
4	FOR THE RT	4,934	@User thanks for the rt. :)
5	THIS IF YOU	3,723	RT @User: RT this if you hate it how cute guys are always jerks. -_-

Considering the most common clusters for RT, we see a similarly prominent relationship between RT and IF. The most common n-gram for RT in HERMES is RT IF YOU (Table 3). Interestingly, THANKS FOR THE (N2), the most common 3-gram in HERMES (Zappavigna 2012) is an expression of thanks for socially promoting a user via retweeting (or the Follow Friday meme[8]):

8 'Follow Friday' is a Twitter meme with the function of "promoting other people on Twitter—anyone you think your followers should also be following for any reason" (Horovitch

RT @ User1 ....
@User2 Thanks for the RT and have a great day

In light of this general relationship between contingency relations and retweeting practices, I will now explore some more specific patterns in meaning.

5 Common Contingency Relations in HERMES

The most common 3-grams involved in if-then contingency relations are shown in Table 4. As this table suggests, YOU is a very frequent collocate, with users proposing bonds in relation to an imaginary persona, perhaps an archetypal follower of their tweets. For instance, N 58 calls this persona to retweet their tweet if they share a positive appreciation of a celebrity. I will explore this type of pattern later in this chapter in relation to Justin Bieber fans. RT occurs in two of the 3-grams (N = 58, n = 388) and is highly associated with the other 3-grams shown, as the examples sample suggest (Table 4).

TABLE 4 *Common IF 3-grams in HERMES*

N	3-gram	Example
48	IF YOU WANT	RT @User @User If you want funding to create a community food growing project in London look at this http://bit.ly/5a6g1V
58	**RT IF YOU**	**RT @User: Rt if you think @Selenagomez is gorgeous. :]**
88	IF YOU ARE	RT @User: RT if you are the #1 Ariana BIGGEST FAN ;D
103	IF YOU HAVE	RT @User: RT if you have more than a hundred photos of @justinbieber saved on your computer! = SO TRUE!
230	IF YOU DON'T	If you don't know the person, DON'T add them! ;-)
379	IF YOU THINK	RT @User: Retweet this if you think Ashley Cole is stupid.
388	**RT THIS IF**	**RT @User: RT this if u think tht @justinbieber should have is own tv show!! i would wach it every day lol**

2009). The concept centres upon users mentioning in a tweet people worthy of such subscription each Friday.

Tweets containing the 3-gram RT IF YOU typically invite the reader to re-share the tweet if they meet some criteria specified by an if-then contingency relation (as explored earlier). The most common items in R1 are THINK, LOVE, WANT, HAVE, ARE, and all appear to construe aspects of a persona aligned with the tweeter (Table 5). The examples shown in Table 5 have been selected as instances that express what the persona of a Justin Bieber fan *thinks, loves, wants, has*, and *is*.

TABLE 5 *Common items in R1 for RT IF YOU*

N	R1	Example
1	THINK	RT @User: RT if you think Justin Bieber is the bestest of all best singers ever!!!
2	LOVE	RT @User1: RT @User2 RT if you love Justin Bieber For him not because of his fame! EVERYONE SHOULD BE RTing THIS!
3	WANT	RT @User: RT IF YOU WANT TO GO OUT WITH JUSTIN #bringbiebcrback
4	HAVE	RT @User: RT If you have listened to Justin Bieber today #bringbiebcrback
5	ARE	RT @BieberGasms: SOO HYPED for @justinbieber's BABY video this week!<3 RT if you are too:D

Returning to the notion that interpersonal bonds may be proposed in terms of ideation-evaluation couplings, we may consider contingency in terms of its interaction with these couplings. In many tweets contingency is used as a resource to construe entry criteria to a particular discourse community of retweeters, rather than directly tempering evaluative meaning. In other words it is used as a strategy for establishing alignment with a particular persona, such as someone who positively values Justin Bieber. The following retweet is a response to a call by a user to retweet a post because they agree with the evaluation of Bieber presented:

> RT @User: #JustinBieberSingsWithHisSoul RT this if you love justin bieber and if you agree with me :)

This tweet inscribes the orientation that the original poster wishes the retweeter to adopt, also understood as a criterion for reposting. In order to explain this type of patterning further it is necessary to introduce in more detail systems evaluative meaning proposed by Appraisal Theory (Martin and White, 2005).

6 Appraisal Theory

Evaluation is a domain of interpersonal meaning, where language is used to express attitudes and to adopt stances about other texts. Appraisal Theory argues that the emotional reaction to the world seen in infant protolanguage develops as we are socialised into a culture and into institutions (Martin and White, 2005: 45). Feeling becomes institutionalized as ethics and morality, forming the JUDGEMENT[9] system with which we construe rules and regulations regarding behaviour (top example, Figure 2). Feeling is also institutionalized as aesthetics and value, forming the APPRECIATION system with which we generate assessments based on our reactions to phenomena (bottom example, Figure 2). The sections that follow explain each of the discourse semantic systems involved in making these meanings.

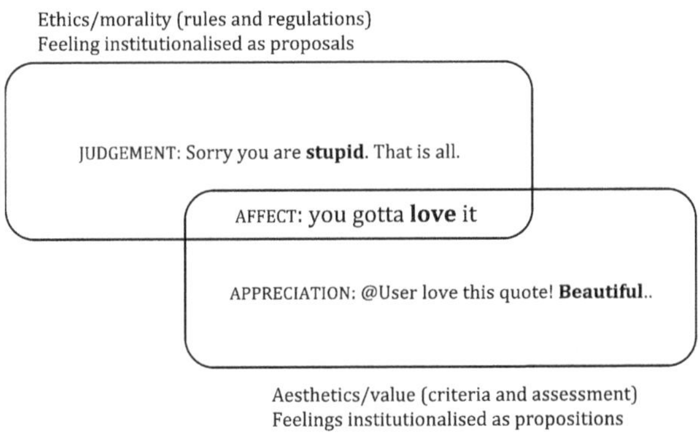

FIGURE 2 *The institutionalisation of AFFECT* (ADAPTED FROM MARTIN AND WHITE, 2005: 45)

Appraisal Theory models evaluative meaning using systems networks that model the choices made in a particular text in light of the potential choices that

9 Appraisal terminology is show in small caps to differentiate it from commonplace terms.

might also have been made. This systemic orientation arose out of the Firthian tradition in linguistics (Firth, 1957). Firth asserted that a distinction needed to be made between structure and system—that is, between syntagmatic and paradigmatic relations in language. Firth's ideas about how the notion of a system might be used to model language were taken up in Halliday's development of system networks. System networks are networks of interrelated options that are organised paradigmatically, in terms of "what could go instead of what" rather than syntagmatically in terms of structure (Halliday and Matthiessen, 2004, p. 22). They are an alternative to modelling language as a catalogue of structures.

Figure 3 provides examples of each region of appraisal as a system network as theorised by Martin and White (2005). The network adopts the convention whereby capitalised labels above the arrows indicate different systems of meaning, and the lowercase labels at the end of each path mark features within systems. A square bracket represents a choice between two options in a system (an 'or' relation), while a brace represents simultaneous choices (an 'and' relation). For example, the ATTITUDE system involves three more delicate systems from which a choice can be made:

- AFFECT—expressing emotion
- JUDGEMENT—assessing behaviour
- APPRECIATION—estimating value

The examples in the boxes are tweets from the Obama Win Corpus, a corpus of tweets about Obama collected in the 24 hours after he won the 2008 US presidential election (Zappavigna, 2011). Each example illustrates a type of attitudinal appraisal. The network may be further specified to greater levels of delicacy depending on the kind of analysis in which it is being used. For example, in this paper I consider instances where the affect system is further specified to include the following subsystems:

- un/happiness (e.g., sad/happy[10])
- in/security (e.g., anxious/confident)
- dis/satisfaction (e.g., fed up/absorbed)

10 These examples are taken from Martin (1992: 49).

In addition, the appreciation system is made more delicate to include:

- reaction (e.g., captivating/dull)
- composition (e.g., harmonious/discordant)
- valuation (e.g., profound/insignificant)

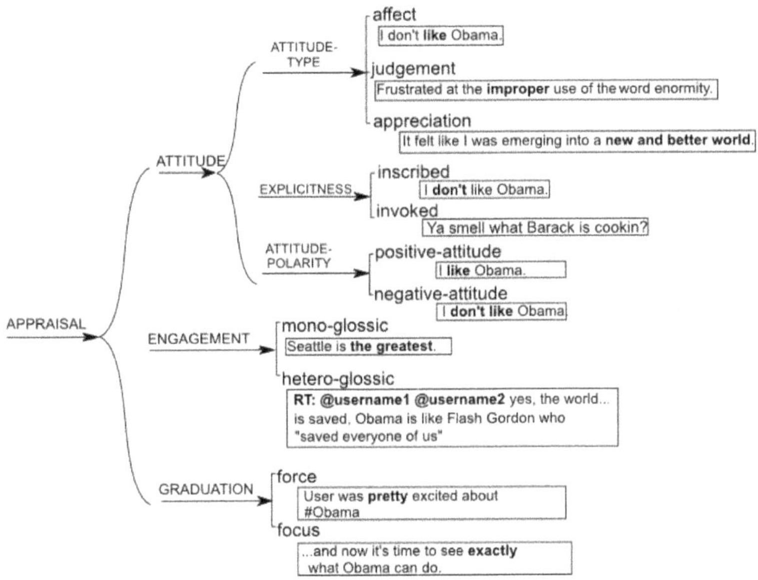

FIGURE 3 *The appraisal system* (ADAPTED FROM MARTIN AND WHITE, 2005 WITH EXAMPLES FROM THE OBAMA WIN CORPUS, ZAPPAVIGNA 2011)

As this network suggests, a full appraisal analysis would also analyse how stances are adopted in a text by considering the engagement system that models how external voices are negotiated in a text, as well as the graduation system that models how attitudes are scaled up and down.

Depending on the target and source of the evaluation, lexis such as 'good' can work with any of the ATTITUDE systems. Consider the difference between JUDGEMENT in the following tweet:

> Thank god is the weekend, time off for **good** behaviour

and AFFECT:

> I feel really **good**, finally reached the 1,000 followers who wanted both!!

or APPRECIATION:

> Got to have some best friend time tonight, pack a few boxes and drink some **good** wine. Going to bed content.

I will now consider two domains in which evaluative systems enter into a pattern with contingency relations: affiliation around the celebrity Justin Bieber and communing around complaints about daily irritations.

7 Beliebers: Bonding around Bieber

> if i could have any wish in the world, it would be for @justinbieber to follow me. <3 so can you please follow me? i'm not giving up. :)

In addition to general users, celebrities also populate Twitter, attracting communities of fans who engage in public performances of affiliation (Marwick and Boyd, 2011). One of the largest such communities concentrates around teen singer Justin Bieber, who in 2011 had a follower base of more than 13 million users, exceeding that of the US president (10 million). This community is frequently parodied by users outside its largely teenage demographic. Bieber fans, many of whom employ usernames of the form *UserLuvBieber*, are mocked as 'beliebers', a reference to their apparent emotional fanaticism manifest in expressions of Bieber-targetted affect (shown in bold) such as:

> RT @User I **love** Justin Bieber's music and I love him
> I **Love** Justin Bieber More Than Anything In The World<3333333333333 <3*8 days*<3
> RT @User: RT this if u **love** Justin Bieber <3
> RT if you are **addicted to** Justin Bieber <33

Such a large user base of committed fans means that Bieber frequently precipitates trending topics. For example the following tweet by Bieber rapidly elevated the phrase 'Latin Girls' to a trending topic on February 27, 2011:

> shoutout to all of Latin America ... i got love for all my Latin Girls

As one user quipped:

> Beliebers run Twitter. Hater or not. You have at least 1 belieber following you.

This user is humorously commenting on the way Justin Bieber fandom polarises opinion on Twitter and how public appreciation of celebrities can create both an in-group rallying around positive values targeted at the public figure and an out-group that mocks those values. The following tweet is an instance of the discourse characterising the latter position:

> Attention all **#Beiber** fans! I am not a fan, in fact I hate the spastic! Don't follow me thinking I am, I'm not! I repeat, I am not!!

Hashtags play a role in coordinating such mass expression of value by focusing this expression around a particular ideational target (for example, #Bieber). In other words, hashtags align users into "overlapping communities of attitudinal rapport" (Martin, 2004: 323).

Retweeting is an important social process within these communities of attitudinal rapport as they are manifest in microblogging. Indeed, Bieber appreciation specifically was highly associated with retweeting practices in HERMES. RT is its most common collocate of 'justinbieber' (and 'justinbieber' is the 84th most common collocate of RT (freq. = 8,256)).

Returning to the three most common R1 items for RT IF YOU in HERMES-RT IF YOU **THINK**, RT IF YOU **LOVE**, RT IF YOU **WANT**—we may gain some insight into the kind of values an authentic Bieber fan is construed as adopting. Consider the 4-gram RT IF YOU THINK (Table 6), where the most common item in R1 is 'Justin Bieber'. This pattern involved tweets such as:

> RT if you think Justin Bieber is hot :)

As Table 6 suggests, these posts have the general structure:

> **RT if you think** + (Justin Bieber + positive appreciation)

Bieber is positively appreciated in terms of APPRECIATION: REACTION with fans rallying around their reaction to his physical form.

TABLE 6 *Positive appreciation collocating with RT IF YOU THINK JUSTIN BIEBER*

RT if you think Justin Bieber	is hot :)
	looks amazing in anything he wears. (: #GodblessBieber
	has awesome shoes
	is the most perfect guy in the world!
	sounded sooo hot in we are the world #biebcrgasm ;)
	is amazing.
	is THE SEXIEST MAN ALIVE!!!
	is the best!!!!!!
	looks incredbile in purple! :)
	is the hottest guy alive end of story ;)
	is so hot you wanna bake cookies on him

Bieber fans also enacted a particular orientation to feeling, most commonly positive AFFECT: HAPPINESS targeted at Justin Bieber (Table 7) and also realized graphologically using the heart symbol <3. This positive sentiment is also directed at the fans themselves as a community centred around Justin Bieber-targetted AFFECT:

> RT if you love the Rest of your big Belieber family <33.

TABLE 7 *Examples of the pattern RT IF YOU LOVE with Justin Bieber as target*

RT if you love	justin bieber and will always support him
	Justin Bieber #biebcrgasm [now 100+ people better retweet this]
	justin bieber nd wish him the best valentines day ever
	JUSTIN BIEBER AND YOUR LIFE CHANGED WHEN YOU HEARD HIS SONGS AND LOVE HIS LYRICS!!!!!!!!!!
	Justin and you tell people all the time #JustinLovesMe not you haha #iloveitwhenjustin
	Justin Bieber! ;) (I'm gonna list whoever retweets this!)
	Justin Bieber more than anything!
	it when Justin Bieber does the hairflip
	Justin bieber's dance moves! espcially in Baby. (:

The 4-gram RT IF YOU WANT gives use some insight into the desires of Bieber fans in relation to the celebrity figure (Table 8). These appear to centre around desire for interaction with the celebrity realized with verbal processes (reply, call, say, sing, tweet, etc.) and desire for the celebrity to increase their artistic output by adopting new channels or travelling to new locations.

TABLE 8 *Examples of the pattern RT IF YOU WANT with Justin Bieber as target*

RT if you want	justin to have his own show
	JUSTIN TO REPLY TO YOU #bringbiebcrback
	JUSTIN TO ... CALL YOU #bringbiebcrback
	JUSTIN TO SAY HE LOVES YOU ;) #bringbiebcrback
	JUSTIN BIEBER IN BRAZIL
	JUSTIN TO RELEASE ANOTHER SONG FROM MY WORLD 2.0
	justin to come to your school!
	TO SING TO YOU #_bieberworld_
	justin to come on and TWEET! #justbieberco #justbieberco

Related to the hope for verbal interaction with the celebrity is the high value assigned to having Justin Bieber as a follower, seen in frequently retweeted posts such as:

> RT if you have Justin Bieber following you <3

Being able to perform this retweet is worn as badge of honour in the fan community, despite the somewhat phatic nature of the following relationship given the volume of fans:

> so happy cant believe that justin is following me

The Bieber fan is likely to construe a set of couplings realised by particular co-patterns of Justin Bieber-related ideation together with a selection of appraisal subsystems. Performing the social relation of being a Bieber fan, in other words enacting a Bieber-fan persona, involves retweeting the micropost based on sharing the bonds proposed through the couplings construed (shown on the left of the following figure).

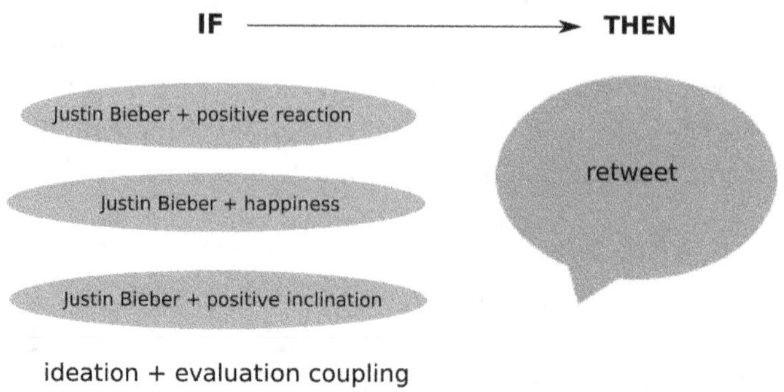

FIGURE 4 *The co-patterning of contingency and coupling in retweets*[11]

We might also consider this retweeting practice in relation to the aggregation afforded by hashtags. Elsewhere I have explored the community-forging function of hashtagging, where hashtags are used to render tweets searchable (Zappavigna 2011). Tweets that can be found by searching for a tag can be thought of as existing in an ambient relation to each other, and the bonds they propose characterise an ambient community aligned in relation to the topic identified by the tag. We can thus think of all tweets containing the tag #justinbieber in this way, contrasting tags where inscribed positive evaluation has bled into the hashtag, such as #ilovejustinbieber (given a positive charge in Figure 5), with hashtags such as #biebersucks, representing communities of dissenting voices (given a negative charge in Figure 5). The contrasting values (analogized as opposing + and—charges in Figure 5) can be seen by comparing the two tweets:

> RT @User RT this if you hate Justin Bieber. || !! #hate
> RT @User: RT if you think justin bieber is the most perfect guy in the world!

The social bonds proposed by Justin Bieber fans are part of enacting a targeted persona, but as we will see in the next section, bonds may be construed by much more general value-ideation couplings.

11 Inclination is a further subsystem of happiness (e.g., miss, long for, yearn for) (Martin 1992: 51).

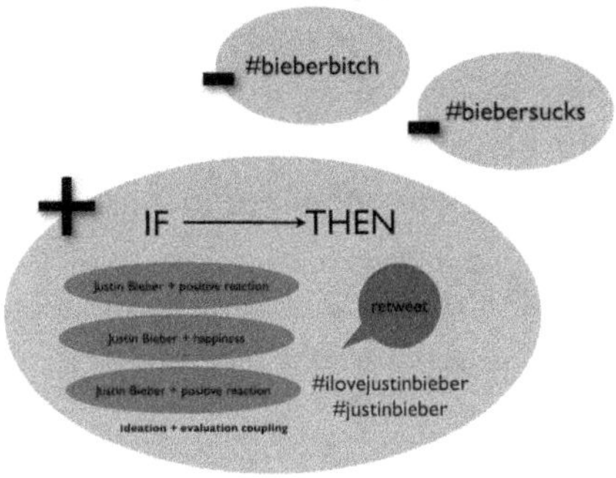

FIGURE 5 *Considering retweeting in relation to hashtagging*

8 Bonding around the Quotidian

Microblogging discourse affords new insight into aspects of everyday life that have hitherto not been readily made public. Personal expression of routine experiences has never been subject to real-time mass dissemination in the way that we are currently witnessing. Twitter provides a forum where these routine experiences may be almost instantaneously broadcast, whether to share a positive moment or to satisfy the very human need to complain. Microposts frequently provide an opportunity for bonding around the quotidian, affording the private realm of daily experience a public audience.

The increasing pervasiveness of this form of personal disclosure arises from the history of online journaling and blogs, where authors often use their own lives as the focus of their material. The microblogger is engaging in a practice that "centers on making the ordinary visible to others" (Oulasvirta et al., 2010, p. 238). A social need to remain in the collective consciousness of the social stream as it unfolds in time seems to motivate this kind of disclosure:

> What needs to be explained is somebody's willingness to stop the current activity, take out the phone, and expend effort to actively create such a "peephole" for others. The key is to understand that a microblogger "exists" through a staccato of one-liners, organized in reverse chronological order such that the most recent one fixes others' interpretation of his or her most current doings.
>
> OULASVIRTA ET AL., 2010, P. 248

In this way microblogging can be seen as an ongoing performance of online identity. Perhaps another significant explanatory factor for the disclosures performed is the human desire for affiliation: we exist within communities of other voices with which we wish to connect. The stances we adopt and the observations and evaluations we share all exist relative to the meaning making of the other members of our social network and to all other potential networks of meaning. In other words, we perform our online identities in order to connect with others.

A very common bond proposed in HERMES tweets was displeasure about commonplace annoyances. Proposals in this domain might take the form (as shown in Table 9):

> RT IF YOU + (negative affect + ideational description of everyday annoyance)

The tweets sampled are part of the #iDoit2 Twitter meme. Memes are collective, formulaic, and usually humorous expressions that propogate virally on the Internet. They often take the form of phrasal templates with empty slots into which users can insert their own items to create variations (Zappavigna, 2012).

TABLE 9 *Concordance lines for tweets expressing negative affect toward common daily irritations*

RT @iDoit2: RT if you	walk into a room and forget what you went in there for #iDoit2
	hate it when people touch you and they have cold hands. #iDoit2
	hate people who walk really slow infront of you and can't get past them. #iDoit2
	hate those people who clap when the plane lands #iDoit2
	can't stand the sound of your own voice on recordings #iDoit2
	stay in the shower longer because you're scared of the cold wave that will hit you when you get out #iDoit2

The #iDoit2 meme is closely related to a larger set of Twitter memes concerned with complaining about life. These memes use hashtags such as #IHATEITWHEN, #AREYOUSERIOUS, #DONTJUDGEME, and #GETOVERIT to express a kind of universal complaint about daily events. Using a hashtag flags the universality of the complaint as it suggests that others share the same experience (and may use the same tag). Expressions of appraisal rather than simple ideational topics occur in the hashtag.

Some of these evaluative hashtag memes employ contingency with the function of activating invoked evaluation in the body of the tweet:

> **#ihateitwhen** someone gets so caught up with the tv they stop in the middle of a statement ...

In this tweet, the AFFECT in the label, #iHATEitwhen, marks the invoked NEGATIVE JUDGEMENT of the behaviour (not paying proper attention to an interlocutor). Tweets conforming to this pattern typically present the event as habitual via modalisation, for example:

> RT @IDoThat2: RT if you **always** say "What?" then realize what they said one second later.

Where negative AFFECT is present, it invokes JUDGEMENT of NORMALITY. In other words, the point is not that you find the daily event annoying, but rather than you are to be positively judged in terms of NORMALITY because you do. The social relation is one of proposing a bond that is shareable because others experience the same problems.

The kind of self-deprecating persona construed in these quotidian bonds made in relation to everyday irritations is closely aligned with the Twitter #fail meme where users will post about something that has gone wrong during their day, for example:

> Painting my nails at 2 in the morning #fail ... forgot I had to wait for this crap to dry :-\

Using Fail in a status update invokes affinity with a putative community of fellow 'failures' who we can imagine posting 'RT if you hate it when you paint your nails before bed and have to wait for them to dry'. The minor incident, inconvenience at waiting for nail polish to dry, reported in this tweet takes on a more global meaning potential via #Fail.

The bonds proposed when retweeting this kind of contingency and coupling pattern, particularly when proposed with hashtags such as #iDoit2, #Ihateitwhen, and #fail, show users aligning around and lightly mocking the common problems of modern life. The ideational concerns that enter into these coupling relations are often encountered alone and are somewhat trivial, awkward moments that are part of the minutiae of life. In this way microblogging offers the opportunity for people to express frustration at such minor adversity that might otherwise be considered too inane to bother communicating face to face.

The hashtag virtually and symbolically binds these expressed couplings together as an assemblage of related bonds. The intimate act of painting nails in the early morning becomes a public act, and the private frustration finds an ambient audience. This is characteristic of a blurring of the public and private seen in social media in general (Boyd, 2010, p. 49). We are oriented by the humorous commonality of the contingencies ('if you think/feel/do') to enact a response to the coupling marked by the hashtag. Just as "Humour connects the micro-interactive, interpersonal contexts of private life with the macro-social contexts of institutionalized public life" (Eggins and Slade, 1997, p. 167), it works to create community from individual, commonplace experience.

As the examples used throughout this chapter suggest, when proposing bonds, tweets will often attempt to render themselves more likely to be found by others sharing the similar couplings of meaning. For instance, consider again a tweet enacting the #iDoit2 meme:

> **RT @iDoit2**: RT if you get annoyed when girls call themselves fat or ugly when they're NOT, and they're just trying to get attention. **#iDoit2**

There are two ways in which this tweet renders itself findable (shown in bold): the #iDoit2 hashtag and the RT directed at the user, iDoit2,[12] with @. Users who are particularly amused by this meme may follow iDoit2 as a way of viewing the retweets directed at this account (which will generally be iterations of the meme). As I mentioned earlier, just how pervasive these kinds of retweeting practices are on Twitter is seen in the most common 3-gram for HERMES, THANKS FOR THE where users are typically thanking others for retweeting their post.

9 Conclusion: Proposing Bonds with Searchable Talk

This chapter has explored the close association between contingency and interpersonal bonds. Microbloggers appear to search for personae that hold similar values to their own. The significance of this social search is demonstrated in

12 iDoit2 is the user who likely instigated this meme and who has proposed the bond in the original tweet alongside the call to retweet the tweet.

practices such as hashtagging and retweeting, which we can think of as the beginning of what I term *searchable talk*. Searchable talk is online conversation where people render their talk more findable and hence more bondable. In other words, it is discourse where users are proposing bonds to an ambient audience in order to create alignments in such a way that they may be automatically found (via means such as hashtags and directed retweets). In order to propose a bond we must construe an orientation to the coupling presented, and contingency relations are one resource of many at the microblogger's disposal. We might think of microblogging services as interpersonal search engines: '*if I do it 2*' then so might you, and we can find each other on Twitter.

This type of contingency relation can be classified under the general class of coherence relations, which other chapters in this volume (Stukker and Sanders, in addition to the introduction by Taboada and Trnavac) have shown have an impact on the interpretation of evaluation.

References

Bakhtin, M.M. 1986. *Speech genres and other late essays*, University of Texas Press.

Bollen, J., Mao, H. & Xiao-Jun, Z. in press. Twitter mood predicts the stock market. *Journal of Computational Science*.

Boyd, D. 2010. Social Network Sites as Networked Publics: Affordances, Dynamics, and Implications. *In*: Papacharissi, Z. (ed.) *A Networked Self: Identity, Community, and Culture on Social Network Sites*. New York: Routledge.

Boyd, D., Golder, S. & Lotan, G. 2010. *Tweet, Tweet, Retweet: Conversational Aspects of Retweeting on Twitter* [Online]. Kauai, HI: Computer Society Press. Available: http://www.danah.org/papers/TweetTweetRetweet.pdf [accessed 24 March 2011].

Eggins, S. & Slade, D. 1997. *Analysing casual conversation*, London; New York, Cassell.

Firth, J. 1957. *Papers in Linguistics 1934–1951*, London, Oxford University Press.

Gruzd, A., Doiron, S. & Mai, P. Is Happiness Contagious Online? A Case of Twitter and the 2010 Winter Olympics. Proceedings of the 44th Hawaii International Conference on System Sciences (HICSS), 2011 Kauai, HI, USA.

Halliday, M.A.K. 1978. *Language as social semiotic: the social interpretation of language and meaning*, London, Edward Arnold.

Halliday, M.A.K. & Matthiessen, C.M.I.M. 2004. *An introduction to functional grammar*, London, Arnold.

Hood, S. 2010. *Appraising Research: Evaluation in Academic Writing*, London, Palgrave Macmillan.

Huang, J., Thornton, K.M. & Efthimiadis, E.N. 2010. Conversational tagging in twitter.

Proceedings of the 21st ACM conference on Hypertext and hypermedia. Toronto, Ontario, Canada: ACM.

Knight, N. 2008. "Still cool ... and american too!": an SFL analysis of deferred bonds in internet messaging humour. *In*: Nørgaard, N. (ed.) *Systemic Functional Linguistics in Use, Odense Working Papers in Language and Communication*.

Knight, N. 2010. Wrinkling complexity: Concepts of identity and affiliation in humour. *In*: Bednarek, M. & Martin, J.R. (eds.) *New Discourse on Language: Functional Perspectives on Multimodality, Identity, and Affiliation*. London; New York: Continuum.

Martin, J.R. 1992. *English text: system and structure*, Philadelphia, John Benjamins Pub. Co.

Martin, J.R. 2000. Beyond Exchange: APPRAISAL Systems in English. *In*: Hunston, S. & Thompson, G. (eds.) *Evaluation in text: authorial stance and the construction of discourse*. Oxford University Press.

Martin, J.R. 2004. Mourning: How We Get Aligned. *Discourse & Society*, 15, 321–344.

Martin, J.R. 2010. Introduction: Semantic Variation. *In*: Bednarek, M. & Martin, J.R. (eds.) *New Discourse on Language: Functional Perspectives on Multimodality, Identity, and Affiliation*. London; New York: Continuum.

Martin, J.R. & White, P.R.R. 2005. *The language of evaluation: appraisal in English*, New York, Palgrave Macmillan.

Marwick, A. & Boyd, D. 2011. To See and Be Seen: Celebrity Practice on Twitter. *Convergence*.

McCracken, H. 2009. *What I Know About Twitter* [Online]. Available: http://technologizer.com/2009/03/15/what-i-know-about-twitter/ [accessed 28 February 2011].

Nagarajan, M., Purohit, H. & Sheth, A. A Qualitative Examination of Topical Tweet and Retweet Practices. Fourth International AAAI Conference on Weblogs and Social Media, 2010 Washington, D.C.: The AAAI Press, 295–298.

Oulasvirta, A., Lehtonen, E., Kurvinen, E. & Raento, M. 2010. Making the ordinary visible in microblogs. *Personal Ubiquitous Comput.*, 14, 237–249.

Page, R. 2011. *Stories and Social Media: Identities and Interaction*, UK, Routledge.

Thelwall, M., Buckley, K. & Paltoglou, G. 2011. Sentiment in Twitter events. *Journal of the American Society for Information Science and Technology*, 62, 406–418.

Trnavac, R. & Taboada, M. 2010. The contribution of (non)veridical rhetorical relations to evaluation in discourse. *37th International Systemic Functional Linguistics Congress*. Vancouver.

Whitelaw, C., Garg, N. & Argamon, S. 2005. Using appraisal groups for sentiment analysis. *Proceedings of the 14th ACM international conference on Information and knowledge management*. Bremen, Germany: ACM.

Zappavigna, M. 2011. Ambient affiliation: A linguistic perspective on Twitter. *New Media & Society*, 13, 788–806.

Zappavigna, M. 2012. *Discourse of Twitter and Social Media: How we use language to create affiliation on the web*, London, Continuum.

Zappavigna, M., Dwyer, P. & Martin, J.R. "Just like sort of guilty kind of": the rhetoric of tempered admission in Youth Justice Conferencing. 2007 Annual Congress of the Australian Systemic Functional Linguistics Association: Bridging Discourses, 2008a Wollongong. Available from: http://www.asfla.org.au/wp.../07/the-rhetoric-of-tempered-admission.pdf.

Zappavigna, M., Dwyer, P. & Martin, J.R. 2008b. Syndromes of meaning: exploring patterned coupling in a NSW Youth Justice. *In*: Mahboob, A. & Knight, N. (eds.) *Questioning Linguistics*. Newcastle: Cambridge Scholars Publishing.

Zhao, S. 2010. Intersemiotic relations as logogenetic patterns: towards the restoration of the time dimension in hypertext description *In*: Bednarek, M., Martin, J (ed.) *New Discourse on Language: Functional Perspectives on Multimodality, Identity, and Affiliation*. London: Continuum.

Zhao, S. 2011. *Learning through multimedia interaction: The construal of primary socials science knowledge in web-based digital learning materials*. PhD, University of Sydney.

Index of Subjects

References to notes are indexed as, for example, 55n2 (page 55, note 2). References to tables and figures are indexed as (respectively) 51t, 207f.

 | DOI: 10.1163/9789004258174_010

Index of Names

References to notes are indexed as, for example, 55n2 (page 55, note 2).

 | DOI: 10.1163/9789004258174_011

www.ingramcontent.com/pod-product-compliance
Lightning Source LLC
LaVergne TN
LVHW010642300926
849161LV00005B/1021
* 9 7 8 9 0 0 4 2 5 8 1 6 7 *